British and American Gardens in the Eighteenth Century

British and American Gardens in the Eighteenth Century

EIGHTEEN ILLUSTRATED ESSAYS ON GARDEN HISTORY

Edited by
Robert P. Maccubbin *and* Peter Martin

The Colonial Williamsburg Foundation
Williamsburg, Virginia

This volume has been published simultaneously as Volume VIII, n. s., 2 of
Eighteenth-Century Life by the College of William and Mary (ISSN 0098-
2601).

Library of Congress Cataloging in Publication Data

British and American gardens in the eighteenth century.

  "Published simultaneously as volume VIII, n.s., 2 of Eighteenth-century
life by the College of William and Mary and the Colonial Williamsburg
Foundation"—T.p. verso.
  Includes bibliographical references.
  1. Gardens, British—History—18th century—Addresses, essays,
lectures. 2. Gardens, American—History—18th century—Addresses, essays, lectures. I. Maccubbin, Robert P. II. Martin, Peter, 1940-
III. Colonial Williamsburg Foundation.
SB457.54.B75   1984   712'.0942   84-4252

ISBN 0-87935-105-5

CONTENTS

Plates follow page 91

American Gardens

Plates follow page 188

Introduction

Peter Martin

As the first essay in this volume demonstrates, British garden history in the last decade has come of age as a discipline in its own right. There has been an explosion of writing on the subject, and the scope has been wide. To quote the editorial in the first number of the *Journal of Garden History* (January 1981) garden history generally concerns not only garden design, but also "iconography, aesthetics, botany and horticulture, technology, social and economic history, conservation and restoration of historic gardens, geography, history of ideas, and the relation of gardens to the history of landscape taste." The second essay in this volume, on the nomenclature of style in garden history, also indirectly suggests the growth of the discipline by considering some of the attending problems of terminology inherent in the rapid rise of this young field. There is every indication that garden history will continue to develop as a discipline and increasingly will become a subject of university academic study.

In light of this "bursting Prospect," it is surprising that American garden history, especially in the eighteenth century, has been neglected. There are fine American garden historians, but they do not write much about their own country's gardens. What has been written has chiefly and narrowly concerned botanists and botany, or garden restoration.[1] One is reminded of this neglect by the program for a conference, "Discovering in Wide Landscape: A Conference on Gardens, Landscape, and Literature," held at Trinity College, Toronto, in August 1983. Notwithstanding the richness of colonial American garden history, of the twenty papers delivered not one was on America. However, two recent and promising efforts in the United States to generate some intellectual and scholarly movement along these lines are the creation in 1981 of the Southern Garden History Society and the establishment of an American garden history section in the American Society of Landscape Architects. It is hoped that the essays on eighteenth-century American gardens and gardeners in this present volume will also encourage scholarly attention to the early efforts of colonials to create gardens in the New World.

One guiding assumption in the preparation of this collection of essays has been that by publishing a number of pieces on eighteenth-century British and American gardens within the same volume, the extent to which colonial gardens and gardening were shaped and determined by Britain could be measured. Also the uniqueness of colonial gardens, owing to climate, resources, and economic conditions, could thereby be more clearly appreciated. The essays on British gardening point up a number of characteristics of this art in the eighteenth century: they include the early classical impetus as apparent in Pope's garden, Switzer's ideas about rural and extensive gardening, the emergence of the *ferme ornée* at gardens like Painshill and Shenstone's The Leasowes, the personal (even psychological) element not infrequently involved in the laying out of a garden, continental influences, the romantic introduction of the volcano, the ascendancy of feeling over taste in the evolution of the landscape garden during the so-called high phase, and the manifestations in late eighteenth- and early nineteenth-century gardens of the American botanical zeal.

Colonial gardening, though it lagged behind British gardening throughout the century in practice and theory by a couple of decades—certainly not by as much as half a century as has for long been believed—was distinguished by an eager awareness of most of these characteristics and the personalities and books connected with them. William Byrd of Westover, Virginia, for example, preened in young manhood on both the rural and urban pleasures of English life, brought to his Virginia plantation in the late 1720s a knowledge of the latest British garden ideas that he had picked up at estates like Cliveden, Whitton Park, Claremont, Euston Hall, Petersham, perhaps Marble Hill, Blenheim, Hagley Park, and Uborn.[2] His library suggests that he also kept up with the British literature of gardening. We do not know that he visited Pope's garden in Twickenham, but a number of other Americans did. Richard Stockton, who owned a country residence called Morven in Princeton, New Jersey, on a visit to England in 1766 made a point of riding over to Twickenham to see Pope's famous garden. He wrote to his wife of his intention to "ride to Twickenham . . . principally to view Mr. Pope's gardens and grotto, which I am told remain nearly as he left them. . . . I shall take with me a gentleman who draws well, to lay down the exact plan of the whole."[3] As for the classical theme, to cite a few examples, John Custis of Williamsburg at least as early as 1740 achieved allusions to Roman mythology by introducing appropriate lead statues within his four-acre town garden; Landon Carter carefully alluded to Horatian semi-retirement at his plantation in Virginia by calling it Sabine Hall; and in May 1743 Eliza Lucas Pinckney acknowledged her "rural taste" in gardens at Crowfield, near Charleston, South Carolina, by describing their "Virgilian" beauty of "Wilderness," fine prospects, and ornamental mounts—one of which was crowned by a "roman temple."[4]

As the essays here collectively suggest, British influences upon colonial pleasure gardening were felt more in some of the more southern colonies than in New England. This was due principally to climate and the greater affluence of planters and town residents chiefly in Pennsylvania, Maryland, New Jersey, Virginia, and North and South Carolina. In the scientific vein, although botanical research and plant exchanges with England were pursued in New England, they were nowhere nearly as intense and precise as in the colonies to the south. This is the one area of American garden history in the century that has been closely chronicled in biographies of colonial botanists, which include accounts of their contacts in England with Sir Hans Sloane, Peter Collinson, Leonard Plukenett, James Petiver, and other members of the Royal Society; it is a subject which comprises a logical and important part of the stories some of our essays tell. So is the sometimes intensely personal character of the ornamental and botanical gardening carried on by some colonists throughout the century—colonists who turned to gardens as one potential way of creating for themselves a more civilized pose in the New World, of feeling closer to the British culture they had either left behind, pined for, or knew only through books and conversation. Common enough to both the New England and southern colonies, the effort was normally beset with discouraging and frustrating obstacles thrown in the way by a paucity of competent practical gardeners and adequate tools, extremes of weather, and the maddening undependability of transatlantic shipments of plants and seeds.

Other examples of British-American gardening links abound, most of which were well established before the last quarter of the century, when Thomas Jefferson made a deliberate study of English gardens in 1786 as he rambled about the English countryside with a copy of Thomas Whately's *Observations on Modern Gardening* in his hands. Indeed, it would appear from his accounts of the famous early and mid-century gardens he saw that he was less impressed by them than were his colonial predecessors. By 1786 gardens like Pope's, Stowe, Hagley, Chiswick, Esher, Claremont, Painshill, The Leasowes, and Wotton seemed to him old-fashioned and cramped, in spite of the classical touches he enjoyed, such as the "Doric temple" at Painshill.[5] Not only that, Jefferson's major garden designing at Monticello—for which he indulged in some sketches of classical temples— took on a patriotic theme after the War of Revolution. Both he and his fellow traveler in 1786, John Adams, felt that the English taste for expensive temples (in spite of his own sketches), statuary, obelisks, and other furnishings was unsuitable for either the American landscape or the new national mood of liberty and equality. As Adams put it, "It will be long, I hope, before ridings, parks, pleasure grounds, gardens, and ornamented farms, grow so much in fashion in America." He was thinking of the grander American landscape: "Nature has done greater things and furnished nobler materials, there; the oceans, islands, mountains, valleys, are all laid out upon a larger scale."[6] Even Horace Walpole prophesied a new spirit of American landscaping in 1775, one that at the beginning of the next century would take the new nation into the era of Andrew Jackson Downing and others of that new breed, the professional landscape gardener. Walpole imagined a declaration of gardening independence: "Some American will . . . revive the true taste in gardening. . . . I love to skip into futurity and imagine what will be done on the giant scale of a new hemisphere."[7]

Colonial Williamsburg Foundation and *New England College, Sussex*

4

————————————————NOTES————————————————

1. Some exceptions are Ann Leighton's general studies, *American Gardens in the Eighteenth Century* (Boston, 1976) and *Early American Gardens* (Boston, 1970); Rudy and Joy Favretti's *Landscape and Gardens for Historical Buildings* (Nashville, 1978), chap. 1; and Richard Beale Davis, *Intellectual Life in the Colonial South, 1585-1763* (Knoxville, Tenn., 1978), II, chap. 7.

2. See *William Byrd of Virginia: The London Diary, 1717-21*, ed. Louis B. Wright and Marion Tinling (New York, 1958), pp. 128, 148, 150, 155, 175, 267-268.

3. The Stockton MSS. are at the Princeton Historical Society; see Alfred Hoyt Bill, *A House Called Morven* (Princeton, 1954).

4. *The Letterbook of Eliza Lucas Pinckney, 1739-62*, ed. Elise Pinckney (Chapel Hill, 1972), pp. 61, 181. In her mind she linked Virgil with Carolina: "I am persuaded tho' he wrote in and for Italy, it will in many instances suit Carolina" (pp. 35-36).

5. *Thomas Jefferson's Garden Book, 1766-1824*, ed. Edwin M. Betts (Philadelphia, 1944), pp. 111-114.

6. *The Works of John Adams*, ed. C.F. Adams (Boston, 1865), III, p. 395.

7. See Walpole's letter to the Rev. William Mason (Nov. 27, 1775), *The Correspondence of Horace Walpole*, ed. W.S. Lewis (New Haven, 1955), XXVIII, p. 234. Without specific application to gardening, Leo Marx has written about the role of the American landscape in generating patriotism during the War of Revolution: see *The American Revolution and the American Landscape* (Washington, D.C., 1974).

"Bursting Prospect": British Garden History Now

Morris R. Brownell

Meantime you gain the Height, from whose fair Brow
The bursting Prospect spreads immense around.
("Spring," 11. 950-51)

James Thomson's lines in *The Seasons*[1] describing the gardens of Hagley Park, Worcestershire, provide an apt appraisal of the state of English garden history after the era of Christopher Hussey and H. F. Clark, two of its most important early historians. The point of departure for this survey of recent research in English garden history is the year 1974, when festschriften dedicated to each of them were published.[2] Hussey's contribution to garden history derives from his articles in *Country Life* on the architecture and gardens of the Georgian country house, essays of "exemplary balance" in the words of Nikolaus Pevsner, some of which were revised and collected in a book Joseph Burke has praised as a "lucid exposition of the background of ideas" in English garden history.[3] Hussey's study of the arts of eighteenth-century landscape, *The Picturesque* (1927), has required modification in the light of more specialized research, but it "has kept its freshness" in the opinion of architectural historians like Pevsner.[4] H.F. Clark is remembered for a monograph on the English garden first published in an academic journal, subsequently revised for publication in a recently reprinted book, which introduced scholarly rigor to a subject that had been the preoccupation of amateurs.[5] Together Hussey and Clark can be considered the founding fathers of modern English garden history.

Recent research in English garden history is the story of the birth of an academic discipline in a field that has been recognized as interdisciplinary since Horace Walpole defined "Poetry, Painting and Gardening," as "the Science of Landscape."[6] Roy Strong remarks that "the researches of literary historians . . . more than any others, have begun to open up the subject for serious consideration."[7] This essay will attempt to characterize the variety and vitality of research in garden history by selecting for discussion representative examples: first, traditional histories of gardens and their landscape architects; second, new horizons opened in studies of the landscape garden in Scotland, Ireland, and France; third, interdisciplinary studies of the garden in relation to painting, poetry, and the theater; fourth, new directions indicated by political, structuralist, and feminist studies of garden design; finally, garden history as growth industry manifested in reprint publications, exhibitions, new journals, and literature for the general reader.

To begin with traditional garden history, the period under review has presented us with two nonspecialist histories of the English garden, and the continuation of a scholarly history of Stowe, Buckinghamshire. Joseph Burke's chapter in the *Oxford History of English Art*, "The Creation of the Landscape Garden," is no mere summary of received wisdom.[8] Burke emphasizes Pliny in Melmoth's translation (1746) as the classical writer who "anticipates the new attitude to the garden." He remarks on the lack of attention to "Continental origins of *le jardin anglais*," declares the theory of Chinese origin of the English landscape garden "misleading," remarks on the "impact of the rococo" in Stephen Switzer's writing, and comments on William Kent's attachment "to the stage effects of Mannerist and baroque garden architecture." Burke compares Stowe to Britain's "national Valhalla," Westminster Abbey, and speculates on the possibility that "a surprising number of the grander images from Gray's *Elegy* can be matched in Lord Cobham's seat [Stowe]."[9] He emphasizes the importance of the pictorial in garden design, believing that "the view that Elizabeth Manwaring overstated the case for pictorial influence is . . . based on a misinterpretation of her thesis."[10] Only two ghosts of garden history haunt Burke's perceptive summary: first, the myth of William Kent's gardening revolution; second, the notion that Pope's interest in garden design was confined to precept rather than practice. Otherwise this thoughtful chapter is free of the uncritical recapitulation of secondary sources that continues to pass for garden history.[11] Christopher Thacker's chapters on the English garden in his popular history are well informed by recent specialized studies, and he includes an interesting comparison of Shenstone to a Chinese eighteenth-century poet-gardener, Yuan Mei. Only rarely does an uncritical commonplace, like the idea of Pope's grotto as a "jackdaw collection," intrude to mislead the general reader to whom this history is addressed.[12]

The most important historical study of the English landscape garden is the continuation of the history of Stowe by George Clarke and M. J. Gibbon that has been appearing since 1967 in articles in *The Stoic*,[13] the basis of a forthcoming book on this paradigm of the English landscape garden. "What makes Stowe unique," George Clarke writes, "is that it contains the whole gardening history of the eighteenth century. All stages of the revolution—formal, irregular, transitional and pictorial gardening, *ferme ornée* and ideal landscape—however they are defined, were represented in this one place."[14] Clarke's discussion of the ha-ha or sunk fence at Stowe, his analysis of the satirical program of the Elysian Fields, and his reassessments of the roles of professional and amateur designers, accompanied by detailed analysis of newly discovered plans, illustrations, and guidebooks from the Huntington Library archives, have transformed our understanding of the Genius of the Place.[15] Modern hermeneutic speculations on the semiotics of garden design discussed below rest on Clarke's detailed reconstruction of this exemplary garden.

Both Clark and Hussey relied on Horace Walpole's Whig interpretation of garden history,[16] which exaggerated the importance of William Kent at the expense of the obscure figure of Charles Bridgeman, his contemporary. Peter Willis's definitive study relieves Bridgeman at last of the incubus of Walpole's judgment, collects the fragments of his biography, and establishes him as "the unsung pioneer in the establishment of *le jardin anglais*."[17] Willis catalogs and documents Bridgeman's works, placing them in the context of the origins of the landscape movement and providing the best-illustrated account of Bridgeman's major achievement at Stowe. Kenneth Woodbridge has given us the most searching revisionist account of William Kent, whom Walpole and Hussey established as a revolutionary advocate of pictorial garden design.[18] From a careful analysis of Kent's drawings Woodbridge establishes the priority of garden architecture rather than painting in Kent's designs, dates his earliest designs in landscape architecture about 1731, and convincingly defines Kent's role as "a catalyst, moving from one improving landowner to another, working empirically, his ideas given piecemeal in sketches."[19] Walpole's legendary champion who "leaped the fence and saw that all nature was a garden" dies hard, but after Woodbridge's analysis we can no longer accept Kent as the Calvin of a reformation in English garden design.

In 1975 Dorothy Stroud published a revised edition of her biography of the third major landscape architect of the period, Lancelot "Capability" Brown, "a complete rewriting of the earlier book" justified by documentary discoveries since 1950, including a new plan of Petworth House, autograph drawings of Burghley House, and new biographical information.[20] The scholarship is not entirely up to date (Joseph Spence is quoted from Singer's rather than Osborn's edition, p. 45), but the book provides a complete chronological survey of Brown's works, listed in an appendix illustrated by a map, and Christopher Hussey's ingratiating preface has been reprinted.

Until recently the study of the landscape garden has been largely confined to England, but our horizons have been expanded by new studies of the landscape garden in Scotland, Ireland, and France. A. A. Tait has given us a careful historical account of the hitherto neglected landscape movement in Scotland. "As a child of the Edinburgh Enlightenment" the landscape movement was imported from England and became naturalized only after "the developing taste for the picturesque encouraged a pride in the countryside and its history."[21] Tait's chapter titles referring to aesthetic categories ("informal," "beautiful," "picturesque," "landscape," and "romantic") are somewhat misleading because the book is little concerned with the aesthetics of garden design. Tait's emphasis is on the historical development of Scottish gardens and the careers of Scottish landscape designers. He provides a valuable chronological list (Appendix 3) of their works in Scotland from about 1730 to 1840.

Tait's principal thesis is a negative one: that the Scottish landscape garden has no parallel to the political iconography of the English garden, which Horace Walpole liked to compare to the English constitution. "There was probably no Scottish parallel with Stowe and its moral and political garden buildings," Tait remarks, "the emphasis was exclusively visual rather than political."[22] Although the book is somewhat short on interpretive ideas, it is rich in new facts about unfamiliar garden designs and their architects, well illustrated with plans, paintings, prints, and aerial photographs. We learn that Pope's apostle of garden design, Joseph Spence, made a Scottish tour in 1760, admired gardens around Edinburgh, and praised an unpublished treatise on gardening by Sir John Dalrymple (ca. 1750) with the remark that "improvements in the thought of Gardening are not confin'd to the Southern Part of this Island." Tait sums up the landscaping of the amateur Sir John Clerk at Penicuik in the statement that "the key to the landscape movement for Clerk and others like him was not political but emotional and literary." He discusses Robert Adam's sensibility to landscape as revealed in watercolor drawings Tait has cataloged, and he introduces us to the figure of Robert Robinson who in the 1760s "was prepared to get himself up as some horticultural Ossian."[23] Tait is not completely successful in distinguishing the naturalized Scottish landscape design from the English, and he ignores the important question of the influence of Scottish gardeners in England—the "Northern Lads" against whom Stephen Switzer fulminates in *The Nobleman, Gentleman and Gardener's Recreation* (1715)[24]—but the book is a valuable scholarly survey of the landscape garden in Scotland.

Edward Malins and his coauthor have written a less scholarly but pioneering account of the landscape garden in Ireland. It surveys garden design from 1660 to 1845, draws widely on literary evidence of unpublished correspondence and travels, but fails to establish an adequate historical context and ignores the evidence of architectural plans. Horace Walpole's famous remark about Capability Brown's reason for refusing a commission in Ireland shortly before he died—because *"he had not yet finished England"*—is quoted to illustrate the absence of professional landscape designers in Ireland.[25] But the authors have much to say about the influence of amateurs, particularly Pope's friends, Swift and Patrick Delaney, whom they credit with the introduction of informal principles of garden design into Ireland, a plausible but unproven thesis. Another implicit thesis of the book is that the "special harmony" of Ireland's landscape garden is the work of the amateur designer, although this too is never argued systematically. The book is full of interesting unconsidered trifles that invite further investigation: Bishop Percy's Dromore landscape with its theatrical painted wooden obelisk; Lord Chesterfield's patronage of the public gardens in Dublin, Phoenix Park; and the English enthusiasm for Irish landscape, evident in George Montagu's letter to Horace Walpole praising Mount Merrion "with such a view of the sea and Dublin as would make even your Thames blush for Richmond Hill and Isleworth."[26]

The most distinguished book on garden history outside England is Dora Wiebenson's study of the landscape garden in France, a book which argues the paradoxical thesis that *le jardin anglais* is as much a French as an English creation.[27] She shows that the French informal garden developed independently of the English, was always adapted to a French context, and modified French ideas of formal design; further that French knowledge of English gardens was often superficial, and that English ideas of garden design underwent a sea change across the channel. Wiebenson modestly describes her own book as "introductory," but her study of the relation of French theory and practice to English yields rich insights into the garden history of both countries.

The French picturesque garden, like the English, has its roots in literature, painting, and the theater. Wiebenson cites Honoré d'Urfé's pastoral romance *L'Astrée* (1608-1628) and Watteau as crucial influences. She interprets d'Argenville as an advocate of picturesque irregularity and traces stylistic development in gardening from irregularity around 1700 to rococo in the 1730s, a development contrasting to the English. (Here I believe she misconstrues Addison as an advocate of rococo opposed to naturalism in garden design.) Her second chapter, "French Opinion on the English Picturesque Garden," demonstrates what "French rococo eyes" saw in English gardens like Chiswick and Stowe: the concept of liberty, Chinese influence, and a cemetery air. A chapter devoted to English gardening theory of Chambers, Whately, and Walpole provides a full discussion of nationalist viewpoints in gardening, Chinese influence, and "the repertoire of theatrical techniques." A chapter on gardening theory in France shows how Watelet, Girardon, and others adapted picturesque garden theory to the formalist aesthetic of the French gardening tradition. A handsomely illustrated survey of particular French gardens illustrates how Chinese, pictorial, and theatrical paradigms were worked out in practice, and makes penetrating observations on such matters as the distinction between the English pictorial and the French theatrical idea of the *ferme ornée*. Wiebenson splendidly fulfills her intention to provide "a coherent framework . . . on which more detailed studies may be based."[28] Her study invites us to explore the interrelations of theory and practice in French and English garden design, to reopen the question of Chinese influence, and to examine the theatrical roots of garden design.

"Interdisciplinary" has become a cant term in the academy, but garden history has emerged in recent years as one of the few genuinely interdisciplinary fields of study. Recent studies reflect intimate relations between garden design and painting, architecture, and poetry. John Harris's catalog of paintings of the English country house offers the garden historian the hitherto neglected source of topographical art for the study of individual gardens and their architects.[29] Harris devoted an earlier book to one of his discoveries, the little known painter of garden architecture, Thomas Robins the Elder (1716-1770), whose paintings of rococo garden architecture in mid-eighteenth-century England have changed our sense of the evolution of garden design.[30] Harris's catalog of country house views helps us to overcome the persistent difficulty confronting the garden historian: the scarcity of visual evidence and the need for adequate indexes of topographical art. John Riely's rediscovery of William Shenstone's watercolor drawings of The Leasowes, which Elizabeth Manwaring had located without realizing their significance, has provided us with valuable visual evidence for study of this prototype of the English *ferme ornée*. The recent catalog of the views of Pope's villa recording more than fifty pictures indicates how informative to the garden historian the complete iconography of a country house can be.[31]

The garden's relation to poetry and the contributions of poets to English garden design have been studied extensively in the period under review. John Dixon Hunt's book on the relations of poetry, painting, and gardening introduces a fresh perspective on the arts of landscape. He insists on the futility of attempting to adjudicate the informality of eighteenth-century gardens through a pre-romantic telescope, arguing that the important question is not "when" but "why" informal design in gardening came to be introduced. His answer is that the informal design reflects a new Lockean psychology with its emphasis on association of ideas, and that informal garden design answered "fresh visions of the human mind."[32] For example, Hunt finds at Pope's Twickenham a psychological landscape in the garden, a "psychological programme" in the grotto, and a habit of psychologizing landscape in Pope's descriptions of gardens in poetry and prose. In his discussion of Pope and other eighteenth-century poets Hunt shifts our attention to poetic and psychological values, restoring a balance that Hussey and Manwaring had weighted heavily towards pictorial values.

Hunt believes that the introspective experience of gardens tutored poets like Pope, and he discounts the influence of topographical verse and the pictorial impulse. My own study of Pope's theory and practice of gardening takes the opposite view: that Pope's poetry and prose reveal a sensibility to the picturesque which distinguishes his theory and practice of gardening from that of his contemporaries.[33] A new book by Peter Martin studies Pope's interest in garden design outside Twickenham in even fuller detail than I did, uncovering new evidence from plans, maps, and local historical archives.[34] Thus garden historians continue to regard Pope as a central figure in the origins of the English landscape garden.

Architecture is inseparably linked to the garden in our term, "landscape architecture," and two recent studies touching on this relationship deserve mention. The first is Michael McCarthy's essay on the attribution of the Temple of Ancient Virtue at Stowe, which leads him to ask the interesting question: "Did neo-classicism in architecture force naturalism in landscape design?"[35] His answer will surprise garden historians relying on Walpole's assumption that concepts of landscape design precede those of architecture when he concludes that "the order of precedence should be reversed."[36] Second, Mark Girouard's *Life in the English Country House*, a study of architectural development in relation to social history, suggests an approach that might be profitably applied to the history of garden design.[37]

One of the most fruitful areas of recent interdisciplinary research concerns the relation of the theater and garden design. Susan Lang's essay in the Hussey festschrift makes the interesting suggestion in an otherwise unreliable summary of the origins of the landscape garden that "the true progenitor of the landscape garden . . . was stage design and its written emanations."[38] John Dixon Hunt has been studying the theatrical origins of the English garden in Italian Renaissance landscape architecture. In a recent lecture on the London garden-theaters Vauxhall and Ranelagh, Hunt showed how verbal and visual motifs combine, how stage and auditorium interchange in the garden encouraging visitors to become actors as well as spectators in garden "scenes." He quotes Horace Walpole's telling remark on a "small Vauxhall" acted at the grotto in the Elysian Fields at Stowe. He discusses Benjamin Nebot's paintings of Hartwell House as cataloged by Harris as "an example of a private garden organized in a series of theatres." He has interesting things to say about the origins of the theatricality of eighteenth-century gardens in English Jacobean masques and the garden scenes of Restoration drama. Many scholars have remarked on the lack of a systematic study of the relation of the theater to garden design. Hunt's work is revealing how enlightening such study will be to garden history.[39]

In addition to traditional historical studies ("perennials"), some examples of new directions ("annuals") deserve mention to characterize political, feminist, structuralist, history of ideas, and aesthetic approaches to garden history. Since George Clarke's groundbreaking article on the iconography of the Elysian Fields at Stowe,[40] political approaches to garden history have yielded promising results. Judith Colton's article on the program of political satire of an important piece of garden architecture at Richmond, Merlin's Cave (1735), provides a penetrating reading of the complex nuances of political satire in the Georgian garden. She makes the intriguing suggestion that Merlin's Cave was carrying on a satirical garden design dialogue with the Temple of British Worthies at Stowe.[41] James Turner's book on *The Politics of Landscape* does not deal with the garden, but in an article he has challenged William Brogden's apolitical characterization of Stephen Switzer, whose view of the garden in *Ichnographia Rustica* (1718), Turner insists, is " 'political' in a general sense."[42] David Jacques has written an essay on an important neglected political garden, Bolingbroke's Dawley Farm,[43] and Richard Quaintance is engaged in a book-length study of the politics of the garden in the later eighteenth century, with chapters on Walpole's Whig interpretation of garden history, William Chambers's Chinese vision of garden design, and the contest between Chambers's Kew and Cumberland's Virginia Water with accompanying graphic and literary satire.[44]

The feminist approach to garden history is represented by an outstanding article by Carole Fabricant, who explores the previously ignored "sexual dimension of Augustan gardening." Reading widely in contemporary gardening literature, she discusses "the gynecological spirit" of botanical studies and the language of natural description in topographical poetry and prose that describes nature "as a coy or seductive maiden, as a promiscuous or chaste consort, as a naked or overadorned damsel."[45] Landscape is continually being characterized as simultaneously titillating and uncontrollable, and the language of natural description reveals "profound interconnections between aesthetic, economic, and sexual forms of possession." Thomson's "bursting prospect" of Hagley quoted at the outset is interpreted as a male owner's possession opening to his private view. In the "Pleasures of Imagination," Addison finds that in landscape he is enjoying conjugal rights over nature. The article is a subtle and convincing study of "certain fundamental interconnections between aesthetics and ideology in eighteenth-century England."[46]

The landscape garden that Hussey was content to study in terms of an eclectic concept of the picturesque has now become the subject of modern structuralist approaches. Ronald Paulson has studied the landscape garden in one chapter of a book exploring the hermeneutics of eighteenth-century visual art and has substituted for the traditional teleology of classic to romantic a shift from emblematic to expressive in the arts, including garden design. Relying on George Clarke, he "reads" the gardens of Stowe as pages from an emblem book, the Home Park surrounding the rotunda as a satire of courtly love, and the Elysian Fields as a satire of Walpolean politics.[47] He follows Kenneth Woodbridge in interpreting the circuitous design of the lake-centered garden at Stourhead as an allegory based on Virgil's sixth book of the *Aeneid*.[48] Both of these interpretations are based on traditional studies of garden iconography, but Paulson presses further in speculations on landscape theory. He applies structuralist linguistic theory to the architecture of house and garden, which he sees as a "sign system"; gardens are construed as sentences, the formal garden "periodic," the informal "paratactic"; features of garden architecture are composed "like words to make new sentences"; parts of gardens are compared to "a page from an emblem book"; the garden is a literary text, a poem, or a painting, which he defines elsewhere as a "Claude structure."[49] Paulson applies principles of affective criticism to the observer in the garden, who reads the emblematic landscapes in an "emblematic meditation" in which space becomes a "metaphor for morality."[50]

The structuralist interpretation of garden design is intriguing, although sometimes the garden itself, patiently reconstructed by a Clarke or Woodbridge, disappears in the hermeneutic mists, as when Paulson confuses Sherborne, Dorset, with Twickenham, Middlesex.[51] Also, interpretations of the same garden text or program will inevitably differ. Thus James Turner's analysis of the program of Stourhead convincingly challenges the claim of Paulson and Woodridge that Stourhead is an allegory of *Aeneid* VI. Turner insists that "the whole lake-landscape is topographically far closer to Virgil's harbor [*Aeneid* I] than to any of the sources in Pliny or Claude put forward by modern critics."[52] But Turner shares Paulson's linguistic assumptions about garden design. "The task of the garden historian," Turner writes, "is like that of the linguist, who studies the structural principles that generate . . . the sentences of a language."[53]

Max Schulz has recently given us a theological reading of the early eighteenth-century landscape garden. Drawing on frequent allusions to rural paradise in contemporary literature of gardening, Schulz finds in the circuit walk of the eighteenth-century landscape garden a paradigm of the pilgrimage of the soul and an anticipation of the romantic theodicy of landscape. He finds pilgrims and pilgrimages at Stowe, Stourhead, and latently in Goldsmith's *Deserted Village* (1770), but Schulz himself admits that the "Edenic impulse" in gardening is "speculative," "not easy to fix," and the argument becomes nebulous when he writes that "the landscape garden thus fulfills, like the temples scattered about its grounds, the requisites of a celestial center, or *axis mundi*, and the contemplative walk around it assumes the repetition of a divine act whereby concrete time is projected into mythical time, and profane space into transcendent space."[54] It is difficult to imagine poets like Pope, much less patrons like Burlington or Cobham, or professional garden designers like Bridgeman or Brown, thinking in these terms.

Kenneth Woodbridge in a recent review and in an essay included in this volume has questioned the usefulness of such terms as "picturesque" in garden history, which have been applied equally to the Trianon, Pope's Twickenham garden, and the landscape of Gilpin's Wye.[55] It is inevitable that definitions like Hussey's continue to be challenged, revised, and modified. Art historical terms in garden history are portmanteau words we must redefine in different contexts. In a distinguished recent essay we have been presented with a new aesthetic category, "singularity," which may have application to garden history. Studying illustrated scientific travel literature of the century, Barbara Stafford has discovered a pervasive interest in the "lone natural object"—odd, isolated, singular—which she claims "was as important an aesthetic category as the Picturesque."[56] If the aesthetics of singularity in natural scenery appear to be irrelevant to the calculated artistry of landscape architecture, the plate illustrating "Le Château de Plessis-Chamand" in *Nouveaux Jardins de la France* (1808) behind a rude arch of rocks shows how effective the juxtaposition of the singular and the artificial in a landscape garden is, and invites us to consider whether taste for singularity influenced the century's garden design.

To conclude with some miscellaneous indications that garden history is "the growth industry of the moment,"[57] consider the evidence of recent reprints, exhibitions, and new journals. John Dixon Hunt and Peter Willis's collection of documents in English garden history, including rare illustrations, gives the garden historian a rich source of carefully edited primary sources.[58] The editors have supplied us with a useful anthology of documents and pictures, including the writings of more than fifty authors from Wotton to Peacock, with an introduction and headnotes that challenge some of our favorite prejudices about English garden history: the painting analogy; the associative syntax; the theatrical theme; and rival claims of professional and amateur designers. John Dixon Hunt, in a related enterprise, has edited with introductory notes a thirty-four-volume facsimile reprint series of books on gardening that includes such rarities as Robert Castell's *Villas of the Ancients Illustrated* (1728), Switzer's *Ichnographia Rustica* (1718), Robert Morris's *Essays Upon Harmony . . .* [of] *Situation . . .* (1739), six descriptions of Stowe (by Gilbert West, William Gilpin, George Bickham, two by Benton Seeley, and one from Defoe's 1742 *Tour*), Walpole's *History* (1771), Whately's *Observations on Modern Gardening* (1770), and William Mason's *English Garden* (1783), to mention a few.[59] Finally, a bookseller's catalog, Weinreb's *Gardens and Landscapes* (1977), unearthed another set of Ripa's *Views of the Gardens of Jehol* whose significance to the landscape movement have yet to be fully assessed.[60]

The Augustan Reprint Society continues to furnish us with reprints of documents important in garden history accompanied by helpful introductions. John Dixon Hunt's introduction to the reprint of William Gilpin's *Dialogue on Stow* describes this early treatise as a "journal of the mind's responses" to an English garden.[61] George Clarke's introduction to George Bickham's *The Beauties of Stow* (1750) in the same series clarifies its confused authorship and tells the story of a battle of guidebooks in the genesis of the first comprehensive guidebook of an English country seat that reveals it to have been a work of piracy and conflation.[62] Richard Quaintance comments on William Chambers's "Chinese myth for the promotion of a change in landscaping style" in the introduction to *An Explanatory Discourse* (1773).[63] Finally, John Serle's *A Plan of Mr. Pope's Garden* (1745), often lacking the fold-out diagram in extant copies, has been reprinted with an introduction detailing the topographical and biographical importance of the *Plan* in Pope's career.[64]

A number of recent and forthcoming art exhibitions will be of interest to the garden historian. The massive exhibition organized by John Harris and Roy Strong at the Victoria and Albert Museum in the summer of 1979 offered an encyclopedic potpourri of "material . . . covering many aspects of the subject,"[65] including some of Thomas Robins's delightful paintings of mid-century rococo gardens cataloged by Harris. A similarly ambitious exhibition was mounted in 1977 in Paris exploring the development of French garden design from 1760 to 1820, including an interesting sequence on English influence illustrated by paintings of François Joseph Bélanger from an unpublished *Carnet de Voyage en Angleterre* (ca. 1774-1778) discovered by Kenneth Woodbridge.[66] The catalog of an exhibition of Scottish landscape painting in 1978 includes a section on "The Country Seat" illustrated with plans and paintings of the development of the gardens of Taymouth Castle, which Robert Burns mistook for "Nature's native taste" in 1787.[67] The Greater London Council exhibition with catalog of the views of Pope's Villa at Marble Hill House in 1980 has already been mentioned. This may be the place to note a recent exhibition organized by Kimberly Rorschach at the Yale Center for British Art in New Haven, "The Early Georgian Landscape Garden" (April 20 to June 26, 1983), which included paintings, drawings, and illustrations of Chiswick, Stowe, Kew, Stourhead, Carlton House, Wilton, Hagley, The Leasowes, Cirencester, Claremont, Esher, Richmond, and Rousham.[68] This exhibition addressed questions that continue to perplex the garden historian: What are the characteristic elements of early Georgian gardens? How are they related to French and Italian gardens? Is the eighteenth-century English garden really more "informal" than the symmetrical seventeenth-century formal garden? How is the garden related aesthetically to the painting?

Another indication of the growing interest in garden history and its arrival as an academic discipline is the appearance in 1981 of a new journal edited by John Dixon Hunt, *The Journal of Garden History*. This is a welcome companion to its predecessor, *Garden History*, the journal of the Garden History Society, which is now appearing in a more scholarly format but remains dedicated mainly to English garden history. The emphasis of the new journal is international and interdisciplinary because "garden history," the editor writes in the first issue, "just like botanical history, sooner or later ignores national boundaries." The new journal has an international board of editors and plans to devote one issue annually to the history of the gardens of one particular country; it will be concerned with such subjects as "patronage, economic and social history, history of ideas, history of science, technology and engineering, architectural history, aesthetics, iconography, horticulture—all . . . topics which garden history must register."[69] In addition to coping with this formidable range of subjects, the journal will publish reviews and new documents.

Roy Strong dedicates his book, *The Renaissance Garden in England*, to the "memory of all those gardens destroyed by Capability Brown and his successors," and blames architects of the landscape garden for the "total obliteration" of the formal garden in England.[70] This explanation is too simple, but Strong is expressing the frustration of every historian of an art that must contend not only with changes of fashion but with "laughing Ceres" who reassumes the land laid out by the garden designer.[71] Despite this handicap, the relatively new discipline of garden history is flourishing and garden historians are busy laying out new designs formal and informal to explain the history of this fascinating art. Eleanor Perényi's recent book, *Green Thoughts*, shows that the literature of the garden has not died in the twentieth century. An opinionated alphabetical salad of anecdote, advice, and observation about gardens, the book is the work of an author steeped in the history, literature, and practical horticulture of the garden. Before World War II she lived in Hungary on an estate with a *jardin anglais*; she has read everything from Henry Wotton to the *Good Earth Catalogue*, and her book is full of perceptive observations, including ideas for research in garden history: she urges a "detailed study" of Hidcote, and a book on "woman's place in garden history."[72] This delightful book reminds us that garden history is not merely the domain of academic inquiry but a subject of enduring human concern. If Thomson's "bursting Prospect" defines its present state, Pope's vision of the unending prospect of humanistic study in the *Essay on Criticism* describes its future.

> Th' *increasing* Prospect *tires* our wandring Eyes,
> Hills peep o'er Hills, and *Alps* on *Alps* arise!
> (ll. 231-32)[73]

University of Nevada, Reno

NOTES

1. James Sambrook, ed., *The Seasons* (Oxford, 1981), p. 47.

2. *Influence Outside the British Isles* (Washington, D. C., 1974), p. v, "To The Memory of Christopher Hussey, 1899-1970"; Peter Willis, ed., *Furor Hortensis: Essays on the History of the English Landscape Garden in Memory of H. F. Clark* (Edinburgh, 1974).

3. Christopher Hussey, *English Gardens and Landscapes 1700-1750* (London, 1967); Joseph Burke, *English Art 1714-1800* (Oxford, 1976), p. 86. For Pevsner's remark, see *The Picturesque Garden and Its Influence Outside The British Isles*, ed. Nikolaus Pevsner. Dumbarton Oaks Colloquium on The History of Landscape Architecture, 1972 (Washington, D.C. 1974), p. v.

4. Christopher Hussey, *The Picturesque, Studies in a Point of View* (London, 1927). For Pevsner's remark, see *Picturesque Garden*, p. v.

5. H. F. Clark, "Eighteenth-Century Elysiums: The Rôle of 'Association' in the Landscape Movement," *Journal of the Warburg and Courtauld Institutes*, VI (1943), pp. 165-189, and Clark, *English Landscape Garden* (London, 1948).

6. "Notes on William Mason's 'Preface' to *An Heroic Epistle to William Chambers (1773)*," in Paget Toynbee, ed., *Satirical Poems by William Mason* (Oxford, 1926), p. 43.

7. Roy Strong, *The Renaissance Garden in England* (London, 1979), p. 7.

8. *Oxford History of English Art*, IX: *English Art 1714-1800* (Oxford, 1976), chap. 2, pp. 39-68.

9. *Ibid.*, pp. 39, 41, 44, 49, 53, 58, 59.

10. *Ibid.*, p. 68n. See Elizabeth Wheeler Manwaring, *Italian Landscape in Eighteenth-Century England: A Study Chiefly of the Influence of Claude Lorrain and Salvator Rosa on English Taste 1700-1800* (New York, 1925).

11. See, for example, the confused summary in David C. Streatfield, "Art and Nature in the English Landscape Garden: Design Theory and Practice, 1700-1818," in David C. Streatfield and Alistair M. Duckworth, *Landscape in the Gardens and the Literature of Eighteenth-Century England* (Los Angeles, 1981), pp. 3-87, and my review in *The Scriblerian*, XIV (Autumn, 1981), p. 48.

12. Christopher Thacker, *The History of Gardens* (Berkeley and Los Angeles, 1979), chaps. 12-14, pp. 181-226, quotation on p. 210.

13. *The Stoic* is the quarterly publication of Stowe School, Buckingham, Buckinghamshire.

14. George Clarke, "The Gardens of Stowe," *Apollo*, XCVII (June 1973), p. 558. In the same issue see Clarke, "Grecian Taste and Gothic Virtue: Lord Cobham's gardening programme and its iconography," pp. 566-571.

15. George B. Clarke, "Military Gardening: Bridgeman and the Ha-Ha, The History of Stowe—VIII," *The Stoic*, XXIV (December 1969), pp. 11-15, and "Moral Gardening, The History of Stowe—XI," *ibid.*, XXIV (July 1970), pp. 113-121.

16. Richard E. Quaintance, "Walpole's Whig Interpretation of Landscaping History," *Studies in Eighteenth-Century Culture*, IX (Madison, Wis., 1979), pp. 285-300.

17. Peter Willis, *Charles Bridgeman and the English Landscape Garden*, Studies in Architecture, XVII (London, 1977). For details, see my review in *Eighteenth-Century Studies*, XII (Summer, 1979), pp. 538-542.

18. Kenneth Woodbridge, "William Kent as Landscape-Gardener: A Re-Appraisal," *Apollo*, C (August 1974), pp. 126-137. For another revisionist account of Kent, see Morris R. Brownell, *Alexander Pope & the Arts of Georgian England* (Oxford, 1978), chap. 7.

19. Woodbridge, "William Kent as Landscape-Gardener," p. 135.

20. Dorothy Stroud, *Capability Brown*, 2nd ed. rev. (London, 1975), p. 7. See the review essay by Ronald Paulson, "Toward the Constable Bicentenary: Thoughts on Landscape Theory," *Eighteenth-Century Studies*, X (Winter, 1976-1977), p. 245, where he describes Hussey's preface as a "brilliant essay . . . largely intact despite the questioning of the revisionist garden historians."

21. A. A. Tait, *The Landscape Garden in Scotland 1735-1835* (Edinburgh, 1980), p. 1.

22. *Ibid.*, p. 5.

23. *Ibid.*, pp. 46, 20, 71.

24. Stephen Switzer, *The Nobleman, Gentleman, and Gardener's Recreation* (London, 1715), pp. xviii-xix.

25. Edward Malins and the Knight of Glin, *Lost Demesnes: Irish Landscape Gardening 1660-1845* (London, 1976), p. 71, n. 22.

26. *Ibid.*, p. 26.

27. Dora Wiebenson, *The Picturesque Garden in France* (Princeton, 1978).

28. *Ibid.*, pp. 27, 54, 99, xviii.

29. John Harris, *The Artist and the Country House: A history of country house and garden view painting in Britain 1540-1870* (London, 1979). See my review essay, "The Garden and the Topographical View," *Journal of Garden History*, I (July-September 1981), pp. 271-278.

30. John Harris, *Gardens of Delight: The Rococo English Landscape of Thomas Robins the Elder*, 2 vols. (London, 1978).

31. John Riely, "Shenstone's Walks: The Genesis of The Leasowes," *Apollo*, CX (September 1979), pp. 202-209; Morris R. Brownell, *Alexander Pope's Villa: Views of Pope's Villa, Grotto, and Garden—A Microcosm of English Landscape*, catalog of an exhibition at Marble Hill House, Twickenham, July 19 to September 28, 1980 (London, 1980).

32. John Dixon Hunt, *The Figure in the Landscape: Poetry, Painting, and Gardening during the Eighteenth Century* (Baltimore, 1976), p. 62.

33. Brownell, *Alexander Pope*, chaps. 3-9.

34. Peter Martin, *"Pursuing Innocent Pleasures": The Gardening World of Alexander Pope* (Hamden, Conn., 1983).

35. Michael McCarthy, "Eighteenth Century Amateur Architects and their Gardens," in Pevsner, ed., *Picturesque Garden*, pp. 33-55.

36. *Ibid.*, p. 44.

37. Mark Girouard, *Life in the English Country House: A Social and Architectural History* (New Haven, 1978).

38. S. Lang, "The Genesis of the English Landscape Garden," in Pevsner, ed., *Picturesque Garden*, p. 29.

39. "Theatres, Gardens, and Garden-Theatres," lecture presented at the annual meeting of the North Eastern Association for Eighteenth-Century Studies, Toronto, 1979. Hunt delivered the Franklin Jasper Walls lectures at the Pierpont Morgan Library in New York in 1981 on the influence of the Italian Renaissance garden on the arts of seventeenth-century England.

40. George Clarke, "Moral Gardening, The History of Stowe—X," *The Stoic*, XXIV (July 1970), pp. 113-121.

41. Judith Colton, "Merlin's Cave and Queen Caroline: Garden Art as Political Propaganda," *Eighteenth-Century Studies*, X (Fall, 1976), pp. 1-20.

42. James Turner, "Stephen Switzer and the Political Fallacy in Landscape Gardening History," *Eighteenth-Century Studies*, XI (Summer, 1978), pp. 489-496. Cf. Turner, *The Politics of Landscape: Rural Scenery and Society in English Poetry 1630-1660* (Cambridge, Mass., 1979).

43. David Jacques, "The Art and Sense of the Scriblerus Club in England, 1715-1735," *Garden History*, IV (Spring, 1976), pp. 30-53.

44. Professor Quaintance's tentative title for the book is *Political Meaning in English Landscaping of the Later Eighteenth Century.*

45. Carole Fabricant, "Binding and Dressing Nature's Loose Tresses: The Ideology of Augustan Landscape Design," *Studies in Eighteenth-Century Culture*, VIII (Madison, Wis., 1979), pp. 109-135, quotation on p. 110.

46. *Ibid.*, pp. 117, 120, 121, 109.

47. Ronald Paulson, "The Poetic Garden," chap. 2 in *Emblem and Expression: Meaning in English Art of the Eighteenth Century* (Cambridge, Mass., 1975), pp. 19-34. Cf. John Dixon Hunt, "Emblem and Expressionism in the Eighteenth-Century Landscape Garden," *Eighteenth-Century Studies*, IV (Spring, 1971), pp. 294-317.

48. Kenneth Woodbridge, "Henry Hoare's Paradise," *The Art Bulletin,* XLVII (March 1965), pp. 83-116.

49. Paulson, "Poetic Garden," pp. 34, 21; Paulson, "Thoughts on Landscape Theory," p. 245.

50. Paulson, "Poetic Garden," pp. 21, 22.

51. *Ibid.*, p. 32, n. 53.

52. James Turner, "The Structure of Henry Hoare's Stourhead," *Art Bulletin*, LXI (March 1979), p. 74.

53. *Ibid.*, p. 70.

54. Max F. Schulz, "The Circuit Walk of the Eighteenth-Century Landscape Garden and the Pilgrim's Circuitous Progress," *Eighteenth-Century Studies*, XV (Fall, 1981), pp. 1-25, quotations on pp. 12, 17.

55. Kenneth Woodbridge, "Irregular, Rococo or Picturesque?" review (with other books) of Dora Wiebenson, *The Picturesque Garden in France*, *Apollo*, CVIII (November 1978), pp. 356-358.

56. Barbara Maria Stafford, "Toward Romantic Landscape Perception: Illustrated Travels and the Rise of 'Singularity' as an Aesthetic Category," *Art Quarterly*, N.S., I (Autumn, 1977), reprinted in *Studies in Eighteenth-Century Culture*, X (Madison, Wis., 1981), pp. 17-75, quotation on p. 64.

57. Robin Gibson, review of "The Garden—A Celebration of One Thousand Years of British Gardening," Victoria and Albert Museum exhibition, Summer 1979, *The Burlington Magazine*, CXXI (July 1979), p. 459.

58. John Dixon Hunt and Peter Willis, eds., *The Genius of the Place: The English Landscape Garden 1620-1820* (London, 1975).

59. John Dixon Hunt, ed., *The English Landscape Garden: Examples of the Important Literature of the English Landscape Garden Movement Together with Some Earlier Garden Books* (New York, 1980).

60. Cataloged and edited by Hugh Pagan, catalog no. 37 (1977), item no. 247, pp. 51-53.

61. William Gilpin, *A Dialogue Upon the Gardens of the Right Honourable the Lord Viscount Cobham at Stow in Buckinghamshire* (1748), Augustan Reprint Society Publication no. 176 (Los Angeles, 1976), p. iv.

62. George Bickham, *The Beauties of Stow* (1750), Augustan Reprint Society Publications nos. 185-186 (Los Angeles, 1977).

63. Sir William Chambers, *An Explanatory Discourse by Tan Chet-Qua of Quang-Chew-Fu, Gent.* (1773), Augustan Reprint Society Publication no. 191 (Los Angeles, 1978).

64. John Serle, *A Plan of Mr. Pope's Garden* (1745), introduction by Morris R. Brownell, Augustan Reprint Society Publication no. 211 (Los Angeles, 1982).

65. Gibson, review of "The Garden," p. 451. Cf. Kenneth Woodbridge, "The British Garden: a partial view," *Apollo*, CX (August 1979), p. 149. For Thomas Robins, see Harris, *Gardens of Delight*.

66. Monique Mosser *et al.*, *Jardins en France 1760-1820: pays d'illusion, terre d'expériences*, catalog of an exhibition at the Hôtel de Sully, Paris, May 18 to September 11, 1977 (Paris, 1977). I would like to thank Professor Basil Guy for calling this catalog to my attention.

67. James Holloway and Lindsay Errington, *The Discovery of Scotland: The Appreciation of Scottish Scenery Through Two Centuries of Painting* (Edinburgh, 1978), chap. 2, pp. 13-21.

68. I am grateful to Professor Judith Colton for sending me a prospectus of this exhibition.

69. "Editorial," I (January-March 1981), pp. 1-2.

70. Strong, *Renaissance Garden in England*, pp. 6, 223.

71. Alexander Pope, *Epistle to Burlington*, line 176, p. 134, in F. W. Bateson, ed., *Epistles to Several Persons*, John Butt, gen. ed., *The Poems of Alexander Pope*, Twickenham Edition, III, ii (London, 1951).

72. Eleanor Perényi, *Green Thoughts: A Writer in the Garden* (New York, 1981), pp. 237, 264. I am grateful to Professor Richard Quaintance for calling this book to my attention.

73. E. Audra and Aubrey Williams, eds., *Pastoral Poetry and An Essay on Criticism, Poems of Pope*, Twickenham Edition, I (London, 1961), p. 265.

The Nomenclature of Style in Garden History*

Kenneth Woodbridge

The history of garden design is bedeviled by problems of nomenclature even more than that of other arts. The reason is partly semantic, in that words lose their precise meaning and become used in a general sense to the extent of being meaningless. A "knot garden," for instance, was originally a garden laid out in continuous interlacing bands, a figure as distinct as the "maze" with which it is often coupled, but it has become a term widely used to denote any compartmented or figured garden of the sixteenth and seventeenth centuries as opposed to the French embroidered parterres. The process can be seen happening in successive editions of gardening treatises such as Thomas Hill's *The Gardeners Labyrinth*, where the text remains the same but the illustrations change with gardening fashion. This occurs, for example, in the diagrams presenting "a proper knot" in 1577 and 1651.[1] John Evelyn used "knot" in his description of the embroidered parterre at the Luxembourg in 1644 and confusion is complete when John James makes the word the equivalent of both "noeud" and "massif" in his translation of Dézallier d'Argenville's *La Théorie et la practique du jardinage* (1712).

Other difficulties arise from the fact that gardens are a composite and complex art and therefore difficult to classify. "The formal system of gardening has suffered from a question-begging name," wrote Reginald Blomfield in 1892. "The formal treatment of gardens ought, perhaps, to be called the architectural treatment of gardens, for it consists in the extension of the principles of design which govern the house to the grounds which surround it."[2]

Blomfield was, of course, speaking as an architect; and history was a justification of practice. For him there were two styles, "Formal" and "Landscape." Alicia Amherst managed without any stylistic characteristics.[3] Edouard André distinguished between *genre*, the character a landscape (either natural or modified by man) is perceived to *have*, and *style*, the imprint *given* to a park or garden by a man's work. He recognized three genres—noble or grand, gay or smiling, picturesque or wild—and three styles—geometric, landscape, and composite.[4]

*This article is the modified version of a lecture given at the Victoria and Albert Museum in June 1979 on the occasion of the exhibition "The Garden."

More recently terms such as "mannerist," "baroque," and "rococo," used to classify styles in other areas of art history, have been taken over to apply to garden design. Marie-Louise Gothein in her monumental *History of Garden Art* uses "baroque" in connection with late sixteenth-century Italian gardens like the Villa d'Este at Tivoli, which are now more frequently labeled "mannerist." She writes of France "adapting the baroque gardens of her country to the requirements of the rococo style." But she uses these terms sparingly and in a general sense without defining them. When she wishes to be specific, she makes qualifications like "straight-lined, architectural or 'formal' garden styles."[5]

When styles are examined closely, one of two things tends to happen: there is either a closer definition leading to the necessity of proposing other categories to harbor what has been excluded; or there is a widening of the concept, as Heinrich Wölfflin did in *Principles of Art History*, in which he was able to regard the whole of the art of seventeenth- and early eighteenth-century Europe as covered by the word "baroque."[6] Such portmanteau words are useful to indicate to suitably programmed minds the area in which communication is taking place. "Mannerist" may then signal "sinuous and elegantly contorted forms, a delight in precious or semi-precious materials . . . a taste for the ingenious and bizarre, complex and ambivalent compositions and all forms of visual wit"; "Baroque," "exuberant decoration, expansive curvaceous forms and an air of solemn, sometimes pompous grandeur"; Rococo, "light, elegant decorative style . . . of freely handled S-shaped curves . . . naturalistic motifs" combined with "unrepresentational ornament" . . . and "a tendency towards asymmetry."[7]

Clearly these bald definitions have had to be qualified and extended to embrace other art forms and the enormous variety that exists within a given period. When it is a question of garden design, the terms can more obviously apply to the architectural accompaniments than to the design of the garden as such. Here, broad trends from the fourteenth to the eighteenth century can thus be summarized as follows:

> from horticultural to architectural emphasis;
> from closed to open form;
> from the obviously artificial to the seemingly natural.

The terms commonly used in connection with these trends are "renaissance," "baroque," and "picturesque." The first is not really a stylistic term at all but a label covering the period when classical canons and motifs (particularly Roman) became generally accepted as stylistic sources. "Baroque," originally meaning misshaped, was used as a term of abuse for architecture that was regarded as breaking the classical rules. In the 1880s it was adopted as a nonpejorative stylistic term. Neither "renaissance" nor "baroque" was used at the time the style developed; they are umbrellas sheltering a mixed bag of characteristics occurring in the art forms of a given period. "Picturesque," on the other hand, differs in having been applied to a style with a specific meaning in the past, that is to say, in relation to the character of gardens or their ornament at the time they were made. Like other stylistic terms, it is now used to cover a variety of tendencies in garden design both in England and in France (*Plates 1 and 2*). The question is, does "picturesque" adequately describe these tendencies, or does it, by creating a mental set, inhibit us from seeing the true nature of what we are trying to understand? In its origins at the beginning of the eighteenth century it meant "that which concerns painting" or "all that is suitable to form the subject of an effective and striking picture." This immediately begs the question, "What is an effective and striking picture?" The answer was implied in the image of the garden as seen through the eyes of seventeenth-century engravers deriving from Paul Bril. When required to make a picture of the "regular," "formal," "architectural" (or whatever you like to call them) gardens of the time, in almost every case the artist added an invented, broken, irregular foreground of figures in a stylized natural setting (*Plate 3*). The irregular and the natural are so essential to the concept of what a picture should be that often these characteristics are extended beyond the foreground to all those parts of the picture that are not architectural. What we are looking at in Nicolas Perelle's engraving of Rueil is not a style of garden but a style of picture. This cannot be sufficiently emphasized.

From the start, however, the concept of the "picturesque" embraces irregularity and is associated with the "natural" as opposed to the "artificial." But these two qualities do not constitute of themselves what is understood by "picturesque." "Nature"—the "natural"—is too vague and varied a concept to be identified with any particular style of garden design. "A garden should owe more to nature than to art, which must only be used to show it off to best advantage."[8] And, "Apparent art, in its proper province, is almost as important as apparent nature. They contrast agreeably; but their provinces ever should be kept distinct."[9]

Irregularity is a quality that belongs to situations, either by reason of the site, as at Saint-Cloud, or due to a conception that cannot be regarded as pictorial, for example, in a plan like Antoine Richard's project for the Petit Trianon (*Plate 4*). If "picturesque" means anything as a style, it is the direct appeal by purely visual means, or, as Christopher Hussey has put it, "An art that addresses the reason, even though it does so through the eye, does not stress visual qualities."[10] Before "Capability" Brown the rational element was of prime importance, both in the sense that gardens were designed with "level and line," as it was put, and because association and allegorical intentions were important. Apart from the fact that "picturesqueness" was denied to both Brown and William Kent by Uvedale Price, to apply it as a stylistic label indiscriminately to all Kent's gardening diverts attention from his true intentions and indeed from the complexities of the situation in which he worked (*Plates 5 and 6*). There are certainly picturesque elements in his garden designs, that is to say, scenes that derive from purely visual considerations. These, however, are equaled by others where rational factors such as implied geometry or association are predominant. So deeply ingrained in the thinking about this period of garden history is the idea that Kent was inspired by the paintings of Claude Lorrain that comparisons have been stretched beyond the bounds of probability, while other sources such as direct experience of Italian gardens, the theater, and the extended vistas of André Le Nôtre have been ignored. Emphasis on a pictorial approach diverts attention from other important characteristics of pre-1760 English gardens. Whether they close straight vistas or are approached indirectly, buildings invite movement—we see them—we want to reach them. Connecting walks are not just a passage from one picture to another; they are in themselves a spatial experience, now open, now closed, at different levels. It is the quality of Kent's spaces that Thomas Whately singles out for praise:

> The walk to the cottage [at Claremont], though destitute of many natural advantages . . . is yet the finest part of the garden: for a grove is there planted, in a gently-curved direction, all along the side of a hill, and on the edge of a wood, which rises above it. . . . The intervals, winding here like a glade, and widening there into broader openings, differ in extent, in figure, and direction; but all the groupes, the lines, and the intervals are collected together into large general clumps, each of which is . . . both compact and free, identical and various. The whole is a place wherein to tarry with secure delight, or saunter with perpetual amusement.[11]

In his penetrating analysis of English gardens of the 1760s Whately gives four of his 257 pages to "picturesque beauty," "a denomination in general expressive of excellence," he writes, "but which, by being too indiscriminately applied, may be sometimes productive of errors." He continues to discuss the differences between painting and gardening, in order to conclude that the term is applicable only to certain objects in nature.[12] A more precise definition of picturesque beauty (rough, broken, irregular) he left to his friend, William Gilpin. By that definition, ruins and gothic architecture are picturesque; classical architecture is not.

Of course, styles are constantly evolving, and do not really fall into the neat categories that this kind of nomenclature suggests (*Plates 7 and 8*). Just as what was once regarded as early baroque is now classed as mannerist, so "rococo," once seen as a phase of late baroque, is now distinguished as a separate style, first used for a specific form of decoration, extended to architecture, then to painting, and now to garden design. Like "picturesque," "rococo" has associations with such qualities as irregularity, asymmetry, and naturalistic. In fact, the term "pittoresque" was used in the eighteenth century of a form of decoration related to the rococo style. In this sense it meant that ornament was composed of figurative elements without regard to regularity or symmetry—like a painter would do it, as it were. "Rococo" as a stylistic term embracing painting refers especially to Watteau and Boucher. Watteau painted garden scenes based on the gardens of the Luxembourg in decay. The pastoral scenes of Watteau, Boucher, and Fragonard have been called "rococo-romantic" as opposed to "classical-romantic" (Poussin, Claude, et al) and the term extended to include such parks and gardens as Rambouillet, the Desert de Retz, Bagatelle, or Parc Monceau. Now there is certainly a close relation between painters like Boucher and rococo decoration. There is also a link between painters and gardens in that the buildings which adorned them were called "fabriques," a term borrowed from the jargon of the studios, meaning ruins, buildings, and other architectural features that painters invented as elements in the composition of a picture. Some *fabriques* such as the Column at Retz or the Pagoda at Chanteloup cannot necessarily be called "rococo," and the cottages in Boucher's pastoral scenes are related to those in Marie Antoinette's Hameau at Petit Trianon and thence to Blaise Hamlet near Bristol, which many would describe as "picturesque."

Here we come to the crux of the "rococo" problem, the firm association of the term with the post-Regency style in France between 1730 and 1760. In gardens I would associate this with a preference for the relatively small and intimate, compared with the grandiose and expansive parks of Louis XIV's era, or what is found in Jacques Blondel's *Maisons de Plaisance* (1738) compared with Dézallier d'Argenville's *Jardinage* (1709), especially in the ornamental details, rather than any radical departure from axiality and a rectilinear scheme in the framework of the garden. Thus there are rococo elements in Blondel's trellis pavilions (*Plate 9*) compared with those of Dézallier, or again in Blondel's designs for parterres compared with those of Le Nôtre.

"Rococo" is used as a stylistic term for a parallel period in England, legitimately for certain forms of furniture and interior decoration, but extended to include fanciful gothic and Chinese styles, which of course included garden buildings. Sir John Summerson clearly differentiates:

> Both the Gothic and the Chinese, in the middle of the eighteenth century, enjoyed a freedom somewhat akin to the Rococo which, from across the channel, sent occasional eddies of influences across Palladian England.[13]

Mark Girouard associates rococo with certain tendencies shared by the members of the St. Martin's Lane Academy, but he does so tentatively:

> Pulled in different directions by their inherited disciplines, by the seduction of the rococo, by the claims of a new liberty, which let them roam in Chinese and Gothic as well as Classic pastures, the artists and architects of the Hogarth set leave one with a synthesis never fully completed. English baroque and English Palladianism on the one hand, English Neo-classicism on the other, all present a clearer image than what—for the lack of a better phrase—one is forced to call English rococo.[14]

I am not sure when the term was first applied to English gardens—I think possibly by Nikolaus Pevsner in his essay, "The Genesis of the Picturesque." Rococo, he says, is "the style *par excellence* of variety, irregularity and the *aperçu*." Writing of the origins of the English landscape garden in the first third of the eighteenth century, he said that the architects and gardeners who created them were brought up in the atmosphere of the early rococo and "could not help interpreting the nature of the Whig, the nature of the rationalist, the nature of the *virtuoso* into a nature of the Rococo." Pope's garden, "with its wiggly paths, its minute mount, its cockle shells and minerals, and its effects of variety on a small scale" would now be called "Rococo more than anything else."[15] And the avenue of cypresses leading to the Obelisk? Hardly a rococo gesture. As for the architects, I can only think of Vanbrugh, Hawksmoor, Archer, Gibbs, and Kent; surely not rococo? Finally, Joseph Burke writes of Stourhead (*Plate 10*), where a temple embodying the classical ideal overlooks a lake whose form is largely determined by the contours of the ground,

> The plan of the lake resembles in shape the outline of a well-known type of rococo girandole mirror. . . . Whereas Stowe has the breadth of at least a fragment of the Roman campagna, Stourhead is Vergilian landscape on a miniature scale; it is rococo-Claudian.[16]

Surely, according to a previous definition, classical-romantic!

And so, in conclusion, back to "picturesque." Wölfflin makes this distinction: "picturesque"—a quality inherent in the object; painterly—a matter of perception, how a thing is perceived. That is, picturesque is an effect; painterly, a method. This is somewhat similar to the distinction between "genre" and "style" made by André. Applied to garden design, when can "picturesque" be regarded as a style? I would say, when the intention is to create a pictorial effect, stressing purely visual qualities, and I would qualify this by saying visual qualities as these were conceived in the late eighteenth and early nineteenth centuries. There are many gardens, like Stourhead (*Plate 11*), which have evolved over a long period. Gardens are not like pictures or furniture—all of a piece. There are some elements that are purely picturesque in intention whose quality is solely to tease the eye; others whose messages are more indirect. Humphry Repton used a pictorial method in his designs even though he introduced regular features in the foreground of his compositions. Was he therefore not "picturesque"? Eighteenth-century writers on aesthetic matters used "picturesque" in a specific sense; are we justified in extending it to subjects they excluded? I do not pretend to have an answer to these questions. Nor do I believe there should be one. Each writer will choose the words that suit him. But the trouble with labels is that they provide a ready-made description that may mislead and thus come between us and a direct response to a work of art. Should we not, where possible, avoid them and, to adapt what Professor Gombrich has written in another context, look at each garden in a period as an effort in its own right, created in a given situation?

Bath, England

NOTES

1. See Kenneth Woodbridge, "The Rise and Decline of the Garden Knot," *Architectural Review*, CLXV (June 1979), pp. 324-329.

2. Reginald Blomfield, *The Formal Garden in England* (London, 1892), p. 2.

3. Alicia Amherst, *A History of Gardening in England* (London, 1895).

4. Edouard André, *L'Art des jardins* (Paris, 1879), pp. 136-140, 148-152.

5. Marie-Louise Gothein, *History of Garden Art* (New York, 1928).

6. Heinrich Wölfflin, *Principles of Art History: The Problem of the Development of Style in Later Art* (London, 1934).

7. *Penguin Dictionary of Decorative Arts* (London, 1977).

8. Dézallier d'Argenville, *La Théorie et la practique du jardinage*, rev. ed. (Paris, 1713), p. 18.

9. William Shenstone, "Unconnected Thoughts on Gardening," from *The Works in Verse and Prose* (1764), quoted in John Dixon Hunt and Peter Willis, eds., *The Genius of the Place* (London, 1975), p. 293.

10. Christopher Hussey, *The Picturesque* (London, 1927).

11. Thomas Whately, *Observations on Modern Gardening* (London, 1770), pp. 48-50.

12. *Ibid.*, pp. 146-150.

13. Sir John Summerson, *Architecture in Britain, 1530-1830* (London, 1953), p. 238.

14. Mark Girouard, "English Art and the Rococo," *Country Life*, CXXVII (January-February 1960),

15. Nikolaus Pevsner, "The Genesis of The Picturesque," *Architectural Review*, XCVI (1944), pp. 142, 146.

16. Joseph Burke, *English Art 1714 to 1800* (Oxford, 1976), p. 63.

Pope's Twickenham Revisited

John Dixon Hunt

It is inconceivable that there is anything left to be written about Alexander Pope's garden and grotto at Twickenham. Yet his villa continues to elude our analysis. So many interpretations have been brought to bear upon it that its legendary scenes have taken on that "chequer'd shade" which *The Dunciad* attributed to critics who pick holes to let in their own illumination.[1] One strong and recent ray of light, Morris Brownell's *Alexander Pope & the Arts of Georgian England*, has argued so forcibly for Twickenham as a "Paradigm of the Picturesque Garden"[2] that it is timely to review the available evidence and attempt once again to "place" Pope's gardens.

It is essential to see Pope's garden and grotto as an expression of traditional ideas, however modified, rather than as the striving after notions which he could scarcely have known and which indeed reached definition only after his death. We are easily led into this latter error because his first commentators, Horace Walpole and Joseph Spence, sought to annex his work to the developments that they saw in garden design after 1750.[3] Eager to champion an English landscape style, early historians (as recent ones) have imposed their teleological patterns upon Pope's endeavors at Twickenham, which in their accounts become a precursor of later Brownian or picturesque modes of landscape. Yet what that garden and grotto declared and what Pope himself constantly articulated on their behalf is a debt to Rome. It is here that we must begin in any search for an adequate version of their meaning.

Pope's earliest garden utterance, in *The Guardian*, no. 173, of 1713, makes clear that it is "the Taste of the Ancients in their Gardens" which guides his own thinking. Martial ("Sed *rure vero, barbaroque* laetatur"), Virgil, and Homer provide him on this occasion with his authority; and having translated Homer's description of the gardens of Alcinous, Pope reminds his readers that Sir William Temple had thought that "this Description contains all the justest Rules and Provisions which can go toward composing the best Gardens."[4] The difficulty, of course, was precisely that ancient gardens had not survived and therefore the language of Homer's description of Alcinous's garden layout and especially of its manipulation of water laid itself open to tendentious interpretation. Unlike the English imitation of classical poetry, unlike even the neo-Palladian emulation of classical, Vitruvian principles, Pope's wish to invoke ancient gardening was constrained by the simple fact that he could not know what it would have been.

But English Palladianism, with which Pope was much involved albeit on the periphery of the movement, provided a model solution.[5] For although architects could and did study classical buildings and ruins, they also looked as much to modern Italian versions of antique architecture. The classical past was thus mediated to the present via Italian Renaissance examples. Palladio's role in this process needs little exposition here, nor does Pope's awareness of it: his library at Twickenham contained busts of both Palladio and his first English disciple, Inigo Jones; that he was aware of the mediating processes of contemporary and Palladian architecture is clear from his compliment to Lady Howard in 1727 on the room in Marble Hill House which was modeled on Palladio's interpretation of a Roman atrium.[6] But what does need comment is the place that garden design occupies within the Palladian revival.

Too often critics have expressed surprise that neo-Palladian mansions came to be set amid the "natural" scenery of the English landscape garden. Yet if the strongly classical provenance of Pope's and some of his friends' ideas on gardens was registered instead of trying to establish their place in *later* traditions of English gardening, that incongruity between Palladian villa and its setting would seem far less significant. This may to some seem "reactionary,"[7] but it has the merits of being both historical and attentive to the interconnections of Pope's concerns. For it would be odd if there were not a relationship between his "neoclassicism as a poet" and his theories and practice as a gardener.[8]

Pope's debts to the idea of ancient gardening are declared everywhere in his writings just as they are acknowledged by his critics, who, nevertheless, seem to be able to make nothing of them. Even Brownell, for instance, can pause in his proleptic commentary on Pope's picturesque taste to note that his description of a garden he had never seen (Bolingbroke's La Source in France) relies upon Horace for its imagery.[9] Certainly, from the classical references in that early *Guardian* essay, through his reading of Pliny's account of his villas, to his late plans for his riverside frontage, Pope's controlling ideas are all classical.[10] In November 1720, not long after he has taken up residence in Twickenham, Pope talks of "My Tusculum"; his allusion to Cicero's country house anticipates by seven years Robert Castell's discussion of Pliny's country retreats and their garden layouts in *The Villas of the Ancients Illustrated*, which was dedicated to Pope's friend, Lord Burlington.

Castell's extrapolation of Pliny's villa designs from his writings, as I have argued briefly elsewhere,[11] is part of Burlington's Palladian schemes; it proceeds by reading the Latin text of Pliny's descriptions in the light of eighteenth-century knowledge of ancient gardening, which—given the virtual absence of significant remains—means in effect projecting upon it the experience of modern Italian gardens and their relationships with classical ruins on the Grand Tour. Throughout the seventeenth century English visitors to Italy admired Renaissance gardens, often in close proximity to Roman remains, and believed the modern creations to be revivals in the true spirit of antique garden art, of which they had read extensively in Latin texts. When travelers surveyed the seven hills of

Rome, they were well aware that the Pincio was the old *mons hortorum* or that the Esquiline had been "famous for the Gardens of Mecanas [Maecenus], so much celebrated by Horace."[12] At Tivoli and Frascati English visitors knew from their reading that they were on territory "much frequented by the ancient Romans, who had their Villa's": Edmund Warcupp's *Italy in Its Original Glory, Ruine and Revival* claimed that the Villa d'Este was worthy of "the greatness and magnificence of the ancients," while at Frascati Richard Lassels explained that "here Cato was born, here Lucullus delighted himself, and Cicero studied."[13] After visiting the modern villas and gardens at Frascati, Ellis Veryard "walk'd out to see the ruins of the ancient *Tusculum*, lying on an Hill about two Miles from the Town, where we found nothing but a great heap of Rubbish, with some few old Walls; and an House almost entire, said to have been Cicero's, where he writ his *Tusculan Questions*."[14] Such identifications say more for the ingenuity of Italian guides, knowing what their visitors wanted, than for rigorous archaeology; but English tourists, doubtless bewitched by being on classical ground, would believe anything, just as they also retained a strong sense of Italian Renaissance gardens as somehow authentic revivals of classical predecessors. And their creative confusions were inevitably the impetus for gardening schemes in England after their return from the Grand Tour—John Raymond, for instance, observed at the Villa d'Este that "this shall be my patterne for a Countrey seat."[15]

The development of the English garden during the first sixty years of the seventeenth century is entirely a history of the steady implementation of Italianate designs, often on the assumption that they had classical authority.[16] James Howell's *Instructions and Directions for Forreine Travell* of 1650 urged the tourist in Italy to note "the trace, forme and site of any famous *Structure*, the Platforms of *Gardens, Aqueducts, Grots, Sculptures*, and such particularities belonging to *accommodation* or *beauty* of dwelling."[17] After the Restoration there was, of course, an alternative taste in gardens derived from France that landed gentry could invoke when they remodeled their estates. But the French taste did not displace the Italian— indeed, there is evidence to suggest that for political as much as aesthetic reasons Italian designs were set up in rivalry to French ones: Timothy Nourse and John Woolridge both championed Italian gardens at the expense of French.[18] And by the early years of the eighteenth century England was just as full of gardens and grottoes modeled upon Italian sources or memories as of designs derived from André Le Nôtre. Now the significance of these long traditions of English admiration for Italianate gardens and their distinct color romanus have never been studied for their contribution to the early English landscape movement. Yet Pope's garden and grotto at Twickenham, like Castell's reconstructions of Pliny's villas, must owe their essential inspiration to these traditions whereby classical villas and gardens, mediated by modern Italian examples, were established upon English soil.[19]

Pope's use of the term "villa" has been interpreted rightly as an indication of his commitment to Palladian ideas. But as he registered in *The Guardian*, no. 173, where he quotes Martial's "Baiana nostri Villa," the word has strong classical associations as well as a meaning that includes house and garden. The word was used throughout the last half of the seventeenth century to signal the classical and modern Italian resonances of a country seat: as Douglas Chambers has shown, the third Earl of Arundel used the word to describe his gardens at Albury, Surrey, sixty-five years before the first instance recorded by the *Oxford English Dictionary*; it was similarly used by John Aubrey in his watercolors of Easton-Piers, Wiltshire, executed in 1669.[20] Since both Albury and Aubrey's gardens were distinctly Italianate, the use of the word "villa" is perhaps designed to underline that characteristic design; Pope's fondness for the same word fifty or so years later is surely because it still retains an Italian coloring both modern and classical.

Like Aubrey, Pope never visited Italy. But we know that he studied Roman antiquities in Johann Georg Graevius's *Thesaurus* and modern buildings in Pieter Schenk's *Romae Novae Delineatio*.[21] It seems inconceivable, too, that he would not have discussed gardens with his friends who had made the Grand Tour—Burlington, William Kent, Joseph Spence. The latter's letters and journals from his first visits to Italy often notice classical remains—he brought Pope some marble fragments from Egeria's Grotto in Rome—classical ruins like Virgil's tomb closely related to modern gardens, and various forms of villa gardens "with statues and fountains sloping down half the side of a hill."[22] In short, the whole ambience of Pope's architectural and gardenist circle was distinctly Italianate.

It remains, therefore, to explore his grotto and garden in the light of these Italian absorptions, contributing to Maynard Mack's elegant and learned survey of their literary associations some sense of their architectural contexts.[23] The grotto is perhaps the last English example of any significance in a line of Italianate creations throughout the seventeenth century,[24] and Pope maintains not only some of the design features that distinguished the grottoes at Wilton, Woburn, or Moore Park but also suggests that he is conscious of the Italian origins of this English tradition of grotto making.

We know that the legends of Numa and Egeria were part of Pope's "Poetical villa" and that he planned to formalize or "complete" those allusions by incorporating a statue of the nymph with an inscription—"like that beautiful antique one which you know I am so fond of."[25] If funds did not permit Pope to execute this idea, we can still have some sense of how it would have looked from Henry Hoare's grotto at Stourhead where such a statue and Pope's verse translation of the inscription were installed. The whole contrivance amalgamated literary sources (classical, in the legends of Egeria and of nymphs presiding over springs of water; modern, in the Latin inscription), classical sculpture (the so-called Cleopatra or Ariadne from the Belvedere sculpture garden in the Vatican, well known through engravings, much visited by tourists, and imitated by such as Hoare), classical remains (the "Egerian Grotto," [*Plate 12*], shown to tourists just off the Appian Way and frequently engraved with a sleeping nymph in its niche), and the many Renaissance imitations of such grottoes and nymphaeums in gardens (Villa Giulia, for instance, or Villa Carpi, both in Rome).[26] Pope's plan, like his later project to install river gods on the lawn beside the Thames, invoked a whole congeries of classical ideas that Renaissance gardens had tried to realize in palpable forms. The nymph (*Plate 13*) and her allusion to the inspiratory powers of such a spring as Pope discovered in his grotto were part of his claim that it was a "Musaeum."[27] It was the place where his muses communicated with his best self, as is suggested in visible form by William Kent's well-known drawing of the poet (*Plate 14*) in the traditional pose of meditation (his chin supported by a hand) and decorated above with images of what appear to be butterflies, emblems of Psyche.

But "musaeum" also signified something of the modern "museum," a role which Pope's grotto performed with its elaborate collection of mineral specimens and rocky souvenirs; it was these that his gardener, John Serle, celebrated after Pope's death in his "Account of the MATERIALS which compose the Grotto."[28] In this aspect of the poet's Twickenham there was also an Italianate component, although one that has received little attention. Seventeenth-century English visitors to Italian gardens not only marveled at their variety and the often intricate contrivances of their grotto work but connected such gardenist entertainments readily with the cabinets of curiosities that were adjacent in the villas. Thus Veryard in Rome at the Villa Ludovisia moves smoothly from admiring the "Garden . . . very artificially disposed into Walks and Terrasses, fill'd with Fountains, wetting Spots, Statues, Urns, Tombs, and other pieces of Antiquity" to the "many stupendious Cabinets of Natural and Artificial Rarities" inside the two palaces;[29] John Ray in his *Observations . . .* of 1673 had shown a similar taste for gardens and museums. It is clear that an interest in the variety and marvels of Italian gardens was equally maintained in those *Kunst-und-Wunderkammer* which most seventeenth-century palaces and villas also possessed. That it is not absurd to think such traditions sustained Pope's grotto-musaeum is perhaps clearer if the role of his aquatic contrivances is considered in this context. For a much admired part of Italian garden experience was the hydraulic machinery and the wondrous effects it produced: Pratolino, north of Florence, and the Villa Aldobrandini at Frascati were both particularly famous for their waterworks. The vogue inevitably passed to England, where as late as 1729 the nurseryman and garden writer, Stephen Switzer, issued *An Introduction to a General System of Hydrostaticks and Hydraulicks*; it is a book that seems to sort oddly with his ideas on garden design if we do not recall the Italian origins of both. Pope, of course, had no hydraulic machinery, but he somehow managed to contrive "three falls of water" in the grotto by 1740 and the *Newcastle General Magazine* in 1748 wrote ecstatically of its waterworks:

> Here it gurgles in a gushing Rill thro' fractur'd Ores and Flints; there it drips from depending Moss and Shells; here again, washing Beds of Sand and Pebbles, it rolls in Silver Streamlets; and there it rushes out in Jets and Fountains; while the Caverns of the Grot incessantly echo with a soothing Murmur of aquatick sounds.[30]

The marvels of Pope's waterworks were of a piece with (if less ambitious than) Italianate predecessors and in conjunction with the mineral specimens and exhibits of his grotto go far to make us understand his claim for Twickenham as a "study for Virtuosi."[31]

But in the same letter to Bolingbroke where he boasts of his musaeum and virtuoso's study, Pope also claims that the grotto is "a Scene for Contemplation." That he means it is an apt setting for his contemplative life—Kent's drawing is again the visual rendition of that verbal meaning—should not distract us from the emphatically theatrical significance of "Scene." About the garden itself both Pope and his friends made similar suggestions—the "multiplied scenes of your little garden" was Bolingbroke's version.[32] Now the connections of gardens and grottoes with theater are intricate. Susan Lang has insisted that the "influence of the theatre" was "the decisive factor . . . in the earlier phases of the eighteenth-century garden," and certainly Pope was fascinated enough by the theater to see natural as well as garden scenery in theatrical terms.[33] But beyond the impact of scene painting on the early English landscape garden was surely the stronger influence of garden and grotto scenery organized and experienced theatrically in Continental gardens. The Italian garden had lent itself increasingly during the sixteenth and seventeenth centuries as a location for dramatic performances, and its shapes and the shapes in which engravers recorded its imagery testify to these theatrical connections. Above all in grottoes, such as those beneath the villa at Pratolino or in the Hall of Parnassus at the Villa Aldobrandini, the hydraulic machinery contrived scenes which with their moving and vocal or musical effects struck many visitors as miniature dramas. Pope's friend, William Kent, had been particularly impressed at Pratolino by the "very fine groto's adorn'd with shells and petrified stone with pretty water works as Galatea coming out of her Grotto drawn by Dolfini."[34] So that Pope would think of both his grotto and his garden in terms of theatrical scenes suggests his recognition of longer traditions of garden and theater than are generally supposed.

Pope's Twickenham was a theater in other ways. Maynard Mack has shown how expertly and effectively the poet invoked his rural retreat in his satires. Just as Kent's drawing catches a dramatic moment of Pope posing as contemplative man, so he presented himself in his poems in various roles, the most pervasive and persuasive of which was undoubtedly that of the "virtuous recluse, the Horatian *beatus ille* figure."[35] For this role his garden and grotto provided the ideal stage, a scene or theater where his public and personal selves could perform. But it was essential to this role playing in both his writings and his private life that his "scenes" were informed by what Mack has termed Pope's "truer, more 'primitive' classicism . . . reaching behind the overlay of time and custom, notably in this instance Italian and French custom."[36]

Such an emphasis would appear to undermine Pope's debts to Italy which this essay has sought to develop. Yet the difficulty, already noted, with any ambition to recover the truer classicism of gardens was simply that its examples no longer existed, so that modern gardenists were forced to re-create Latin literary texts in the light of Renaissance knowledge and practice. (It would follow perhaps that Italian examples, as being somehow nearer to that true classicism, would be preferred to French.) But Pope's work at Twickenham was not a straightforward translation of Italian elements into an English garden and grotto. Like his literary efforts to make Homer and Horace speak good English, his gardening was a matter of finding equally apt English visual idioms for antique and modern Italian forms. Given his mistrust of mere size in the *Epistle to Burlington*, the reduction and miniaturizing of effects in his grotto and "little garden," if not deliberate, acquired a retrospective significance. Pope knew at least by the 1730s that Augustan values could realistically be accommodated in contemporary England only in diminished or adjusted terms: this was as true of Horace's villa life as of Horace's poetry. So I think that we must attend in much of Pope's theoretical and practical gardening to the sense that his achievements at Twickenham registered a skepticism with the relevance to England of Italian schemes.

The grotto may have been in the long line of Italianate grottoes, but its very lack of elaborate hydraulic effects implicitly denies any mannerist extravagence such as Kent had found at Pratolino. Its "truer, more 'primitive' classicism" brought it nearer to realizing the natural ("arte laboratum nulla") grotto of Ovid's *Metamorphoses* III.[37] Similarly, Pope's inability to install the statue of the nymph and the inscription suitably denied him the chance to emulate the luxury of Renaissance gardens, as did the failure to complete his riverside scheme. It is true that nowhere does Pope specifically imply that his unfulfilled projects could have this meaning; yet the garden itself and his attitudes toward it lend some support to that interpretation.

There seems to be some assumption by Pope's commentators that his garden and grotto represented different styles and tastes. But in their creative adaptation of Renaissance imagery to the recovery of classical garden art they are surely of a piece. The color romanus of the garden is clear from its scattered urns, classical inscriptions, statues of "Deities" and "Antike busttos," the obelisk (a significantly Roman item, often noted by tourists in villa gardens), a triumphal arch, and the Shell Temple, which contemporaries recognized as a classical rotunda.[38] The "grove-work" of which Pope spoke so proudly to Spence was also a characteristic feature of Italian gardens, as its quincunx planting was a classical emphasis.[39] The piece of fountain statuary with an inscription that Pope contemplated in 1725 was another Italianate item, but his early *Guardian* essay had also implied the ancient imprimatur for "Fountains . . . disposed very remarkably."[40] Finally, the spaces of Pope's garden, upon which every visitor seems to have commented, were a smaller and less elaborately contrived exercise in Italianate garden management whereby visitors were led about its various and intriguing territory.[41]

Only one important representation of Pope's garden survives, Kent's drawing of the Shell Temple (*Plate 15*), but it captures wittily both the classical tonality of the garden and the fantasy of its creator that was necessarily involved in making antique/Renaissance gardens speak good

English. The fanciful addition of a group of visiting classical deities suggests very neatly the visionary attitude of Pope himself to the garden and grotto. We have it on his own testimony[42] that he surrendered himself there to dreams and visions; but the whole complex of garden, groves, and grotto was but the realization, as best he could with limited resources and space, of a dream of a classical villa. Kent's drawing simply extrapolates Pope's fantasies and realizes them in an image of a slightly improbable antique scene with two diminutive Georgian figures.

Perhaps nowhere do Pope's ambitions for his villa (*Plate 16*) as well as his due sense of their wishful potential reveal themselves as clearly as in the scheme for his Thames riverside communicated to Joseph Spence in 1743.[43] It involved statues of two river gods, as direct an allusion to classical literature and sculpture as could be made, and, furthermore, one that was frequently employed in Renaissance villa gardens; there were also to be little temples, terms, busts, and two inscriptions. The whole complex has been interpreted by Mack as an elaborate testimony to Pope's sense of his place in a tradition of accommodating classical poetry to new, local situations or, in Mack's words, "of enlarging and enriching the national culture by causing to be poured into it the great works of classical antiquity." The Latin inscriptions from Politian's *Ambra* and Virgil's *Georgics* alluded to river gods, who, once installed beside Pope's own Thames, would testify to the place of his own poetic career in the continuities of classical and Renaissance poetry. Mack, following Spence's modern editor and Spence himself, focuses attention upon Poliziano; but besides his Latin poem, *Ambra*, which is devoted to praise of Homer, there was a poem in Italian with the same title by Lorenzo the Magnificent himself. And this *Ambra* refers to the little river that runs near Lorenzo's villa at Poggio a Caiano and is to be seen in the upper left-hand corner of Gustave Utens's lunette (*Plate 17*). Joseph Spence actually visited this villa in the early 1730s on his first Grand Tour.[44] It seems inconceivable that Pope's invocation of *Ambra* in one of his riverside inscriptions was not intended to signal how his own villa beside the Thames maintained in an English setting, however modified, the potent traditions of villa life which the Renaissance had revived on the basis of their knowledge of classical literature. Maynard Mack thinks this may be "pursuing the edge of analogy too far," but I hope I have shown that such an implication would have been entirely in keeping with the carefully structured allusions to antique and modern Italy which Pope's Twickenham everywhere seems to have proposed to its attentive visitors.

University of Leiden

NOTES

1. James Sutherland, ed., *The Dunciad*, IV, line 125, p. 354, in John Butt, gen. ed., *The Poems of Alexander Pope*, Twickenham Edition, V (London, 1943). See also the poem to John Gay, where the phrase is used explicitly about his garden, *Minor Poems*, ed. Norman Ault and John Butt, Twickenham Edition, VI (1954), pp. 225-226.

2. (Oxford, 1978), p. 118. Brownell uses the phrase as the title of chap. 5. I have reviewed Brownell's book at length elsewhere and shall not repeat here my objections to his methods of garden history. See "Pope: 'Practical Poetry' and Practicing Poetry," *Review*, III (1981), pp. 155-164.

3. Joseph Spence, *Observations, Anecdotes, and Characters of Books and Men*, ed. James M. Osborn (Oxford, 1966), I, item 603; Isabel Wakelin Urban Chase, *Horace Walpole: Gardenist* (Princeton, 1943).

4. John Dixon Hunt and Peter Willis, eds., *The Genius of the Place: The English Landscape Garden 1620-1820* (London, 1975), pp. 204-206, quotation on p. 206.

5. Brownell's chap. 11 surveys Pope's involvement with the Palladian movement. *Alexander Pope*, pp. 276-293. See also Charles Beaumont, "Pope and the Palladians," *Texas Studies in Literature and Languages*, XVII (Summer, 1975), pp. 461-479, and James Sambrook, "Pope and the Visual Arts," in Peter Dixon, ed., *Alexander Pope* (Ann Arbor, 1972), pp. 142-171.

6. George Sherburn, ed., *The Correspondence of Alexander Pope* (Oxford, 1956), II, p. 436.

7. This is Brownell's opinion. *Alexander Pope*, p. 147.

8. A. Lynn Altenbernd seems to think otherwise. "On Pope's 'Horticultural Romanticism,' " *Journal of English and Germanic Philology*, LIV (October 1955), pp. 470-477. But in support of the interconnections between Pope's ideas, see Howard Erskine-Hill, "Heirs of Vitruvius: Pope and the Idea of Architecture," in Howard Erskine-Hill and Anne Smith, eds., *The Art of Alexander Pope* (London, 1979).

9. Brownell, *Alexander Pope*, p. 139. Brownell frequently alludes to Pope's classical gardening references but makes nothing of them.

10. For Pope's reading of Pliny, see Sherburn, ed., *Correspondence*, I, p. 508. For his riverside project, see the end of this article.

11. John Dixon Hunt, *The Figure in the Landscape: Poetry, Painting, and Gardening during the Eighteenth Century* (Baltimore, 1976), pp. 93, 98-100.

12. Ellis Veryard, *An Account of Divers Choice Remarks . . . Taken in a Journey* (London, 1701), p. 160.

13. *Ibid.*, p. 205; Edmund Warcupp, *Italy in its original glory, ruine and revival* (London, 1660), p. 309; Richard Lassels, *The Voyage of Italy* (Paris, 1670), pt. ii, p. 307.

14. Veryard, *Account*, p. 28.

15. John Raymond, *An Itinerary contayning a Voyage made through Italy in the yeare 1646 and 1647* (London, 1648), p. 167.

16. For an account of the first forty years, see Roy Strong, *The Renaissance Garden in England* (London, 1979).

17. James Howell, *Instructions and Directions for Forreine Travell* (London, 1650), p. 58.

18. Timothy Nourse, *Campania Foelix* (London, 1700), p. 299; John Woolridge, *Systema horti-culturae: or, the art of gardening*, 3rd ed. (London, 1688), pp. v, 1-2, 4.

19. The connections of the early English landscape garden with the long traditions of English interest in Italian garden design and of Italianate gardens in England was the topic of the Franklin Jasper Walls lectures that I gave at the Pierpont Morgan Library, New York, in 1981. These lectures, of which the present article is a fragment, are being extensively revised for publication.

20. Douglas Chambers, "The Tomb in the Landscape: John Evelyn's Garden at Albury," *Journal of Garden History*, I (January-March 1981), p. 38; John Aubrey, Bodleian MS, Aubrey 17, fol. 2.

21. Spence, *Observations*, item 557; Geoffrey Tillotson, ed., *The Rape of the Lock and Other Poems, Poems of Alexander Pope*, Twickenham Edition, II (London, 1940), p. 237n.

22. Joseph Spence, *Letters from the Grand Tour*, ed. Slava Klima (Montreal, 1975), esp. pp.

22, 109, 114, 377, quotation on p. 114.

23. Maynard Mack, *The Garden and the City: Retirement and Politics in the Later Poetry of Pope, 1731-1743* (Toronto, 1969), esp. chaps. 1-3, pp. 3-115. It seems important to try and see how literary *topoi* concerning gardens were mediated by actual garden experience and practice.

24. Strong, *Renaissance Garden in England*, pp. 138-143. See also Strong's study for a discussion of grottoes at Wilton, Woburn, and Moore Park.

25. "Poetical villa" is a phrase quoted by Brownell from a pamphlet attack on Pope. *Alexander Pope*, p. 48. On Egeria, see Mack, *Garden and the City*, pp. 69-74. For Pope's remark on the statue, see Sherburn, ed., *Correspondence*, II, p. 296.

26. On nymphaeums at these villas, see David R. Coffin, *The Villa in the Life of Renaissance Rome* (Princeton, 1979), and Otto Kurz, "Huius nympha Loci: A pseudo-classical inscription and a drawing by Dürer," *Journal of the Warburg and Courtauld Institutes*, XVI (1953), pp. 171-177.

27. Sherburn, ed., *Correspondence*, IV, p. 262.

28. John Serle, *A Plan of Mr. Pope's Garden. . .* (London, 1745; reprint ed., New York, 1982), pp. 5-10.

29. Veryard, *Account*, p. 194.

30. Mack, *Garden and the City*, p. 42.

31. Sherburn, ed., *Correspondence*, IV, p. 262.

32. *The Works of the late Right Honourable Henry St. John, Lord Viscount Bolingbroke* (London, 1809), V, p. 80.

33. S. Lang, "The Genesis of the English Landscape Garden," in Nikolaus Pevsner, ed., *The Picturesque Garden and Its Influence Outside the British Isles* (Washington, D. C., 1974), p. 27. Brownell also glances briefly at Pope's theatrical appreciation of scenery.

34. Bodleian MS, Rawl. D. 1162, fol. 3.

35. Mack, *Garden and the City*, p. 233. For further discussion of Pope's role playing, see James A. Winn, "Pope Plays the Rake: His Letters to Ladies and the making of the *Eloisa*," in Erskine-Hill and Smith, eds., *Art of Pope*, pp. 89-118, and Dustin H. Griffin, *Alexander Pope: The Poet in the Poems* (Princeton, 1978). I have treated the relationship of gardens and theaters somewhat discursively in "Theatres, Gardens and Garden-theatres," in Inga-Stina Ewbank, ed., *Essays and Studies* (London, 1980).

36. Mack, *Garden and the City*, p. 57.

37. Lines 157-161, quoted *ibid.*, p. 58.

38. See the Newcastle visitor on the Shell Temple, *ibid.*, p. 239. For the "Deities" and busts, see the Twickenham inventory, *ibid.*, pp. 244ff.

39. For Pope on groves, see Spence, *Observations*, item 611. For the presence of groves in Italian gardens, see Elisabeth MacDougall, "*Ars Hortulorum*: Sixteenth century Garden Iconography and Literary Theory in Italy," in David R. Coffin, ed., *The Italian Garden* (Washington, D. C., 1972), pp. 41-46. See also Irving N. Rothman, "The Quincunx in Pope's Moral Aesthetics," *Philological Quarterly*, LV (Summer, 1976), pp. 374-388.

40. For the fountain, see Sherburn, ed., *Correspondence*, II, p. 297; for the *Guardian* essay, see Hunt and Willis, eds., *Genius of the Place*, p. 207.

41. From Henry Wotton onward Italian gardens were always praised for their invitations to visitors to explore them. For Wotton, see Hunt and Willis, eds., *Genius of the Place*, p. 48.

42. Sherburn, ed., *Correspondence*, I, p. 163; II, p. 115.

43. Spence, *Observations*, item 620. For Maynard Mack's commentary on this project, see *Garden and the City*, pp. 37ff.

44. Spence, *Letters*, p. 124n: "One of the Great Duke's seats, from whence there is one of the richest prospects of a vale that can be in the world." No wonder Pope would want to invoke it in the equally famous Thames valley.

An Eighteenth-Century
View of Pope's Villa

Arthur J. Weitzman

Alexander Pope's villa in Twickenham has long been an object of interest both to literary scholars and an artistic public who have regarded his house, its location, and garden a masterpiece of unpretentious and modest living in an age of callous opulence.[1] Ironically, in later years the poet's fame and example made Twickenham a "center of wealth and fashion"[2] and attracted suburbanites. Successive owners were indifferent or more likely ignorant that the villa was meant by Pope to be a standing indictment of men like Walpole and Marlborough who built costly monuments to vanity, such as Timon's villa in the *Epistle to Burlington*.[3] After Pope's death, the estate passed into the hands of Sir William Stanhope, who "improved" the villa out of recognition by subsequent enlargements and decorations. They were defended on these spurious grounds:

> The humble roof, the garden's scanty line,
> Ill suit the genius of a bard divine;
> But fancy now displays a fairer scope,
> And STANHOPE's plans unfold the soul of Pope.[4]

Pope may well have resisted such a compliment.

With two exceptions, views now extant of the house date from this later period of improvement. In a recent display of these pictures held at Marble Hill House (July 19-September 28, 1980), only Peter Andreas Rysbrack's 1735 depiction afforded enough detail to determine the dimensions, layout, and style of the house Pope lived in. An earlier painting by Peter Tillman (ca. 1730) is essentially a vast panoramic landscape, although it shows Pope's villa in its unadorned state without porticos.[5] It is therefore of some significance to have another picture possibly done before the years 1747-1749, when the first non-Popean improvements were made on the exterior of the house by the river side of the property. One such view has now come into my hands, a pen-and-ink and wash drawing depicting the building and the immediate grounds that front the Thames (*Plate 18*).

The sketch itself measures 7 1/2" by 5 1/2" on a thick sheet of paper 17 3/4" by 11 1/2", which has no watermark and is wove paper; it could date from the eighteenth century. Underneath the picture is written, "Pope's Villa Twickenham," and below that these words are lightly penciled: "Taken from an invitation card sent by Pope to invite his friends to dinner." On the back in pencil in a different hand is "By George Hilditch R.A./ (Rev. Canon F. Smythe)." That is, Canon Smythe (whose identity is a mystery) attributes the drawing tentatively to George Hilditch, a nineteenth-century painter who specialized in landscapes in the Richmond-Twickenham area.[6] The clerk in the shop where I acquired this drawing (Walter Spencer in Upper Berkeley Street, London) informed me that the drawing was bought in a folder containing other sketches by Hilditch.

There are good reasons for doubting this attribution. For one, there is no evidence that Pope asked his friends to dinner by writing invitations on a card with a picture (engraving?) of his house. No invitation cards have come down to us, nor have I discovered any references to this method of invitation in the eighteenth century. Second, it is unlikely that Pope would have resorted to what is, after all, a rather pretentious vanity in ownership. Quiet enjoyment, not conspicuous consumption, was part of his ideal of the good life. And finally the picture itself is an unlikely example of Hilditch's art. The drawing of Pope's villa is sunny and lively with a clear sense of directive detail—just the opposite of Hilditch's usual shadowy contours and romantic suggestiveness.

This leaves us with two other possible means of transmission: it was drawn from real life, or it is a copy of some existing representation as claimed in the subscription. However tempting the former theory, no internal or external evidence is available to support it. There is, on the other hand, strong internal evidence for its being a copy of an engraving of a lost drawing of 1735 by Peter Andreas Rysbrack, the only engraving of the villa published in Pope's lifetime. In contrast with later views of the house,[7] Rysbrack's depiction, which may be viewed at Orleans House, Richmond, reveals some notable similarities to the sketch considered here. Significantly, my drawing shows the building presumably before the novelties of 1747-1749. (Our perception of the house's exterior is in part due to Rysbrack's conception as engraved by Nathaniel Parr (1735) and corroborated by another copy by T. Smith (?) in the *Newcastle General Magazine* [January 1748], which Brownell and Mack think is based on Rysbrack's original drawing.) Such novelties as the low waterside hedge, a shifted riverside opening, the curving shrub on the right with a spaced series of busts leading to a river house, the parallel fencing on the left, and finally the addition of a wall to the right side of the house—all of these improvements are absent from the Rysbrack engraving and my drawing. Not only are the main features of the house and grounds the same in the lack of improvements, but the accidentals of these two pictures are compellingly similar. I refer to the angle of vision, the shadows cast by the sun, the arrangement of people disembarking from a boat (despite eight figures in the drawing compared to nine in Rysbrack), the decorative swans in the water, and, what is most conclusive, the suggestion of a small boat in pencil on the right of the drawing corresponding to a low-lying boat by the two trees in the Rysback version. Perhaps the copyist, sketching first in pencil, thought to include the small boat but in carrying out the design in ink neglected this detail. My theory of origin thus takes into account the assertion that the drawing is taken from another view and the internal evidence of dependence on Rysbrack. There remain still the mysteries of when the drawing was executed and by whom.

Northeastern University

NOTES

1. Maynard Mack, *The Garden and the City: Retirement and Politics in the Later Poetry of Pope, 1731-1743* (Toronto, 1969).

2. "Letter of Description of Pope's Villa," *The Topographer*, I (1789), p. 471.

3. Kathleen Mahaffey argues and Maynard Mack agrees that Timon's villa was the fictional counterpart of Walpole's Houghton. "Timon's Villa: Walpole's Houghton," *Texas Studies in Literature and Languages*, IX (Summer, 1967), pp. 193-222; *Garden and the City*, pp. 272-278. Morris Brownell's candidate is Blenheim: *Alexander Pope & the Arts of Georgian England* (Oxford, 1978), pp. 305-325. The most recent identification is Chatsworth: Pat Rogers, "Timon's Villa Again," *British Journal for Eighteenth-Century Studies*, II (Spring, 1979), pp. 63-65.

4. These verses were recorded on a marble tablet that remains in the garden.

5. The catalog for this exhibition, which includes many reproductions in black and white, was put together by Morris Brownell. *Alexander Pope's Villa: Views of Pope's Villa, Grotto, and Garden—A Microcosm of English Landscape* (London, 1980).

6. George Hilditch (1803-1857) developed a local reputation for his romantic landscapes and exhibited often at the Royal Academy. His works are part of the collections of the dukes of Devonshire and Sutherland and the earls of Dysart and Wharncliffe. George C. Williamson, ed., *Dictionary of Painters and Engravers*, 4th ed. (New York, 1904), III, p. 45.

7. See reproductions in Brownell, *Alexander Pope's Villa*, p. 30 passim.

The *Ferme Ornée* and
Changing Attitudes to Agricultural Improvement

William A. Brogden

The *ferme ornée* is an interesting minor aspect of eighteenth-century affairs. Everybody knows and is supposed to be amused by Marie Antoinette's toy farm at Versailles, and by how charmingly silly it was—not at all "real," and certainly not relevant to its time and place. However, the *ferme ornée* originally had a much more serious purpose than to provide a setting for "playing at farmers"; the farm-like way of gardening, as it was also called, contributed significantly to the development of the landscape style.

The term *ferme ornée* first appeared in the appendix of just under one hundred pages that Stephen Switzer had added for the second edition of *Ichnographia Rustica*, originally issued between 1715 and 1718. In further promoting the merits of his Rural and Extensive Gardening, Switzer asserted,

> This Taste, so truly useful and delightful as it is, has also for some time been the Practice of some of the best Genius's of *France* under the Title of *La Ferme Ornée*. And that *Great-Britain* is now likely to excel in it, let all those who have seen the Farms and Parks of *Abbs-Court, Riskins, Dawley-Park* now a doing, with other Places of like Nature declare.[1]

These remarks were published in 1742, but there is reason to point to a somewhat earlier date of composition. The passage, "It must be observ'd in the first Place, That the forgoing Volumes were publish'd some ten or twelve years ago,"[2] suggests 1728 or 1730, whereas his reference to the *Villas of the Ancients Illustrated* ("published by an ingenious Gentleman lately deceased")[3] suggests 1729, the year of Richard Castell's death. There is, too, the fact that the very occasion for mentioning the term was in relation to Riskins, Buckinghamshire, the small estate of Allen, Lord Bathurst. A description of the estate had appeared in 1727 in the *Practical Kitchen Gardiner* which was dedicated to Bathurst, but the promised plate had been left out.

I suggest therefore that Switzer wrote the appendix to complete a projected second edition in 1729, and that, whether because of his extensive business, the constant flow of pamphlets, or the publication of his great *Introduction to a General System of Hydrostaticks and Hydraulicks*, he postponed its issue.

I have no evidence that the French had laid out ornamental farms in the first quarter of the eighteenth century. They may have farmed in a tidy, even pretty, fashion; but knowledge of early eighteenth-century French gardens is inconsistent with Switzer's assertion. It may be that he concocted the term and then fathered it on the French in the hope of making his idea more acceptable. He had done so before.

But what did Switzer mean by his use of the term? Simply, it was the employment of fields, kitchen gardens, orchards, and pasture very near the more polished parterre or central walk: it was a literal mixing of the pleasurable and profitable parts of a country life. It was also small: between two hundred acres and, at a maximum, six hundred acres. It need have no formal significance in laying out gardens: indeed, the "regulated Epitomy" of Riskins (*Plate 19*) follows very closely what is thought of as the French pattern. The enclosures are defined by trees and disposed to either side of a central canal (shown in Switzer's illustration as straight and axial, but in fact it was serpentine, which Bathurst was very proud of). If cornfields were to be substituted for the woodland at Wrest Park, Bedfordshire, or the cabinets and theaters at the Tuilleries replaced by beds of turnips, the formal effect would be roughly the same.

However, Switzer apologized twice about this plate, and had done elsewhere about others, that the scale of an octavo book allowed him only to hint at designs in plan. But in words he was fuller. In the 1727 account of Riskins he referred to the type as "a villa or kitchen garden where its produce is rais'd promiscuously up and down in fields, where there is choice of ground proper for all kinds of vegetables, sometimes by plowing only."[4] These fields or quarters were to be connected together by hedge-row walks leading to the central canal, which was to be flanked by a pair of pleached lime (or elm) walks, "kept down so low that they may not shade the quarters."[5] The shape of the fields was a matter, apparently, of debate. Switzer had had occasion in 1718 to assert that irregular fields were as useful as square ones: he repeated the point, but it never completely convinced:

> Thro' the fields there are half-standard fruit trees planted, which form, some circular [i.e., serpentine], others straight diagonal lines, with no other art or labour than the sowing the edges with parsley, time, or other sweet and fragrant herbs.[6]

At each corner of the fields were to be little pieces of "Wood in the form of a labyrinth."[7] In the main walks sheep were to be kept,

> who will serve instead of mowers, little gates being fix'd wherever you enter the quarters, to keep them from going in there; and on top of the terraces that surround the building, there may be a little grillade of iron, or a low pallisadoe of wood, to keep them from coming up too near to the house.[8]

In writing about Riskins and the *ferme ornée* Switzer was reinforcing his case of Rural and Extensive Gardening. Originally proposed in the second decade of the century, this style had an architecturally formal, though very simplified, setting for the house and dependencies consisting, usually, of Avenue, Parade, Court-yard, House, Parterre, Avenue. This formal setting was meant to be contiguous to the rest of the estate (or farm), and, in the parterre feature especially, there was to be a strong visual connection to the surrounding countryside, however used. In this general prescription, as in the *ferme ornée*, a network of hedgerow walks, and in very large schemes rides, connected all parts of the design. At intersections were to be placed fragments of garden, that is, flower beds, statuary, or perhaps even simple fountains (*Plate 20*).

The idea was that the simplicity of the walks with their wild flowers and nut bushes, the occasional decoration with the productivity and liveliness of the enclosed fields (be they given over to turnips, corn, or pasturage), and, in Switzer's terms, the general correspondence of everything together would, with the pompous "main line," please everybody, be cheap to make and keep, and would certainly establish Roman virtues in Great Britain.

Switzer pursued this idea further and, especially in the 1720s, became interested in agricultural improvement in all its aspects—the drainage of heavy unproductive land, the breaking down and nourishment of soils, the perfection of seeds, and the rediscovery from ancient texts (particularly of Virgil) of the "lost" principles of husbandry. And to this end he established a sort of club of improving landowners and gardeners in England, and became a member and correspondent of the rather grand and aristocratic Society of Scotch Improvers.

The extent of gardens laid out in this style, on present evidence, appears to be (excluding the early Grimsthorpe and Cirencester because of their great size) Riskins, in some form from 1708, but mostly second and third decades; Abb's Court, Surrey, for Lord Halifax, and Dawley-Park, Middlesex, for Lord Bolingbroke—late 1720s; Stowe, Buckinghamshire, for Lord Cobham (this is rather stretching it, but this is a place mentioned by Switzer in 1727, obviously because of the ornamented encircling walk around the "captured" Home Park); Sugnal, Staffordshire, for Lord Glenorchy, from 1733; Woburn Farm, Surrey, for Philip Southcote, from 1734; Penicuik, Midlothian, for Sir John Clerk of Penicuik, (?) 1735-1740; Farnborough, Warwickshire, ca. 1745; Mickleton, Gloucestershire, with Warlies, Essex, both mentioned by Shenstone; and, of course, Shenstone's own The Leasowes, from 1745 onward.

But even before the famous *ferme ornées* were created, at Woburn Farm and The Leasowes, a very significant part of the idea, at least for the likes of Lord Bathurst or Stephen Switzer, had begun to wane. From the late 1720s onward it is observable that agricultural improvement and garden making pursued different courses.

In the 1730s and 1740s improvement is no longer, in itself, sufficient inducement for a man to make a "pretty landskip of his possessions," as Addison had phrased it. Certainly from the time that Pope looked through the gate of the botanical garden at Oxford and observed that "all gardening is like landscape painting—like a landscape picture hung up," a new force is apparent in garden making: a preoccupation with art, and, consequently, taste, and subsequently a reduction of the principles of garden making to those of art, and, specifically, landscape painting.

The practical effect of the growing apart of the agricultural savant and the dilettante is not very pronounced in the 1730s or 1740s, but after mid-century it is an important distinction: the estate improver is, generally, visually naive or experimental, whereas the connoisseur of landscape is visually very self-conscious and conforming.

To a degree this shift can be seen at Woburn Farm and The Leasowes, both of which follow the prescription set up by Switzer, except that they, like Riskins, largely dispensed with the formal setting for the house: in both, the linear garden, or walks, ties all together into a sensible whole. Woburn was on the small side, some one hundred and fifty acres with eighty acres in pasture and thirty-five each in tillage and "garden." Unlike Riskins, which is on flat land, Woburn was laid out on and partly under two sides of a hill.

Woburn was indeed the ornamented farm. Not only was there a large proportion of arable land, but

> the lowing of the herds, the bleating of the sheep, and the tinklings of the bell-wether, resound thro' all the plantations; even the clucking of poultry is not omitted; for a menagerie of a very simple design is placed near the Gothic building; . . . and the cornfields are the subjects of every rural employment, which arable land, from seed-time to harvest, can furnish.[9]

Thomas Whately does not in his account say "how absurd it all is, however touching," although one suspects censure is not far away. For him the *idea* of a farm has become inappropriate: it is *too* rustic to please, even though his description shows Woburn Farm to have been thoroughly delightful (*Plate 21*).

The Leasowes was begun some ten years afterward by the poet William Shenstone. Its situation, west of Birmingham, is topographically richer than either Riskins or Woburn. Shenstone apparently got the inspiration for a *ferme ornée* from a friend whose kinsman had taken "hints" from Southcote. The essential difference with Shenstone's place was, in Whately's words,

> It is *literally* a grazing farm lying round the house; and a walk as unaffected and as unadorned as a common field path, is conducted through the several enclosures.[10]

Now, a *ferme ornée* that is merely a grazing farm is not, in terms of the history of garden making, a farm at all, for even the heroic landscape gardens of Lancelot Brown were diversified with cattle or sheep. And the proportion of open ground to woodland at The Leasowes was the same as that of, say, its later contemporary Croome Court in the same county. As Whately incisively put it,

The ideas of *pastoral poetry* seem now to be the standard of . . . simplicity; and a place conformable to them is deemed a farm in its utmost purity.[11]

But when the ideas of pastoral poetry contribute very largely to informing the landscape style of gardening, where is the distinction?

In fact, agricultural improvement, and by the time of Shenstone's death in 1763 the *ferme ornée*, too, had done their work. Initially, improvement through the means of the extended garden was one of the ways for garden design to expand to something approaching the scale of the landscape. In the 1720s and 1730s the forms proper to the improved estate began to be esteemed in their own right as capable of producing agreeable associations of ideas, or, latterly, as contributing to make "real landscapes" very like those which the leaders of fashion were beginning to hang in their houses. So what originally had been a liberation from garden design to landscape design was brought back into a new sort of garden making, that of the landscape garden (*Plates 22 and 23*).

Then with the self-consciousness of a critic of a fine art Thomas Whately could write in 1770:

Though a farm and a garden agree in many particulars connected with extent, yet in *style* they are the two extremes. Both indeed are subjects of cultivation; but cultivation in the one is *husbandry*; and in the other *decoration*: the former is appropriated to *profit*, the latter to *pleasure*: fields profusely ornamented do not retain the appearance of a farm; and an apparent attention to produce, obliterates the idea of a garden.[12]

Scott Sutherland School of Architecture, R.G.I.T, Aberdeen

NOTES

1. Stephen Switzer, *Ichnographia Rustica*, 2nd ed. (London, 1742), III, Appendix, pp. 8-9.
2. *Ibid.*, p. 2.
3. *Ibid.*, p. 8.
4. Stephen Switzer, *The Practical Kitchen Gardiner* (London, 1727), p. 421.
5. *Ibid.*, p. 422.
6. *Ibid.*, p. 424.
7. *Ichnographia Rustica*, III, Appendix, p. 10.
8. *Kitchen Gardiner*, p. 424.
9. Thomas Whately, *Observations on Modern Gardening* (London, 1770), p. 181.
10. *Ibid.*, p. 162. Italics mine.
11. *Ibid.*
12. *Ibid.*, p. 160.

The High Phase of English Landscape Gardening

Mavis Batey

The English landscaped garden flourished in the relative peace and prosperity of the mid-eighteenth century and reflected the ideas of the dilettanti Whig aristocrats. The century saw great changes politically, socially, and in the ascendancy of feeling over taste. Reaction to aristocratic landscaping was inevitable. Taste was collective and handed down from the top, leaving the imagination only a passive role.[1] Feeling was individual and spontaneous and fostered creative imagination. Landscape gardening, which involved fundamental attitudes to the environment and society, came under attack from several sides. It maneuvered and adapted to the new prevalent romantic attitudes and entered its high phase at the time of Capability Brown's death in 1783.

Its new lease of life was brought about by the growing obsession with picturesque theory. In the mid century landscaping was largely left to the professionals and some gifted amateurs, and little was written down about its theory or practicalities. In the 1780s and '90s there was a flood of theorizing. The picturesque attitude was sparked off by the Reverend William Gilpin,[2] who really had no intention of being involved with theories on landscape gardening. He was the promoter of picturesque travel (*Plate 24*). Obsession with landscape painting had already been fostered by the dilettanti returning from the Grand Tour infatuated with the scenery that Claude and Poussin had painted. Gilpin encouraged the home tour for a much wider public. Roads had greatly improved and it soon became a favorite pastime, and with so much unrest in Europe even the grandees were forced to take it.

The craze that Gilpin started is well described by Jane Austen in *Northanger Abbey* where her fashionable Tilneys were seen to be "viewing the country with the eyes of persons accustomed to painting and deciding on its capability of being formed into pictures." Tourists in search of this picturesque beauty could capture the picture-worthy scene on their sketchpads on the spot or in their special landscape mirrors. When Gilpin was a schoolmaster at Cheam he encouraged the boys to develop a picture imagination; he got them to underline passages in Virgil that they thought would make good paintings and then sent them out to look for paintable spots near the school.[3] In the school holidays he set off to remote parts of Britain in search of picturesque beauty himself. When he was persuaded by his friend, the Reverend William Mason, to publish these picturesque tours, they were written in the down-to-earth and easy-to-understand language that he had used on the boys. Jane Austen's young heroines reveled in it. Gilpin had already published an *Essay on Prints* in 1768 for the guidance of the new public who could afford prints at a shilling a time; and when the picturesque tours in which he evaluated natural scenery were later published, the appreciation of scenery and the enjoyment of pictures became inseparably linked.

Nuneham Courtenay, near Oxford, is an example of a landscaped garden that was laid out on the lines of a Gilpin picturesque tour.[4] The landowner, the second Earl Harcourt, was a patron of the picturesque. He obtained the secret of aquatinting from Paul Sandby in order to give more evocative landscape illustrations for Gilpin's tours and encouraged other artists to forsake Italian landscape and paint the picturesque homeland. In 1777 the earl had inherited from his dilettante father a mid-century landscape garden laid out with prospect in mind. "A bird's eye view from a Knight's terrace" was how the new garden adviser, the Reverend William Mason, author of *The English Garden,* described it. The landscape was soon to be broken down into a series of pictures by judicious planting. The River Thames was no longer to appear as a silvery streak but as a number of separate water features in different pictures. The curving terrace round the hill became a gallery of Thames landscapes, featuring the windings of the river, Radley village, Abingdon church spire, the White Horse Hills, and a view over the water meadows to the domes and spires of Oxford. Gilpin had pointed out that the native Scotch pine could be used as a foreground tree in the same way as Claude had used the Stone pine allowing distant views to be seen through its branches, whereas a tree with dense foliage would merely blot out the view it sought to frame.

Earl Harcourt wrote his own guidebook of his picturesque Thames tour pointing out the "stations" where the visitor should pause and take out his sketch pad or mirror. In typical Gilpin manner he wrote: "On the left there is a narrow opening that admits a view over the underwood, and the trees in the foreground, apparently uniting with a clump in the garden below, leading the eye to the other masses of wood till it reaches Oxford, which is framed by trees and shrubs."[5] Lord Harcourt had offered Gilpin the living of Nuneham so that he could cooperate in his picturesque schemes, but Gilpin preferred to accept a New Forest living where he could observe forest rather than park scenery.

Gilpin's *Remarks on Forest Scenery,* published in 1791, did much to turn opinion away from the great Brownian landscaped parks, which embodied the concept of stabilized beauty. Smooth, round forms, gradual deviations, serpentine lines, clear margins, and the elimination of nature's "false accidents" were beautiful but not picturesque. It was ruggedness and sudden deviations, catching lights on uneven surfaces that a painter really liked; and, as Salvator Rosa had demonstrated, nature's false accidents in the way of blasted trees were particularly picturesque. Gilpin showed in *Forest Scenery* the natural beauties to be found in the "skirts of the forest," the brushwood, twisted trees, broken banks, and exposed roots of trees as well as the picturesque forms of the forest trees themselves.

The observations on natural as opposed to stylized plantings, and on forest streams as opposed to artificial pieces of water, were linked in the 1790s to his previous comments on the character of regions highlighted in his *Picturesque* tours. The tourist had been taught to analyze landscape and to see how variously nature worked up the scenery in the different regions visited. This bred a new sense of regionalism and respect for the character of the Lakes, the Highlands, the Wye, the Peaks, and so on. Capability Brown and his followers worked to a formula that was applied indiscriminately in Wiltshire or Derbyshire and showed no respect for regional characteristics. Jane Austen, who was "enamoured of Gilpin from an early age,"[6] captures the moment when taste turned away from improved nature. She had undoubtedly read Gilpin's *Remarks on Forest Scenery*, having herself lived on the borders of the New Forest for a time, and evidently approved of his criticism of one Brownian landscaped garden in the area that had scooped shaven lawns out of the forest, dammed a forest stream to make a piece of water, and thrown a Chinese bridge across it.[7] Mr. Darcy at Pemberley had no such "awkward taste"; his trout stream flowed through a natural glen and it was "crossed by a simple bridge, in character with the general air of the scene." This marked Mr. Darcy as a man of feeling, and when Elizabeth Bennet was asked by her sister when she had first fallen in love with him, the heroine replied, "I believe I must date it from my first seeing his beautiful grounds at Pemberley." Being right-minded on picturesque taste was, as Jane Austen playfully suggested, of paramount importance in the 1790s.

A veritable paper war on landscape gardening had been begun by two Herefordshire squires, Uvedale Price and Richard Payne Knight, in 1794. The former in his *Essay on the Picturesque* developed Gilpin's practical ideas for looking at scenery into an aesthetic theory, defining the intrinsic quality in objects which was picturesque on the lines of Burke's *Philosophical Enquiry into the Origin of Our Ideas of the Sublime and the Beautiful*. The aging pioneer of the picturesque professed indifference for the abstractions, and his friend, the elderly Reverend William Mason, wrote to him, "O Mr Gilpin. Repent! Repent! The number of Coxcombs that you have made surpasses credence. Everybody now talks about Picturesqueness. What a word to break the teeth of those who have any, which you know is not my case, so I am easy about the matter."[8]

Payne Knight in his didactic poem *The Landscape* (1794) was sharp in his criticism of Brownian landscaping, the "bare and bald" system in which great houses sprung up out of the turf, banks of rivers were left naked, and all vestiges of habitation removed from the park. Even before Brown's death in 1783 William Chambers[9] had condemned his green acres as insipid and Goldsmith had deplored the social aspects of Brownian landscaping that involved the removal of villages from parks in *The Deserted Village* (1770).[10] Brown had many imitators and there is no doubt that the master's formula for clearing slopes to expose undulating landforms, planting clumps of trees and perimeter belts, and damming streams to make a piece of water in the line of beauty was not always copied with the same happy results. Payne Knight, living in an ironmaster's rugged Herefordshire landscape, was critical of landscape improvement undertaken not only by Brown but by the up and coming Humphry Repton, whom he accused of taking on Brown's mantle.

Knight's home of Downton Castle (*Plate 25*) was one of the first examples of a picturesque relationship between architecture and scenery. Begun in 1775 and situated picturesquely above the River Teme, its irregular form was inspired not so much by the gothic past as by the "mixed" buildings in the background of the paintings of Claude and Poussin. William Gilpin, remembering his old home at Scaleby Castle on the Borders, had always emphasized the picturesque nature of irregular gothic buildings and Price and Knight had stressed their architectural values; but it was Walter Scott who put real life blood into gothic when his Waverley novels appeared in the 1820s. Walpole's Castle of Otranto was only gothic in mood and contained no architectural descriptions, but Scott's castles were associated with authentic architecture in stirring historical scenes and fed the imagination already visually prepared for irregular architecture by the writings of Gilpin, Knight, and Price. The Scots baronial mansion, in imitation of Tully Veolan in Waverley, with its angle turrets, crow-stepped gables, and battlements, sprang up, seemingly overnight, in England and Ireland. An Arcadian setting with smooth lawns and pastoral landscape was clearly not in keeping with romantically picturesque castles. Tully Veolan was approached by an avenue, and from a balustraded terrace a stone flight of steps led down to an ornamental garden from which could be seen the picturesquely ruined castle of the former barons of Bradwardine.

The Brownian landscapers had removed all traces of old formal gardens found round the house, severing its connections with the past. When feeling ousted taste there was a new respect for the past that went beyond mere visual appreciation of a scene and established that true pleasure in perception was derived from the "train of reflections" in the mind.[11] Price had bitterly regretted the destruction of the old garden at his home at Foxley and saw the modern system of landscaping as a poor substitute for the rich formality of the old school.

Uvedale Price was anxious to find a professional practitioner who would develop practically the ideas for a new type of gardening that he had called for in his *Essay on the Picturesque* in 1794. He wanted to find a painter-gardener who would apply picturesque principles to the improvement of real landscape and take into account the romantic attitude concerning the relation of the house and its surroundings. Humphry Repton, who had already begun to practice his profession, was his first choice. He was invited to Foxley and taken for a tour of the Wye and his picturesque reactions tested. In a published reproof Price wrote: "I shall always remember with pleasure the hours we spent together on the Wye . . . but I could not help observing at the time with much concern how lightly you treated the idea of taking any hints from any part of a natural river towards forming an artificial one . . . I cannot recollect amidst all the romantic scenes we viewed together your having made any allusions to the works of various masters which might naturally have occurred to a person who had studied or even observed them with common attention."[12] Repton went his own way to become an extremely successful landscape gardener and Price turned his attention elsewhere.

This time it was William Sawrey Gilpin who in 1803 was given the Wye test and passed it with flying colors. It was not surprising that he reacted picturesquely to the scenery since he had attended his uncle's school at Cheam, had made the Wye tour, and made the aquatints from his uncle's drawings. For the Reverend William Gilpin's *Picturesque Tour* he had, as instructed, "analyzed the Wye, and considered separately its constituent parts"[13] and then rearranged them to suit the rules of painting. For Price he was asked, as Repton had been, to consider how the natural beauties of the Wye could be adapted to the improvement of real landscape. Although W. S. Gilpin showed interest in the idea that there was an affinity between landscaping and the rules of painting, he did not at that time wish to set up as a picturesque landscape gardener since he had a considerable reputation as a landscape painter and Repton, in spite of his break with Price, was the accepted authority in the field of landscape gardening.

When Repton died in 1818, W. S. Gilpin, then fifty-eight, reconsidered the matter and contacted Price who immediately put him in touch with many landowners who were indulging in picturesque building schemes that called for a sympathetic landscape treatment. He was just in time for the castellated houses going up in the wake of the Waverley novels. Kinfauns Castle in Perthshire was given a characteristically Gilpin picturesque landscape. William Gilpin on his Scottish tour had found the area somewhat "lacking in picturesque objects" and for painters had suggested that for a composition they should "add trees to the foreground, tufted woods creeping up the sides of the hills, a castle upon some knoll and skiffs upon the lake."[14] His nephew, taking Price's advice, extended these ideas from the sketch pad to real landscape. Kinfauns Castle was sited on the hill with a backing of woodland, the lower slopes deciduous and the upper Scotch pines, and he planted up the rocky surfaces above the River Tay insuring that the trunks of the trees rose boldly from steepest declivities. In 1827 Gilpin visited Ireland and advised on picturesque landscapes for Crom Castle, Enniskillen, and Castle Blaney. In 1832 he restored the landscaped garden and flower garden at Nuneham, which had been laid out with picturesque intention as early as the 1770s.

William Sawrey Gilpin's last commission was Scotney Castle in Kent (*Plate 26*), which he first visited in 1836 at the age of seventy-four at the request of Edward Hussey, a devotee of Price and picturesque theory. Instead of planning a landscape around the existing house, a new one was built on the hill and the old one left as a picturesque ruin in the valley in true Tully Veolan manner. The quarry from which the stone for the new house was taken lent itself to picturesque planting. As a foreground to the picture Gilpin designed a bastion-shaped architectural feature that would also serve as a viewing point for the picturesque moat-encircled castle ruin in its woodland setting. It was here that Christopher Hussey grew up and wrote his book *The Picturesque: Studies in a Point of View.*

W. S. Gilpin was not in the mainstream of gardening ideas that were to influence the nineteenth century, however. As John Claudius Loudon pointed out when he issued the collected edition of Repton's books in 1840, the Brownian school was not followed by the picturesque school but by Repton's school of landscaping. Repton's greatest influence was through his writings and it was by his books that he himself said he wished to be remembered. He was a landscape consultant and his clients carried out the work themselves and not always as he would have liked it. His most famous commission for the Prince Regent at Brighton Pavilion was not carried out, but his ideas for it could be read in his published *Designs* even before Loudon republished them in the collected works.[15]

It was by means of his Red Books that his ideas were, as he said, "diffused over the kingdom." His method was to paint a picture of a place as he found it and by means of a hinged flap show what it would look like after his improvements were executed. He was a great admirer of the Reverend William Gilpin and his drawings are Gilpin's kind of picturesque. The plans and recommendations were bound with red morocco and Repton's greatest advertisement was that the handsome volumes were left on library tables to be seen by envious landlords. Extracts from them were published in his printed books beginning with *Sketches and Hints on Landscape Gardening* in 1794, and by 1806 Repton calculated that over a million and a half of his explanatory sketches were in circulation.

Repton worked in a time of economic depression during the Napoleonic wars. His ideas of improvement were of necessity more flexible and less grand than those of his predecessor Brown. He talked of the "feasibilities" of the place,[16] rather than of its "capabilities." The comfort of the owner was the first consideration; he abandoned the use of the ha-ha, deploring the idea of the cattle coming up to the windows of the house. Dress grounds were advocated in the immediate vicinity of the house. At Rosehill in Sussex, where he followed Brown, he illustrated in his "before" sketch ladies with skirts blown over their heads and umbrellas inside out; when Repton improvements were made they were walking comfortably in a sheltered shrubbery and grassed-in flower corridor.

Repton also catered for the new interest in horticulture, which had been reflected in the founding of the Royal Horticultural Society in 1806. He paved the way for Loudon's gardenesque ideas and villa gardening. It was Repton's "natural and graceful style" which could assimilate Loudon's gardenesque style that was adapted to North America by Andrew Jackson Downing in the 1840s.[17] Downing owned all Loudon's books and made practical all the picturesque and romantic ideas that had been bandied about for decades across the Atlantic. It was largely a question of scale. Downing emphasized the importance of guiding simple cottages as well as mansions by picturesque principles (*Plate 27*). The arguments about picturesque theory were long forgotten but its legacy of visual appreciation was permanent.

Honorary Secretary, Garden History Society

NOTES

1. For the passive imagination, see Joseph Addison, *The Spectator*, essays nos. 411-421.

2. C. P. Barbier, *William Gilpin: His Drawings, Teaching and Theory of the Picturesque* (Oxford, 1963).

3. Gilpin Virgil notebook, Bodleian MS, Eng. Misc. C 388, fol. 135; Mavis Batey, "Gilpin and the Schoolboy Picturesque," *Garden History*, II (Spring, 1974), pp. 24-26.

4. See *Nuneham Courtenay, Oxfordshire. A short history and description of the house, gardens and estate*, 2nd ed. (Oxford, 1979), p. 28.

5. Simon Harcourt, "A Description of Nuneham," *Harcourt Papers*, ed. E. Harcourt (London, 1876), III, p. 206.

6. Reported by her brother Henry Austen in his biographical notice in *Northanger Abbey*.

7. William Gilpin, *Remarks on Forest Scenery and other Woodland Views* (London, 1791; reprint, Richmond, Eng., 1973), p. 22.

8. Bodleian MS, Eng. Misc. D 571, fol. 224.

9. William Chambers, *A Dissertation on Oriental Gardening* (London, 1772).

10. Mavis Batey, "Oliver Goldsmith: An indictment of landscape gardening," in Peter Willis, ed., *Furor Hortensis: Essays on the history of the English Landscape Garden in memory of H. F. Clark* (Edinburgh, 1974), pp. 57-71.

11. For the theory of association see esp. Archibald Alison, *Essays on the Nature and Principles of Taste* (Edinburgh, 1790).

12. *Essays on the Picturesque* (London, 1810), III, p. 45.

13. *Observations on the River Wye* (London, 1782), p. 15.

14. William Gilpin, *Observations relative chiefly to Picturesque Beauty made in 1776 on several parts of Great Britain; particularly the High-lands of Scotland* (London, 1789), II, section XXX.

15. Humphry Repton, *Designs for the Pavilion at Brighton* (London, 1808).

16. *Sheringham Red Book* (Norfolk, 1812; facsimile ed., London, 1976).

17. Downing's first influential publication was his *Treatise on the Theory and Practice of Landscape Gardening, Adapted to North America; with a View to the Improvement of Country Residences* (New York, 1841).

Parnell's Garden Tours:
Hagley and The Leasowes

James Sambrook

The better-known documentary sources for the history of English landscape gardening in the mid-eighteenth century can, at points, be usefully supplemented by recently rediscovered journals written in 1762-1763 and 1769-1770 by an Irish visitor to England, John Parnell (1744-1801),[1] later Sir John, chancellor of the Irish exchequer, great-nephew of Thomas Parnell the poet, and great-grandfather of Charles Stuart Parnell.

In his eighteenth year Parnell traveled to England to hear William Blackstone's law lectures at Oxford and to visit the most celebrated great houses and gardens. His manuscript journal, "An account of the many fine seats of nobles I have seen, with other observations made during my residence in England in 1763," survives and is now in the Folger Shakespeare Library, Washington D. C.[2] This account runs in diary form from October 1762 until it breaks off abruptly at October 23, 1763; but it is almost certainly an edited transcript in view of the evenness and neatness of the hand, the neatly displayed title page dated December 1763, and the occasional reference to later events, such as the election of John Wilkes's successor as M.P. for Aylesbury in January 1764. Possibly it was intended for publication, since Parnell on several occasions addresses his readers and offers advice to would-be garden visitors.

It is not certain when Parnell returned home after this visit to England. He was admitted a student to Lincoln's Inn in January 1766 and in the same year proceeded to his degree at Trinity College, Dublin; he was M.P. for Bangor in the Irish Parliament during the session 1767-1768, and, on the evidence of a reference to Italy in the 1769 "Journal," he must have taken the Grand Tour, probably at some time in the years 1764-1767. From May 1769 to April 1770 he made a second extended visit to England, apparently with the purpose of enjoying the seasons in Bath and London and traveling about the country to gather ideas for the improvement of his own estate in Ireland. The fragmentary "Journal of a tour thro' England and Wales, Anno 1769," in three volumes, survives and is now in the British Library of Political and Economic Science in London.[3] This "Journal" is written in a hasty scrawl, mostly day by day and rarely more than a week after the events described. Its main purpose seems to have been to serve as Parnell's personal aide-mémoire in his plans for the improvement of his own house and grounds and the management of his farms in Ireland, for it is full of memoranda about English farming methods and implements and the manner in which he might employ them, and contains dozens of drawings of farm implements, fences, gates, and buildings, as well as of garden features seen in England or planned for execution in Ireland.

On the occasion of his first journey Parnell landed near Chester on October 29, 1762, proceeded directly to Oxford, and remained there, apart from a brief visit to London, until Blackstone's lectures ended on March 27, 1763. Then he spent a short time in Bath before going on to London to keep his law terms. He remained in and around London until June 2, visiting the regular sights of the City and Westminster, and those a little further afield, such as Wanstead, Richmond, Windsor, Hampton Court, and Kew, the last of which he gives a full description. At the beginning of June he made a short expedition to Stowe, then on June 7 he took lodgings in the village of Thorp, between Chertsey and Egham, as a convenient center from which to visit the more celebrated gardens of this area. In this section of his journal the detailed, illustrated accounts of Woburn Farm and Painshill are particularly informative for the modern garden historian.[4] Parnell remained at Thorp until September 27, when he took an outing to Wilton and Stonehenge before returning to Oxford on October 3 in time for the resumption of Blackstone's lectures. Toward the end of October he made an expedition to Hagley Park and The Leasowes but his journal breaks off without written descriptions of those gardens.

The second recorded visit began at Holyhead on May 11, 1769. He traveled in a fairly leisurely way to London, taking note of farming improvements (including those on Arthur Young's experimental farm at North Mimms) and visiting several gardens, including Shugborough, which is the subject of a long, detailed description with maps and drawings. From London he visited Painshill, Esher, Claremont, and Woburn in the space of three days in June before going to Bath, probably later that month. From Bath he made excursions to Stourhead and Fonthill in late September. In November he returned to London, whence he made more excursions to see improvements in the Windsor area again. In February 1770 he returned to Bath, then in April began the return journey to Ireland, visiting Hagley and The Leasowes on the way and describing them fully. He sailed from Holyhead on April 27.

In his second tour of England Parnell is far more concerned with the practical details of agricultural improvement than he was in his first tour. This appears, for instance, in the striking contrast between his two accounts of Woburn Farm. In 1763 he concentrates attention on the garden buildings, most of which lay to the west of the house, and curtly observes that the farmlands to the east are dull: in 1769 he says hardly anything about the buildings but writes with delight and copious details concerning the way that the farm fields were laid out and managed. The changed emphasis is accounted for partly by Parnell's desire not to repeat observations made in the 1763 account, but mainly by his overriding interest in farming. Park and pasture were regular constituents of the landscape garden, but what struck Parnell most forcibly at Woburn was the brilliant success with which a working arable farm was incorporated into a beautiful garden. It was in the eastern half of the garden that the fields were plotted and pieced to create a scheme that was as visually pleasing as it was agriculturally sound. In a sense, these two descriptions complement one another just as the two elements implied in the term "ornamented farm" were intended to. These accounts of 1763 and 1769, taken together, do not only provide the most detailed written description yet discovered of Southcote's work, they convey a lively and vivid sense of just what made Woburn Farm so distinctive and so exciting for visitors in the age of agricultural improvement.

Parnell was not so favorably impressed by grander gardens such as Stowe or Longleat, where the flatness of the park left it "destitute of the romantic beauties of a more varied place of ground" and created difficulties in the management of water:

> The water at Longleat has been an unmeaning, long, narrow canal passing within about fifty yards of the house. There is a fall or two introduced in it, which though rather formal is very pleasing, as the ground wants something of the sort to enliven the scene.[5]

One might be tempted to speculate that "unmeaning" is a hasty mistranscription of "unmeandering" were it not that Parnell repeatedly alludes to meaning or lack of meaning in all kinds of garden features, although particularly of course with reference to such more obviously iconographic objects as temples and monuments. Here, for instance, he writes of the Bristol Cross at Stourhead:

> It is one of the most elegant pieces of ancient Gothic workmanship I ever saw, and must have been an exquisite ornament to an ancient city as Bristol, but the wise mayor and aldermen disposed of it to Mr. Hoare who paid for the carriage and putting up about £300. It stands within his grounds but appears as belonging to a little village with a neat parish church just without them. This was the very spot above all others to place this neat building in, which would have wanted meaning as a mere garden building.[6]

In the Bristol Cross Parnell found an associative decorum that he thought was lacking in, for instance, the Temple of Apollo or the statue of Neptune in his car with sea horses below the Temple of Flora.

Decorum, propriety, and meaning characterize the location of buildings in Charles Hamilton's landscape at Painshill:

> The Hermitage is the best adapted to its proper place of any in England. The part it's in, though a mere plantation of Scots fir, larch, cedar and pines mixed with birch on the wildest part of the heath which comes into the improvement on that corner, has really the air of a wild forest, the ground amidst the trees so rough not a little contributing. Here also is the gothic tower, fit edifice for a wild forest. But from it you enter ground dressed and clumped with flowering shrubs, sweet trees and flowers, like the Elysian Plains, and in it a

temple with all the elegance about it of ancient Greece. See here what propriety in ornamental buildings: not a root-house in a rosary nor a "Doctor Clarke in a Hermitage."[7]

Parnell's sense of decorum underlies his enthusiasm for gothic forms which, as he acknowledges, may not be "correct, but are in a sense natural." Slender gothic pillars "are much more beautiful than the massy piers we generally find in modern buildings," he declares, and continues, "nothing convinces me of this more than comparing the aisles of Salisbury Cathedral, with that of St. Paul's in London: one looks like only a tall vault or hollowed rock, the other like a fine well grown grove of straight trees, contributing their branching heads, to form a close shade." He admires Esher Place, Henry Pelham's seat, as "a noble old Gothic building," and he is charmed by a Mr. Bateman's house at Old Windsor. Mr. Bateman "has built his house like an old abbey amidst tall elms and limes which give it a most venerable appearance. On one side an open cloister or gothic colonnade shows you several ancient chairs, tables, pictures, reliques, etc.; on the other side of the house is a neat flower garden, with an hermit's cell in it, and at the end the parish church, which being Gothic as most in England are gives the whole a true abbey-like appearance. This gentleman amuses himself amongst these whimsical scenes: sometimes reads like an hermit in his cell, and at other times drives his '*snowy flocks afield*' like a primitive shepherd."[8] One is left with the impression that the gothic parish church somehow gives meaning, decorum, and even truth to what on the face of it is the romantic absurdity of Mr. Bateman acting the part of hermit or Hebrew patriarch.

Parnell is a connoisseur altogether typical of his age in his taste for romantic landscape, natural or man-made, and for all things gothic. As the ship carrying him for the first time to England passed Chester Bar he noted that "the moon shone very bright, and as I could distinguish the Welsh coast it appeared vastly beautiful: romantique rocks, woods, and glens, interspersed with meadows, etc." The Hot Wells near Bristol were "as romantic a pretty spot as ever I beheld, surrounded with perpendicular mountains covered with trees that seem each to have its root in the top of another." He was more impressed by Ralph Allen's quarry than by the improvements at Prior Park, for the quarry "has a very romantic appearance, the parts which have been worked out are planted with fir that ornament it much." He found that the "new-contrived ruin" at Woburn Farm

> inspires all that awe so natural to ruined grandeur, when one conceives it might have been the mansion of greatness or wisdom now reduced to dust. The walls are all overgrown with ivy which hangs in festoons and branches from the top of the one entire spire. One thing I wished away which was a cypress that grew formally up against the wall like a clipped yew.[9]

Evidently Southcote's formal cypress was less decorous in its situation than Allen's romantic fir plantation. The stirrings of romantic fancy that

Parnell experienced at the sight of the gothic ruin in Woborn Farm were felt elsewhere: in Westminster Hall for instance, where "the lawyers walking to and fro are but a bad substitute for so many armed knights preparing for a tournament."[10]

Quotations in the last two paragraphs above are taken from Parnell's account of his visit to England in 1762-1763, but the journals of 1769-1770 reveal no weakening of romantic enthusiasm. In Hatfield House, for instance, "the great hall for entertainment of knights and barons bold shows the hospitality, as the noble chapel with the fine stained glass does the religion of our ancestors," and at Stourhead "the walk enters a sort of ruined castle and, winding up one of the turrets, goes along a passage which you find to be over the high road, as the passages round a fortified town are carried over the great gateways, only all seems in ruin, grass etc. growing extremely romantically in every interstice of this whimsical building."[11] In his two descriptions of Conway Castle on the outward and the inward journeys of 1769-1770 Parnell deploys the current, approved aesthetic terms, "sublime," "beautiful," and "picturesque"; he reveals the close association between taste and feeling in his curious suggestion as to why the beholder should be more affected emotionally and morally by gothic ruins than by classical ones; and he shows himself as a kind of practical romantic in his memoranda and sketches for improvements to be set in hand on his own estate in Ireland:

> Conway Castle and the romantic ivy-towered walls were the only objects particular pleasing to me. . . . I do not think there is to be seen anywhere a more stupendous ruin. . . . It has an effect on the beholder . . . such as I do not recollect to have often felt from the finest remains in Italy. In the one you meet the decay of elegance and magnificence, a thing however affecting is still considered as the certain consequence of over-refinement; but here we see that the most solid strength, the most gigantic masses of mere useful stonework, and their foundation too a rock, are not proof against all-decaying time. Add that the wildness of the country and the size of the building with few breaks or ornaments has all the effect on the beholder which the *Sublime* can produce, an effect ever found stronger, especially in its first impressions, than the *Beautiful*. . . . Memorandum: I am determined to make the very most of my great battlemented walls and build up the turrets. Nothing so magnificent as castles founded on steep rocks on wooded ascents. . . . I took notice that the battlement walls of the small round towers were apparently supported by rounded modillions at intervals, double their own breadth, much as I drew those in the little design for my granary. This pleased me, as two or three have told me they are not a gothic ornament. But I knew at the time they were the properest for a castle whose ornaments as well as several parts differ extremely from the gothic churches which those gentlemen had taken their ideas from. In small buildings a brick rounded at the end thus would just do.[12]

After "thus" he draws the outline of a brick half-rounded at one end to give the effect of a modillion, or corbel. In his union of the practical and the whimsical Parnell seems to typify the taste and sensibility of his class and age. His appetite for romance is as strong as his sense of reality, and he is not aware of any contradiction between the two.

The rest of the present article is devoted to Parnell's comments on Hagley Park and The Leasowes in the "Journal," April 1770. From references in this journal it is evident that Parnell had visited both gardens once before: in the case of Hagley this visit was certainly on the morning of October 23, 1763, because the account breaks off under that date, just at the beginning of a description of the place, at a page on which Parnell has sketched the front and side elevations of the new-built Hagley Hall; his visit to The Leasowes was almost certainly on that same day. The 1770 visits were made on April 18 when Parnell was traveling from Bath to Holyhead where he intended to take ship home to Ireland after a year's stay in England. He wrote up his journal accounts of the two gardens in an inn room at Chester two or three days after the visits, with Dodsley's description of The Leasowes[13] and Young's very recent description of both places[14] either before him or very much in his mind, so that the observations he makes are intended to be supplementary to theirs.

Young had said nothing about the area northwest of Hagley Hall, in the angle between the Halesowen to Birmingham and the Stourbridge to Bromsgrove roads, so Parnell offers a description, keyed to a sketch map (*Plate 28*):

> The house is situated about three hundred yards or more from the Stourbridge road. It is in the park which is separated from a little lawn that joins the road by sunk pales which, except just the breadth of the approach to the house by a side avenue, is continued quite across the park which is here however not above 2 or 300 yards wide. The approach is through a double row of elm, lime and horse chestnut, sweeping round the little lawn to the road and, after you pass through the park gate, continuing close to the pales, which enclose a little shrubbery and plantation behind it to hide the offices. The sweep of these trees keep them out of the way of the view from the house and prevent their being formal. The house communicates with the offices by a sunk road, about 50 yards, entering into the passage which leads quite the length of the house and communicates with all the under-offices. The kitchen and servants' hall are both under the house. The shrubbery I mentioned hides the stables, behind which lie the farm-yard, the barn crossing it. Behind these is a little field marked E in the plan into which a little building with a coarse-cut stone portico opens and serves as a dairy, the other half opening into a little pleasure garden and serving as a small green house from whence you may enter the dairy. The shrubbery G entirely surrounds the gardens and screens them from the view of the house. N.B. pales never look ill when trees are planted close behind them, the branches growing through them, or so close and hanging over in such a manner that they become concealed in a little time and lost in the trees behind them. This is never the case with a stone wall, unless when covered with ivy.[15]

This passage is from the opening of Parnell's description of Hagley; at the end of the description he makes a few supplementary observations:

> The walled gardens, for there are two or three of 'em adjoining, are very good: the espalier trees trained to upright stakes at about ten inches asunder, but kept firm in their place by one continued rail nailed on their tops. There is also two or three little flower gardens, with a basin of goldfish, one of 'em prettily introduced in the shrubbery terminated with a little Doric portico which serves as a greenhouse for the hardier exotics and opens into the dairy. At the side of this little garden is an urn with a great clump of evergreens behind it.[16]

Parnell's map is orientated with east at the top, and, like all the maps in his journals, is wrongly proportioned. The ha-ha, which exists today without its sunk pales, was in fact much closer to the house than to the Stourbridge road, although Parnell's map suggests the reverse, and the whole area between the Birmingham road and the private road to the house was much wider than is indicated on the map. Nevertheless, the map and written description together enable us to recover the location and appearance of several garden features that have now disappeared: the fruit and flower gardens, the shrubbery, the pigeon house (on the map), and the eclectic, dual-purpose, back-to-back building, with its Doric portico into the greenhouse on one side and "coarse-cut stone" portico into the dairy on the other.

Some remarks by Young[17] evidently provided the text for Parnell's general observations on the character of Hagley Park at the beginning of his account:

> The great beauty of Hagley is the great diversity of the ground in view, all gently swelling or rising pretty steep, with valleys between the hills well-covered with fine old wood, and the vales either dressed finely in little lawns or watered by little streams, in one part thrown down in four or five cascades and forming basins between them which in some points of view appear one piece of water. In all they are made to resemble nature much as possible, but I must confess fail in this point, one or two views excepted; for, as the ground falls much, the heads to these little basins are raised high of consequence, and the water which supplies them being but a small stream . . . the cascades do not play constantly, and when they do, though they are broken in a very pleasing manner, yet in order to spread them they are kept so thin on the board over which they fall that, just in that part, they are as apparently forced as in any old fashioned flights of stone step cascades. It is a pity there is not more water coming down this little valley as the pains Lord Lyttelton has been at deserves a better water.[18]

Although he does not attempt to duplicate Young's sequential account, it is evident that Parnell took the same circuit as Young, walking in a northeasterly direction away from the house beside the little stream that still runs alongside the church, and then turning away to the left to climb a gentle slope to the statue of Frederick, Prince of Wales, still standing. Parnell adds a note about the planting behind this statue, and further detail (not in Young) concerning the planting of the steep ridge southeast of the house:

> The ground rises gently behind the house at about 300 yards. Just under a close piece of wood and evergreens is placed a column to the late Prince of Wales. . . . The ground rises pretty steep near the side of the house of the opposite end to the stables. On it open wood, old trees and some spotting trees, etc., and pretty high up on the hill a clump of all larch paled round.[19]

He adds significant information, not in Young, about the stream with "four or five cascades" (the one still running beside the church):

> From the little valley where the cascades are runs the stream which supplies them, through the lawn down towards the house, the course neatly paved with pebbles and the margent kept neatly turfed. It looks cool and very pretty. I think nothing more pleasing than such a little stream, and [it] should never be neglected where it can be procured . . . Lord Lyttelton's stream enters a row of small stew ponds covered over with rails, locked down occasionally, from whence it goes underground to the kitchen and other offices in the house, and thence serves the stable yards, etc., etc. In the stews any fish may be kept a week or fortnight for the house use. As the stream passes constantly through them the fish are purged of any muddy taste they might have had before.[20]

Unlike most of the men who published descriptions of gardens in the eighteenth century, Parnell was himself a landowner and improver. Young, of course, prided himself on being a farmer (and was admired as such by Parnell, who visited his experimental farm at North Mimms), but in his description of Hagley Park he is far less alive to questions of practicality and profit than Parnell is. After the stew ponds that insure that even the most picturesque piece of water is brought to use, Parnell mentions the management of the parkland on either side of the Birmingham road for pasture and hay:

> Part of the park, viz. that to the left of the little valley [i.e., south of the Birmingham road], is divided by moving rails about half as high again as common slatted hurdles for sheep. This part of the park is kept for hay every second year. This is a piece of good management almost universally observed in the best parks in England. The part lying on the other side of the Birmingham road is well dressed and ornamented with three or four buildings, such as a Doric temple of six columns, a small obelisk on the highest part of the ground without any wood behind it, and a rustic building on pillars in a piece of wood which serves as a hovel for cattle. But though these buildings are placed here to give this ground its due share of ornament, yet little real utility has been sacrificed to beauty, the old enclosures having

been all preserved, but the hedges kept either plashed or neatly clipped.[21]

The obelisk and Doric temple (James "Athenian" Stuart's Temple of Theseus) remain today, although the "rustic building," perhaps made of wood, has gone. All the superstructure of Thomson's seat, on a swell of ground ornamented with trees between the house and the Birmingham road commanding fine views inside and outside the park, has now disappeared too, so it is useful to have Parnell's drawing (marked "Fig. A" on *Plate 29*). Whately misleadingly describes the building as an "octagon seat," and Heely refers to its "octagonal form."[22]

The regular circuit of Hagley Park from Thomson's seat followed a generally clockwise direction, serpentining through groves and glades, past Jacob's Well, the eight-columned Ionic rotunda, and the urn to Pope (all of which survive today in various states of ruin), and gradually ascending to the sham castle at the highest point of the park, on the slopes of the Clent Hills. In his description, however, Parnell turns directly to the castle:

> [From Thomson's seat] you get a view of the tower on the top of the opposite hill, peeping through old oak and beech, or as Milton would say "bosomed high in tufted trees." The principal object in this ruin is the high ruined tower and staircase adjoining to fit. The tower is the habitation of the keeper and is four stories high. There are three other towers, supposed in ruins, which serve, one for a cow house, one for a turf house and the other a poultry house, the walls which connect them forming a square yard as in the plan (figure B). The ruin was built on a hill which on three sides commanded a most extensive prospect of Worcestershire and Shropshire, the bottom of which was finely wooded by nature, but towards the top there has been beech planted.[23]

The castle survives, only slightly more ruined than when it was built, but Parnell's description and drawings (*Plates 29, 30, and 31*) give particulars of its use that are not found in other accounts. His other drawings are even more interesting because they depict garden buildings that have not survived and are not fully described in published accounts. Three of these buildings, a "seat of contemplation," a hermitage, and a "cave of grotto work," lay close to the second important piece of water, the stream which ran, and still runs, close to the southernmost boundary of the park. Young's account of them[24] is filled out a little in Parnell's written description, and a great deal more in his drawings:

> From the ruin you pass by a small pond, made by banking up a little stream at the head of a valley. The walk runs near the park pales with a little wood on the right hand which springs from the valley. Here in a spot looking only to the wood you meet a seat dedicated to Contemplation [figure C, *Plate 31*], and soon after (but in a spot where from the door you command a pleasing view of Worcestershire) you arrive at the hermitage, a little square building of roots and stumps and

covered over with turf [figure D, *Plate 32*]. Crossing the head of another small pond in the valley you come to a little rustic alcove formed in front of stumps of wood, arched at top and turfed over [figure L, *Plate 32*], and, as it is built against the side of a bank, scarce visible behind: the inside moss stuck on the stones, at top the moss fastened on with laths and nails, the seat of round unbarked sticks, inch and a half diameter, nailed on about two inches asunder.[25]

Parnell does not mention or draw the "cave of grotto work." This cave, like the three buildings he does depict, has disappeared now.

Following the same route as Young, Parnell turned to his right and climbed up the side of the little valley to Milton's seat (now no longer to be seen, although its site is clear enough). His account adds little to Young, although he does draw attention to an artfully sited farmhouse, ignored in descriptions by others:

From this, winding up a pretty steep hill you come to a seat which overlooks all the park and a vast tract of variegated country. Here you see that the house is situated at a narrow extremity of the park, which is that spot no broader than the ha ha at the front of the house, about 300 yards. This is the spot where Lord Lyttelton has judiciously put up the inscription from Milton: "These are thy glorious works," etc. You have amongst others a pleasing object in view, a smooth swelling hill planted with clumps of Scotch fir, and in a little enclosure just under one of them a neat white farmhouse placed here on purpose in full view of Hagley.[26]

Continuing the regular circuit, Parnell descended toward the principal watercourse through the middle of the park:

From this seat you wind through a great old wood by the side of a little lawn to a small building [figure E, *Plate 33*]. This takes in a view of a little Ionic temple at the head of a lawn, the valley of flowering shrubs and cascades mentioned before, and, full in front on a swell of ground ornamented with trees, you see the first building I mentioned. Winding down to the bottom of the little lawn and passing by giant oak, some 18 feet circumference, you enter the valley paled in from the park and continue your walk by a little pebbly brook which gushes into the valley by a cascade about ten feet high and continues its course through scattered flowering shrubs to the first cascade into one of the string of basins which are terminated at bottom by a small Palladian bridge, from whence the view of the several falls down this little valley thickly wooded at each side has a very good effect. This scheme of an elegant little pleasure ground in the centre of a bold and extensive park is particularly pleasing, as each enhances the other's beauty by contrast.[27]

Parnell's account of this highly ornamented area in the middle of the park lacks the detail of Young's, but the inscription added to his drawing (*Plate 33*) enables us to identify the small building as one referred to by Young as "the seat inscribed *Quieti et Musis*." From what both Young and Whately say about its location, we can further infer that this is also the "Doric Portico called Pope's Building" mentioned by Heely and Whatley.[28] This building has now disappeared: its precise location is not certain, but presumably it was sited somewhere on the northwest facing slopes of the ridge that runs from the sham castle to Milton's seat.

Parnell saw Hagley when George Lyttleton was still alive and when the park was probably at its best. By contrast, Shenstone's more famous ornamented farm nearby had begun to decline. Parnell, like Young, viewed The Leasowes after it had passed through the hands of some owners very different from Shenstone, but he is far more informative and less discreet than Young concerning recent possessors and the decay of the grounds:

> This poor place is fated to ill luck with its possessors, none of those taking it appearing to me in the least fit for what I may call so *poetic* a place. In the name of order, decency, etc., etc., what has Captain *Turpenny* of Birmingham and Powell of Liverpool or any other trafficking West Indian slave master to do with urns, inscriptions, mottoes, shady recesses dedicated to poets, muses, etc., etc.? . . . Poor Miss Dolman's urn is quite destroyed. It should have been ever preserved for the sake of the elegant Latin inscription on the pedestal, but as the lovers' walk in which it was placed is in a ruinous state I was not suprised that the deity of the walk should herself suffer by all devouring *time* and his follower *neglect.* . . . The old Gothic seat [*Plate 34*] with the inscription "Oh ye who bathe in courtlie blysse" is nearly fallen down.[29]

This gothic seat is numbered 20 on the map in Dodsley. Another gothic seat, marked 30 on Dodsley's map, and sketched by Parnell (*Plate 35a*) was apparently in good order.

Although Young had made few observations on The Leasowes, Dodsley had given a detailed account of the regular tourist circuit for taking in Shenstone's improvements, so Parnell makes no attempt at duplication. Declaring that, unlike Dodsley or Young, he will attend as much to the means as to the effects of landscape gardening, he explains at great length Shenstone's methods of concealing the bounds of his fields (perhaps considering such explanation all the more necessary because hedges appear as the most prominent feature on the map that accompanied Dodsley's published description):

> Both Dodsley and Young have said so much of the Leasowes that I have little to say even for my own satisfaction with respect to its beauties, but with respect to the disposition of its grounds, how he has managed to mix the utile dulci, I think I have made myself master of that which has often puzzled me to conceive, as from Shenstone's writings I should have concluded he had thrown his whole domain into an open lawn, whilst at the same time I knew his circumstances could not well have afforded such an expensive disposition of his farm. This made me more desirous of seeing the Leasowes than any other consideration. I well remembered from the time I had been

there before . . . what beautiful scenery, what romantic cascades, occurred to us in several parts; but as I was then no farmer, at best no practical one, it never occurred to me to attend to the *means* which produced this agreeable tout ensemble, content as I was with the pleasure the *effect* gave me. . . . His land is (contrary to what I expected) as much divided as necessary, but he has well concealed the divisions by making use of some part of the improvement to answer that purpose, not merely as a hedge but as it were accidentally. Thus the first glen you meet at the Priory gate, thickly wooded and consequently concealing the hedge which fences it in, divides the lawn from a pasture field on one side, as the little wooded glen with the cascade to Lord Stamford forms a division on the other side the lawn. The little serpentine river[30] from the house to the head of this cascade, together with the house and offices, divides the lawn in front from that at the back of the house. As the private road to some outland is also brought down through a part of this back lawn, and being planted on each side with a neat plashed hedge and sufficiently below the fence to be concealed, it appears only a skirting plantation to the house and offices instead of a disagreeable eyesore, which it would do less artificially managed. The small piece of water which supplies the cascades in the first or Priory glen makes another division. The rest of the land, consisting of swells with small valleys, is divided artfully in the valley so that the eye overlooks the hedge, except in one or two places where very fine thorn hedges are suffered to appear; but as they rather skirt the view than cross the eye they have a pleasing effect and add to the variety of the scene. I cannot express how much I was pleased with this natural and at the same time most judicious division of the grounds. It suffered nothing obtrusive to hurt the sight, as Shenstone somewhere expresses it; at the same time it avoided the poorness of having all thrown into an expensive lawn, which would have ill become the character of a ferme ornée as Mr. Shenstone studied to make the Leasowes. Where a large swell has at its bottom a strip of flat meadow, just immediately under the swell runs a thorn hedge: this cannot hurt the eye from any part of the swell, as it overlooks it at once. By those judicious strokes a farm may at once be enclosed and at the same time preserve all the beauty of an extensive lawn. All his woodworks were fenced by a small grip [i.e., ditch] and neat stake hedge or plashed thorns on top of the bank. The fields in general did not exceed four or five acres Irish.[31]

Parnell notes that where fences are used they are used with great economy, and interestingly links the dearth of new plantation with the aesthetic disadvantage of fencing young trees. He praises economy also in Shenstone's little seats, and here too Parnell's descriptions and drawings add some detail not found in accounts by others:

Through the whole improvement you may perceive Shenstone had not in his power to expend the sums in embellishing his farm he would have done had fortune been more bountiful to him. Consequently his seats are often such as he would never have put up could he have afforded others, two or three excepted which I think are really pretty enough to have a place in any improvement in other places. Two small wooden pillars, mostly gothic, supporting a roof just broad enough to shade you from a summer shower is the usual building you meet. These, and the back all of wood. In one or two places he has formed a pretty rural-looking seat and clump all in one by planting a clump of about 10 yards diameter and paling it in this shape [*Plate 35b*]. The pales at A which serve to fence that side of the clump are run in about two or three feet so that the plantation projects at your side, and they answer at once as a fence to the trees and as a back to a seat placed at A. The trees growing over at top and sides soon form an agreeable shade over the seat, more so than any artificial cover would be, except in very heavy rain. In some places the corners of fields are taken off with a circular paling and closely planted within. This forms a charming well shaped back-screen for a building which, if white, is shown off to great advantage by the dark green of firs, hollies, etc. behind it. The pales of those plantations in angles run as at AA [*Plate 35c*]. In the margent B the little building before the plantation.[32]

Dodsley had enthused over the cascade that ran down toward the root house inscribed to Lord Stamford: "The eye is presented with a fairy vision, consisting of an irregular and romantic fall of water . . . a more wild and romantic appearance of water, and at the same time strictly natural, is what I never saw in place whatever."[33] Young, too, found the cascade "astonishingly romantic."[34]

Parnell, as he had done at Hagley, reminds himself that there is more water available on his estate in Ireland for the creation of such effects, and observes, as Young had failed to do, by what artificial means the romantic dashing and sparkling effect of the waters was achieved: "The first cascade, I mean the long one to Lord Stamford, is nothing to what I might have in the Bounds Brook, especially if I made a small reservoir. The trees were mostly natural wood. The criss-cross dashing of the water formed by flagstones and dams built purposely, not by the roots of trees as I at first imagined." Parnell also adds some detail, not in Dodsley and Young, concerning the root house near the foot of the cascade, and provides a sketch (*Plate 34*): "The root seat dedicated to Lord Stamford was only a sort of concave screen, about a yard and a half thick and sodded at top. The narrow door through it has a very pretty effect. It is a good sort of seat where one would wish any view excluded till immediately at it."[35]

Hagley and The Leasowes are relatively well-documented landscapes, but Parnell's descriptions contribute significant information not available in the better-known published accounts. Parnell's value lies perhaps in his combining the roles of practical landowner and romantic connoisseur so that his principle of decorum is applied unself-consciously to the provision of fresh fish and fruit as much as to the siting of a sham-gothic priory or castle. The improvement of an estate is a matter equally of aesthetics, sentiment, and business. Parnell's easy union of the pragmatic and the romantic reminds us, perhaps, that landscape gardening is a curiously mixed art form.

University of Southampton

NOTES

1. *Dictionary of National Biography*, s.v. "Parnell, John."

2. Shelfmark MS, Ma. 11. Extracts are quoted by courtesy of Lord Congleton and the Folger Shakespeare Library, Washington, D.C.

3. Shelfmark MS, Coll. Misc. 38. Extracts are quoted by courtesy of Lord Congleton and the British Library of Political and Economic Science, London.

4. "Wooburn Farm in the 1760s," *Garden History*, VII (Summer, 1979), pp. 82-101; "Painshill Park in the 1760s," *ibid.*, VIII (Spring, 1980), pp. 91-106.

5. "Journal," II, pp. 69, 71. In this and all other quoted extracts from Parnell's manuscripts, I have modernized spelling and capitalization and have supplied punctuation.

6. *Ibid.*, pp. 85-86.

7. *Ibid.*, I, pp. 162-163. "Nor in an Hermitage set Dr. Clarke." Alexander Pope, *Epistle to Burlington*, line 78, p. 140, in F. W. Bateson, ed., *Epistles to Several Persons*, John Butt, gen. ed., *The Poems of Alexander Pope*, Twickenham Edition, III, ii (London, 1951).

8. "Account," pp. 212, 147.

9. *Ibid.*, pp. 7, 63, 60, 163.

10. *Ibid.*, p. 76.

11. "Journal," III, p. 10; II, p. 90.

12. *Ibid.*, III, pp. 130-133; I, pp. 7-8; III, pp. 133-134.

13. Robert Dodsley, "A Description of The Leasowes," in Robert Dodsley, ed., *Works in Verse and Prose of W. Shenstone, Esq.* (London, 1764), II, pp. 333-371.

14. Arthur Young, *A Six Month's Tour through the North of England* (London, 1770), III, pp. 342-361.

15. "Journal," III, p. 65-66.

16. *Ibid.*, p. 76.

17. Young, *Six Month's Tour*, III, p. 361.

18. "Journal," III, pp. 68-69.

19. *Ibid.*, pp. 66, 68.

20. *Ibid.*, pp. 71-72.

21. *Ibid.*, pp. 72-73.

22. Thomas Whately, *Observations on Modern Gardening* (London, 1770), p. 197; Joseph Heely, *Letters on the Beauties of Hagley, Envil and The Leasowes* (London, 1777), I, p. 221.

23. "Journal," III, pp. 73-74.

24. Young, *Six Month's Tour*, III, pp. 353-354.

25. "Journal," III, p. 74.

26. *Ibid.*, pp. 74-75.

27. *Ibid.*, pp. 75-76.

28. Young, *Six Month's Tour*, III, p. 356; Whately, *Observations*, pp. 198, 201; Heely, *Letters*, I, p. 205.

29. "Journal," III, pp. 85, 101, 103.

30. Dodsley's map shows only a disconnected piece of water, below and to the left of number 18, but all the references in his written description are to a long serpentine stream. *Works*, II, pp. 348, 350, 352.

31. That is about seven or eight English statute acres. "Journal," III, pp. 88-89, 93-96.

32. *Ibid.*, pp. 106-108.

33. Dodsley, *Works*, II, p. 341.

34. Young, *Six Month's Tour*, III, pp. 343-344.

35. "Journal," III, pp. 103, 115.

Nature as the Bride of Art:
The Design and Structure of Painshill

Michael Symes

The landscape garden of Painshill, Cobham, Surrey, is, at the time of writing, about to be restored after years of neglect and deterioration. The Painshill Park Trust has been established with a view to re-creating as far as possible Charles Hamilton's original layout so that once more this jewel among eighteenth-century gardens may live and glow. Quite apart from its importance to garden historians, therefore, Painshill has a special topical interest which makes it important that its history be explored and understood.

Painshill, formed by the Hon. Charles Hamilton between 1738 and 1773, is a subtle, complex and rewarding garden, rich in many of the elements that contribute to eighteenth-century landscape gardens but unique in its particular combination and use of those elements (*Plate 36*). In some ways it was a landscape in the freer and more natural style promoted by Alexander Pope and William Kent,[1] who had popularized the concept of irregular (although controlled) form and the mode of composing landscape as a series of carefully calculated set pieces. Hamilton was certainly acquainted with Kent's work: two of Kent's major works, Claremont and Esher Place in Surrey, were only a few miles from Painshill, and Kent had also advised Lord Lincoln and Philip Southcote on Oatlands, Surrey, and Woburn Farm, Surrey, respectively. Hamilton had connections with both places (which were also close by). He was a friend of the anecdotist, author, and garden designer Joseph Spence, and made comments on the layout of Oatlands to Spence; and Southcote was with Hamilton a mutual friend of Spence and of Stephen Fox, later Lord Ilchester. Southcote was also related to Lord Petre, to whom Peter Collinson wrote about Painshill.

Three of these estates were early enough possibly to have influenced Hamilton. Claremont had a lake, an island, a temple, and a belvedere that is an obvious candidate for the source of Hamilton's watchtower; Esher Place had a grotto, a hermitage, and a thatched house (Hamilton's hermitage was thatched); Woburn Farm had gothic buildings, a ruined chapel, alcoves, and bridges; and the fourth, Oatlands, had a grotto decorated by the builders of several grottoes, the Lanes, although their involvement there was later than at Painshill. In addition to these architectural features, Hamilton could have learned much about the management of trees and water, the framing of visual compositions, distancing and perspective, and all the practicalities of the art of landscaping.

Hamilton appears to have followed many of Southcote's ideas on design, as recorded by Spence. He put into effect Southcote's precept that a garden should not be so open that it could be comprehended at one glance, and Painshill was contrived so that one continually looked down to the lake and across and up to a hanging wood, as Southcote recommended. Southcote also thought that buildings should be placed on rising ground, and those at Painshill were certainly in prominent positions. This last point is, however, common to most garden theorists of the time.

It is unfortunate that we have no firsthand record of Hamilton's intentions. It is, nonetheless, possible to arrive at a number of conclusions from contemporary commentators and from the work of other designers and garden theorists. The first thing to be said is that in 1738 the idea of the free form landscape was still in its infancy (and even Kent himself never outgrew formality altogether), and that Hamilton turned out to be a creative innovator in a number of respects.

The main effect that Hamilton sought was naturalness. There were some formal areas at Painshill, such as the straight walk leading from the bastion overlooking the vineyard hill to the Sabine statue in its "amphitheatre" of shrubs and trees (Parnell's word)[2] and thence to the gothic temple, but most of the pleasure grounds and all of the open landscape park anticipated the idealizing of nature implicit in "Capability" Brown's designs. Joseph Warton observed that Pope's dictum that nature should never be forgot was not put into practice until the 1740s: "The best comments that have been given on these sensible and striking procepts, are, *Painshill, Hagley,* the *Leasowes, Persefield, Woburn, Stourhead,* and *Blenheim;* all of them exquisite scenes in different styles, and fine examples of practical poetry."[3] The Reverend Stephen Duck, rector of Byfleet and sometime curator of Merlin's Cave at Richmond, described Hamilton and Spence as "nature's children,"[4] and Hamilton's natural approach was widely recognized.

The unobtrusive use of art at Painshill was frequently commented upon. Elizabeth Montagu paid a visit in 1755: "Pray follow me to Mr. Hamilton's: I must tell you it beggars all description, the art of hiding art is here in such sweet perfection, that Mr. Hamilton cheats himself of praise, you thank Nature for all you see, tho' I am informed all has been reformed by Art."[5] This foreshadows similar comments made about Brown's landscapes. Uvedale Price approved thoroughly of the style:

> Among many circumstances of more striking effect, I was highly pleased with a walk which leads through a bottom skirted with wood; and I was pleased with it, not from what *had,* but from what had *not,* been done; it had no edges, no borders, no distinct lines of separation; nothing was done except keeping the ground properly neat, and the communication free from any obstruction; the eye and the footsteps were equally unconfined, and if it is a high commendation to a writer or painter, that he knows when to leave off, it is not less so to an improver.[6]

Price goes on to praise Hamilton's use of the art that conceals art.

Many others continued to praise the natural appearance of the grounds:

> There may be scenes, says an author who describes it, where Nature had done more for herself, but in no place that I ever saw has so much been done for Nature as at *Pains-hill*. The beauty and unexpected variety of the scene, the happy situation, elegant structure and judicious form of the buildings, the flourishing state, uncommon diversity, and contrasted groupage of the trees, and the contrivance of this water &, will not fail to awaken the most pleasing sensations.[7]

The natural effect was not achieved lightly: the lake had to be excavated, and much planting was undertaken to convert an area of barren heath, woods, and fields (but including some formal gardens) to the place of elegance and beauty that it became under Hamilton's guidance.

An important concept behind the structure of Painshill is that of "mood." Shenstone considered that garden scenes could be categorized as sublime, beautiful, or melancholy, and put this into practice in his own *ferme ornée* at The Leasowes. Lord Kames, discussing the parallels between gardening and architecture, wrote in 1762 that local areas within a garden could evoke special moods and thoughts: "Gardening, beside the emotions of beauty from regularity, order, proportion, colour, and utility, can raise emotions of grandeur, of sweetness, of gaiety, of melancholy, of wildness, and even of surprise or wonder."[8] He thought that several emotions should be inspired in turn: "A ruin affording a sort of melancholy pleasure, ought not to be seen from a flower-parterre which is gay and chearful. But to pass from an exhilarating object to a ruin, has a fine effect; for each of the emotions is the more sensibly felt by being contrasted with the other."[9] To the eighteenth-century sensibility a landscape garden was not only an attractive place to look at and walk about in, but it could be a broad experience that stirred the visitor's mind and imagination as well.

Painshill is an associative garden, but not a literary or allegorical one. There is nothing comparable to the specific literary references at The Leasowes, with its inscriptions and texts, to the emblematic and political groupings at Stowe, or to the Aenean progress at Stourhead. But there are deliberate evocations of mood and of associations of different cultures, and Hamilton played on the sensibilities of his visitors. Geoffrey and Susan Jellicoe have described Hamilton's theme as

> poetic as the allegory at Stourhead: out of an unpromising scene to make an artificial landscape that would tell the story of past civilizations and their place in the great wilderness of nature. In contrast to Stourhead, he made it linear—a study in time and movement as in a Chinese scroll. The symbolic objects were to be revealed in progression along a broad, sinuous and island-studded river apparently without beginning or end.[10]

This interesting interpretation claims for Hamilton the instincts of a poet without being a man of letters.

In the gardens we find the creation of a series of moods as well as the provision of a number of differing visual effects. Particular atmospheres were conjured up—near the hermitage, gloom; near the Temple of Bacchus, cheerfulness; near the ruined abbey, sadness or awe. Painshill was an emotional and mental experience akin to a poem, which gave additional meaning to Warton's phrase "practical poetry," mentioned earlier.

Painshill is often described as a "picturesque" garden insofar as it represents a series of visual compositions. The term is misleading, as Kenneth Woodbridge tells us elsewhere in this volume, both because the concept of the picturesque itself changes through the eighteenth century and also because it is dangerous to press the painting analogy too far when dealing with gardens. At Painshill Hamilton demonstrated both smooth and rugged "picturesque" styles, as characterized by Claude and Rosa respectively; but rather than think of the scenes in the gardens as paintings or quasi-paintings it may be preferable to use some other term such as "set piece," not least because of the theatrical nature of some of Hamilton's effects.

It has often been claimed that Hamilton deliberately tried to reproduce landscape painting of the school of Claude, Poussin, or Rosa, either by copying or using the same style, in nature's own materials. Uvedale Price made capital out of the notion in 1794, but it was only to be expected that, because he admired Painshill, he should try to make it fit his "picturesque" theories. The basic tenet was that created landscape should follow the same rules in its making as landscape painting. Price wrote: "I have always understood that Mr. Hamilton, who created Painshill, not only had studied pictures, but had studied them for the express purpose of improving real landscape. The place he created (a task of quite another difficulty from correcting, or from adding to natural scenery) fully proves the use of such a study."[11]

The same idea was taken up by the Reverend John Mitford in his edition of the works of Thomas Gray, published in 1858. In a letter to Wharton dated August 13, 1754, Gray advises Wharton to visit Painshill. Mitford added a footnote: "Mr. Hamilton formed many of the beautiful scenes in the grounds at Painshill from the Pictures of Poussin and the Italian Masters: the Waterfall at Bow-wood, the seat of the Marquis of Lansdowne, is from a Picture of G. Poussin."[12] The latter claim seems quite likely, for the Bowood cascade does resemble Gaspard's view of the falls at Tivoli, but this does not necessarily mean that Hamilton copied specific paintings at Painshill. The likelihood is, rather, that Italian campagna paintings generally were one of a number of influences on him. He was a keen collector of Italian paintings, including works by Panini and Maratta, but he also knew the Italian countryside at firsthand from his two visits there. When he came to create his garden, it would be understandable if he had tried to include some elements that suggested or embodied those qualities and characteristics that he absorbed while in Italy, in terms both of landscape and the use of buildings within a landscape. He may well have used the techniques of perspective and distancing to be found in landscape painting (but also in architecture and theatrical scenery). It is salutary, however, to bear in mind George Mason's caveat: "If HAMILTON by studying pictures improved his real landscape, it is to be remembered that he was *previously* a gardener. His thoughts were engaged by their favourite pursuit, which saved them from being cramped and vitiated by painting prejudices."[13] This reminder of Hamilton's considerable horticultural interests puts the matter in a needed perspective.

Hamilton used a wide selection of styles to achieve his effects, and it is clear that the range constituted a major attraction. The separate associations evoked, combined with the visual kaleidoscope of scenes, furnished the essential charm of Painshill: its variety. Almost every commentator has mentioned this quality, summed up in the topographical historian E. Brayley's words: "There is a great diversity of surface at Painshill, and its fame is owing in a considerable degree, to that circumstance."[14] Thomas Whately, writing in 1770, gives the credit to Hamilton rather than to nature. He makes many perceptive and interesting remarks, and—most important—shows the insight and reactions of a visitor in Hamilton's own day. Among his comments on the design are the following: "But Painshill is all a new creation; and a boldness of design, and a happiness of execution, attend the wonderful efforts which art has there made to rival nature. . . . Throughout the illustrious scene consistency is preserved in the midst of variety; all the parts unite easily."[15] This is followed by a description of the plantations and the varying scenery.

The key is Whately's comment on consistency. It was Hamilton's aim to achieve a range of different kinds of effects that did not appear incongruous when juxtaposed. Whately considered that Hamilton had managed to create this unity in diversity, and that the overall effect was twofold, beauty and grandeur. The visitor who expected variety and a series of fresh and differentiated prospects was not disappointed. At Painshill he would find varying colors, perspectives, declivities, different views of the lake, contrasts of light and shade, thick and sparse woodland, a medley of effects of sun and light through the day, numerous species of shrubs and trees, and an assortment of styles of landscape and architecture.

The essence of variety is contrast, and George Mason noted how the banks of the lake were contrasted with the "wild rusticity" on the other side of the arch, with a thicket in between to separate the two types of scenery.[16] In his garden Hamilton demonstrated Pope's ideas not only with contrasts of light and shade, the management of suprises, and the concealment of the bounds, but also by consulting the genius of the place. Hamilton's landscape had few natural advantages, so in shaping it he determined his own "genius loci." He used the elements of hills, woods, and water with great skill and success. With regard to concealment of the bounds, Hamilton brought in the Surrey landscape to the south and the views stretching over Cobham to the east; from the terrace near the house one could see across the River Mole to the land on the other side, which appeared to be part of Hamilton's landscape. Another aspect of his art of concealment was the formation of the lake in such a way that it could not be seen all at once and sometimes gave the appearance of a river, sometimes of a lake, and sometimes of a canal (*Plate 37*).

The only evidence we have of Hamilton's own stated thoughts on design is in Spence's account of what he said about another estate: "At Oatlands they had done *just the contrary* to what they ought to have done: they had planted the low grounds close and left the hill quite naked."[17] The opposite was achieved at Painshill, where the "hanging wood" of trees stretched along the hill above the water wheel to the forest clothing the upper parts of the hermitage hill, while broad, open lawns swept down to the lake.

One particular means of securing contrasts was by choice of plantings. The hermitage hill was planted with evergreens thickly massed, while (for example) the park had clumps dotted about. Hamilton used flowers and colorful shrubs away from the house in a way that was most unusual for the time. Only Southcote at Woburn Farm and Richard Bateman at Old Windsor (and Lyttelton, to a lesser extent, at Hagley in the West Midlands) used color to anything like the same degree; and it is significant that, apart from Hamilton's almost certain knowledge of Woburn Farm, he knew Bateman through mutual friendship with Henry and Stephen Fox. There is also a possible connection with Lyttelton, who was secretary to the Prince of Wales, although at an earlier period than when Hamilton worked for him. Shrubberies, or separate groups of shrubs, were to be found in the following areas: near the house, around the Sabine statue, on the descent from the gothic temple toward the lake, in front of the Temple of Bacchus, and on grotto island. The splashes of color added variety and illumination to the scene.

Let us look at some of the "set piece" areas as they appeared in Hamilton's design. One such area was the Roman mausoleum, standing in a patch of unkempt grass. The mausoleum was intended to have a somber effect, to remind the visitor of transience and decay, and its immediate surroundings were intended to sound a corresponding note. The agricultural writer Arthur Young's impression was as follows: "Through the arch, the river appears winding in a proper manner, that is, dark and gloomy, around a rough piece of grass, which has a consistent appearance."[18] Although he went on to complain that in another direction the views were too smooth and attractive, the point is made that there is a connection between the artifact (the mausoleum) and its surroundings. This was the area described by George Mason as "wild rusticity," as mentioned above.

Another example of a "set piece" is grotto island. The grotto is an amazing creation, and in most places would have stood on its own, as at Oatlands, for instance. But at Painshill the island is scattered with constructions of tufa ranging from an elaborate arch to small clusters of stone, giving the effect that the material was to be found naturally there. The outcrops of the tufa both prepare the visitor for the grotto and contribute to the atmosphere of the whole island, which is a dramatic entity, all the more mysterious and alluring for being an island and therefore cut off emotionally and literally from the rest of the gardens.

A further example is the area from the cascade toward the water wheel. This part of the lakeside scene may owe something to Rosa: the cascade was a "natural" construction of branches and boulders, although more than one commentator considered that the latter were placed in rather too regular a state of disorder. Arthur Young gives a picture of the cascade against its background: "in a very just taste. The water gushes in five or six streams, out of tufts of weeds growing in the rock; over it bends the trunk of an old oak, from side to side, which has an exceeding good effect; and the trees rising to a great height above all, finish the scene very completely."[19] In addition to the rocks that were used in the cascade, a number lay dispersed on the sides of the walk leading westward from the cascade: as with the grotto island, the idea was thus created of a whole area, or mini-area, in which rocks "naturally" occurred.

Hermitage hill was powerfully evocative of a particular mood. The wood, according to Whately,

> about the hermitage . . . is thickened with trees of the darkest greens; a narrow gloomy path, overhung with Scotch and spruce firs, under which the fern seems to have been killed, not cleared, and scarce a blade of grass can grow, leads to the cell; this is composed of logs and of roots; the design is as simple as the materials; and the furniture within is old and uncouth; all the circumstances which belong to the character, are retained in the utmost purity, both in the approach and the entrance.[20]

The key to the mood is the word "gloomy," when the surroundings reinforce the central conception of the hermitage, a place for meditation and retreat.

This part of the estate was categorized by Horace Walpole as exemplary of the savage or forest garden:

> I mean that kind of alpine scene, composed almost wholly of pines and firs, a few beech, and such trees as assimilate with a savage and mountainous country. Mr. Charles Hamilton, at Painshill, in my opinion has given a perfect example of this mode in the utmost boundary of his garden. All is great and foreign and rude; the walks seem not designed, but cut through the wood of pines; and the style of the whole is so grand, and conducted with so serious an air of wild and uncultivated extent, that, when you look down on this seeming forest, you are amazed to find it contain a very few acres.[21]

To achieve this alpine effect Hamilton used trees not from Italy or Switzerland but mostly from North America. Yet again there is evidence of Hamilton's skill as a designer and as creator of illusion, the forest appearing to be larger than it was, like the lake.

Hamilton's use of illusion spread to the other elements: Parnell mentioned the lawn, or park, being made to appear doubly large by cleverly placed plantings (see reference in note 2). Although there is no evidence to suggest that Hamilton was influenced by the theater, his ingenious handling of materials to create illusion, as well as the "set pieces," has something strongly theatrical about it.

From the dark pine woods forest, Hamilton takes us to the watchtower to get a view above the woods and then leads us out of the wood to a site that was designed to provide a complete contrast, visually and emotionally. Once again it is Whately who provides the best picture of the scene that presents the Temple of Bacchus in its setting (*Plate 38*):

> The situation is on a brow, which commands an agreable prospect; but the top of the hill is almost a flat, diversified however by several thickets, and broad walks winding between them; these walks run into each other so frequently, their relation is so apparent, that the idea of the whole is never lost in the divisions; and the parts are, like the whole, large; they agree also in style; the interruptions therefore never destroy the appearance of extent; they only change the boundaries, and multiply the figures; to the grandeur which the spot receives from such dimensions, is added all the richness of which plantations are capable; the thickets are of flowering shrubs; and the openings are embellished with little airy groupes of the most elegant trees, skirting or crossing the glades; but nothing is minute, or unworthy of the environs of the temple.[22]

The temple was a light, pleasant building, cheerful as befits the god of wine, in a cheerful, colorful setting. Aside from the "set pieces," another aspect of the design is the "to and from" positioning of many of the buildings. They were focal points of interest when viewed from a great or less distance, and were also vantage points from which particularly fine views could be seen. From the gothic temple, or even from lake level by the ruined abbey, all the features in the western half of the grounds were visible, including the tower rising above the trees (*Plate 39*). Correspondingly, the gothic temple could be seen from the rear portico of the Temple of Bacchus. Placed mostly on some kind of brow or eminence, the buildings represented a point of pause from which to enjoy a panoramic view in contrast to the smaller self-contained set pieces.

The gardens at Painshill were not house-centered, which puts them in a small category of independent grounds including Rousham and Stourhead. In the days of formal design the house was almost always at the heart of any garden layout, and later in the eighteenth century even many of the Brown landscapes also showed the house as the focal point. But at Painshill the landscape was everything (partly through necessity, Hamilton's house being so small and of such little interest) and bore little relation to the house. The buildings played their own parts in the scene, not serving merely the role of extension and projection of the house that the garden architecture assumes, for instance, at Castle Howard and Sezincote in Gloucestershire.

Hamilton aimed at creating an ideal, composite landscape of beauty, surprise, and variety. It appealed to the eye, the mind, and the feelings.

Overall, a unity bound the various styles, a unity that had its basis in respect for the character of the different parts of the garden. As a union of the painter's eye with the practical interest of the planter, it fused successfully the real and the ideal, and this original creative landscape achieved a magical balance between art and nature.

University of London

NOTES

1. For the work of Pope and Kent, see Morris R. Brownell, *Alexander Pope & the Arts of Georgian England* (Oxford, 1978), and Peter Martin, *"Pursuing Innocent Pleasures": The Gardening World of Alexander Pope* (Hamden, Conn., 1983).

2. John Parnell, Irish politician, whose accounts of Painshill are contained in James Sambrook, "Painshill Park in the 1760's," *Garden History*, VIII (Spring, 1980), pp. 91-106. Other valuable scholarship on Painshill is in Alison Hodges's articles: "Painshill Park, Cobham, Surrey (1700-1800)," *ibid.*, II (Autumn, 1973), pp. 37-68; "Further Notes on Painshill, Cobham, Surrey: Charles Hamilton's Vineyard," and "Painshill, Cobham, Surrey: Further Notes on the Water-Wheels," *ibid.*, (Autumn, 1974), pp. 77-80 and 81-82; and "Painshill, Cobham, Surrey: The Grotto," *ibid.* (Spring, 1975), pp. 23-28.

3. Joseph Wharton, *An Essay on the Genius and Writings of Pope* (Dublin, 1782), II, p. 244.

4. Reverend Stephen Duck, *Caesar's Camp; or, St. George's Hill; a poem* (London, 1755), line 16.

5. Emily J. Climenson, *Elizabeth Montagu, The Queen of The Bluestockings: Her Correspondence from 1720 to 1761* (London, 1906), II, pp. 75-76.

6. Uvedale Price, *An Essay on the Picturesque* (London, 1794), p. 277.

7. O. Manning and W. Bray, *The History and Antiquities of the County of Surrey* (London, 1809), II, p. 768.

8. Henry Home, Lord Kames, *Elements of Criticism* (Edinburgh, 1774), II, p. 432. See also John Dixon Hunt, *The Figure in the Landscape: Poetry, Painting, and Gardening during the Eighteenth Century* (Baltimore, 1976), esp. pp. 39ff, 84, 113-120, 192 on the topic of emotional response to gardens.

9. Hunt, *Figure in the Landscape*, p. 437.

10. Geoffrey and Susan Jellicoe, *The Landscape of Man: Shaping the Environment from Prehistory to the Present Day* (New York, 1975), p. 242.

11. Sir Thomas Dick Lauder, ed., *Sir U. Price on the Picturesque* (Edinburgh, 1842), p. 230.

12. Thomas Gray, *Works*, ed. John Mitford (London, 1858), III, p. 120n.

13. George Mason, *An Essay on Design in Gardening* (London, 1795), p. 206.

14. E. W. Brayley, *A Topographical History of Surrey*, rev. and ed. Edward Walford (London, 1878-1881), II, p. 21.

15. Thomas Whately, *Observations on Modern Gardening* (London, 1770), pp. 186, 188.

16. Mason, *Essay*, 1768 ed., p. 29.

17. Joseph Spence, *Observations, Anecdotes, and Characters of Books and Men*, ed. James M. Osborn (Oxford, 1966), I, item 1104.

18. Arthur Young, *A Six Weeks' Tour through the Southern Counties of England and Wales* (London, 1768), p. 189.

19. *Ibid.*, pp. 189-190.

20. Whately, *Observations*, p. 190.

21. Horace Walpole, "On Modern Gardening," in *The Works of Horatio Walpole* (London, 1798), II, p. 541.

22. Whately, *Observations*, p. 191.

The Volcano:
Culmination of the Landscape Garden

Christopher Thacker

In the gardens of the sixteenth and seventeenth centuries, it was not uncommon to build an artificial hillock, a mount as it was called. Such a mount might be set in or near the center to give a view over the garden as a whole, or alongside the enclosing wall, to give a view outside as well. Depending on the size of the mount, there might be a building—an arbor, a belvedere, even a banqueting house—on the top. For symmetry, two mounts might be built, at matching corners of the garden, or even four of them.[1] Symmetry is indeed a quality associated with these mounts, both in their position and in their design. Contemporary illustrations show them with geometrical plans—square, octagonal, circular—and mostly pyramidal elevations, all given architectural and sometimes military formality by terraces, regular rising paths, or flights of steps. Their entire idea is "artificial" and runs parallel to the formality of the gardens in which they appear. Although their remnants today are generally irregular in outline, and often appear more "shapeless" from the trees that grow on their slopes—as at New College, Oxford, or at Lyveden New Bield or Boughton, both in Northamptonshire—their creators do not seem to have intended them to look like real and "natural" hills at all.

When, in 1712, Joseph Addison suggested that "a Man might make a pretty Landskip of his own Possessions,"[2] he was rejecting much of the formality of the seventeenth-century garden. Instead, he was urging the adoption of a more "natural" kind of garden, incorporating aspects of the rural scene. Probably Addison had in mind the creation of a slightly "embellished" countryside—he says that "the natural embroidery of the Meadows" might be "helpt and improved by some small Additions of Art"—resembling not so much untouched nature as the carefully presented, near-ideal aspects of nature seen in landscape painting.

In the second half of the eighteenth century, the old formal gardens had been largely discredited and the new landscape gardens had become more and more "natural." Indeed, some were even *wild*, incorporating that fearsome yet thrilling quality of the *sublime* which Edmund Burke had explained to the public in 1756 in his *Philosophical Enquiry into the Origin of Our Ideas of the Sublime and the Beautiful*. As the fashion advanced, some gardens grew wilder and wilder until they embraced the ultimate and hitherto unthinkable wildness, the volcano. Earlier, in contrast, Addison's "pretty Landskip" would not have included a volcano. In 1700 he visited Naples, and his comments on Vesuvius are purely factual and statistical. Doubltess he was, as we might say, *interested* in the volcano, but he expresses no admiration.[3] His attitude is in this respect no different from that of the polymath Athanasius Kircher, whose *Mundus subterraneus* (1665, followed in 1669 by a digest in English, *The Vulcanos: or Burning and Fire-vomiting Mountains*) expresses immense curiosity about this aspect of God's creation, but still shows that Kircher thought volcanoes were dangerous and horrid.

Interest in volcanoes was immensely stimulated by Sir William Hamilton (1730-1803), who was posted to Naples as British Envoy in 1764. In the next fifteen years, Vesuvius erupted frequently, and Hamilton became a passionate vulcanologist, ascending Mount Vesuvius over two. hundred times, and acquiring a villa on the lower slopes (the Villa Angelica, near Portici) from where he might observe the eruptions with facility, and where he might entertain numbers of his friends and visitors, who, like himself, were interested in the volcano. Hamilton wrote copiously on the subject, his publications extending from his *Observations on Mount Vesuvius . . . Letters Addressed to the Royal Society* (1772) to the three volumes of the *Campi Phlegræi*—two volumes published in 1776, the *Supplement to the Campi Phlegræi* in 1779. The *Campi Phlegræi* were lavishly illustrated by the Italian Pietro Fabris, whom Hamilton encouraged to draw and paint the many aspects of the volcano and its eruptions in meticulous detail.

Hamilton himself saw the volcano with the eyes of a philosophe. It was for him a part of the material world, exceptional maybe, but still a phenomenon to be studied, measured, and rationally comprehended. It was also a unique background for his other interests—archaeology, music, literature, politics—shown excellently by Dr. Charles Burney, the musicologist, who was among Hamilton's guests at the Villa Angelica on Friday, October 26, 1770. Burney wrote of this occasion:

> After dinner we had music and chat till supper. . . . As soon as it was dark our musical entertainment was mixed with the sight and observation of Mount Vesuvius, then very busy. Mr. H. has glasses of all sorts and every convenience of situation etc. for these observations with which he is much occupied. . . . The sight was very awful and beautiful, resembling in great the most ingenious and fine fireworks I ever saw.[4]

Burney's words link "music and chat," "entertainment," and "fireworks" with the "awful and beautiful" sight of the eruption. Others—for example the artist Pietro Fabris and the English painter Joseph Wright of Derby— see the eruptions in a more sublime light, but still linked, *tant soit peu*, with entertainment. Fabris's nocturnal paintings show the volcano in spectacular form, a manifestation of nature's terrible and irresistible power. But they also show human beings watching the eruption as if it were an alarming yet admirable stage effect. One painting shows the spectators promenading along a convenient arched quayside while they watch (*Plate*

40). Another shows the king of Naples accompanied by Hamilton himself, explaining and demonstrating to his royal guest the awe-inspiring yet comprehensible phenomenon, and a third shows a woman on her knees, holding up a relic to propitiate the volcano, while by her side a man gestures in frenzied excitement—it is the lurid and terrifying climax to a melodrama.

Wright of Derby was Hamilton's guest at the Villa Angelica in October 1774, and witnessed and depicted an eruption of Vesuvius while he was there. Most of his stay in Italy was spent in Rome, where he painted several views of the "Girandola," the fireworks display given from the Castel Sant'Angelo. When he returned to England in 1775 he continued to paint canvases depicting one scene or the other; and twice, in 1776 and 1778, he exhibited pairs of paintings, *Vesuvius* and the *Girandola,* as if to stress both "entertainment" which was a part of the volcano's eruption, and the volcanic excitement of the fireworks display.[5]

While Hamilton was studying Vesuvius and he and his literary and artistic protégés were establishing the volcano as a sublime, glorious, instructive, and entertaining phenomenon, one writer in England was, in theory at least, linking the volcano with the garden. Sir William Chambers (1723-1796) had in 1757 published his *Designs of Chinese Buildings, Furniture, Dresses, Machines, and Utensils,* one section of which referred to the Chinese "Art of Laying Out Gardens." He claimed that the Chinese divided their garden scenes into "three different species," viz. the "pleasing, horrid, and enchanted," and Chambers gave most attention to "their scenes of horror." In their nature these corresponded closely to what Edmund Burke, the year before, would have termed the "sublime." Chambers does not mention volcanoes here, but in 1772 he enlarged this section on gardens to form his *Dissertation on Oriental Gardening.* Here again he divides Chinese gardens into three categories, "the pleasing, the terrible and the surprising." Among the scenes of terror the Chinese have "deep caverns in the rocks, and descents to subterraneous habitations, overgrown with brushwood and brambles." Above these deep caverns, "to add both to the horror and sublimity of these scenes" the Chinese

> sometimes conceal in cavities, on the summits of the highest mountains, founderies, lime-kilns, and glass-works; which send forth large volumes of flame, and continued columns of thick smoke, that give to these mountains the appearance of volcanoes.[6]

This is not the place to discuss how much of what Chambers wrote came from firsthand experience of China. It is enough to remark that China has no volcanoes, while Chambers himself spent some years in Italy in the 1750s, visiting Naples and the region of Vesuvius more than once. He was acquainted with Burke, and by the 1770s he would have known, seen, approved, or laughed at many of the grottoes that were being built as wild, subterranean adjuncts to English landscape gardens—including, for example, the "deep caverns" and "subterranean habitations" of Sir Francis Dashwood's Hell-Fire Caves at West Wycombe in Buckinghamshire (ca.

1750), and the lakeside grottoes built for Charles Hamilton at Painshill in Surrey by Joseph Lane in the 1760s. While Dashwood's infernal labyrinth was carved in the solid chalk of the hill beneath the church of St. Lawrence, Hamilton's grotto-work was made from "pierre antidiluvienne," "pre-diluvian stone," a holed and pockmarked tufa which looked so weather- and water-worn that it might be imagined to date from before the Flood. While Dashwood's caves suggested the flames of damnation, Hamilton's grottoes reminded the visitor of the Old Testament cataclysm. Discreetly, of course.[7]

So far as I know, no English garden was given a volcano of the "Chinese" sort that Chambers describes. But one was built in Germany, and still survives (*Plates 41 and 42*). It is in the huge landscape park at Wörlitz, near the town of Dessau, now in East Germany. The best contemporary account of the park at Wörlitz is by Carl August Boettiger, *Reise nach Wörlitz 1797*, edited by Erhard Hirsch (Wörlitz, 1976).

In its origins and its component parts this volcano is directly descended from Hamilton and from Chambers. It was the creation of Prince Leopold Friedrich Franz von Anhalt-Dessau (1740-1817), who traveled extensively in Europe before and during his long span of garden enthusiasm. In England twice in the 1760s, and making a fourth visit in 1785, he knew Chambers personally, admired his work as an architect, and possessed his *Dissertation on Oriental Gardening*, which was translated into German in 1775. Prince Franz had also traveled to Italy, visited Naples, was friendly with Hamilton, and had been an honored guest at the Villa Angelica, and he possessed Hamilton's writings on volcanoes.

The volcano that he built was begun after 1788 and was more or less completed by 1790. Called "der Stein," "the rock"—or "Vulkankrater," "Vulcan's crater"—it occupies an island some three hundred yards in circumference, on a branch of the main lake, and its cone rises up prominently in the flat terrain to a height of about eighty feet. But it is not a natural hill carved or excavated to look like a volcano; it is entirely man-made, and it is hollow, so that it may "erupt" when the proper materials are ignited inside. Its volcanic effects were best observed at night, and were achieved in two ways—by sending out fire and smoke, as Chambers said the Chinese had done, and by pumping *water* over the lip of the cone, so that it would flow in a gleaming, cascading sheet down the outside of the cone, and pass over red-tinted glass ports set in this cone, which would be illuminated from the inside. In this way a reddish light would gleam through the tumbling water, making it look as if a stream of molten lava were pouring down the flank of the volcano.

But this was not all that the "Stein" could offer. In itself a garden wonder, it was and is still an extremely complex creation, incorporating lavish references to other wonders of the ancient and the natural world. The approved way to approach the "Stein" was to come down the lake by boat. You would land at its foot in a cave-like recess—a grotto, adorned with fragments of basalt columns, reminiscent of those in Fingal's Cave, discovered in 1772 by Joseph Banks on the island of Staffa in the Hebrides, and seen instantly as a relic of a volcanic convulsion in the earth's earliest days. In the wall of the grotto was a door—and, with some trepidation, you stepped inside the volcano.

The most lively description of this strange, mainly underground visit is by Prince Charles de Ligne, who was there soon after the "Stein" was built. I translate from his French:

> Jumping from one's boat, you plunge into caves, catacombs and scenes of horror, through fearsome darkness and stairways. You emerge for a breath of air, right into a fine roman amphitheatre.
>
> And now new fears seize you, you wish to escape, and must, perforce, climb up a narrow stairway. The darkness becomes more complete . . . a sudden brightness dazzles your sight . . . a door opens; light gleams from a beautiful statue in the middle of a room, and you realize . . . that it has come through yellow, star-shaped panes in the roof of this chamber, and that an Etruscan entablature is set in the velvet blackness of the stones forming the walls. . . .
>
> You are still less than a third of the way through the tour. . . .
>
> A dwelling on another peak of this very rock. . . . It is a house which looks most simple and straightforward from the outside. Inside it is utterly magnificent, the whole of *Herculaneum*. . . .[8]

Much of this underground visit recalls Chambers, whose *Dissertation* of 1772 suggests that Chinese gardens "sometimes" had "subterranean vaults, divided into apartments, where lamps, which yield a faint glimmering light, discover the pale images of ancient kings and heroes." Elsewhere, Chambers claims, there were "dark passages cut in the rocks, on the side of which are recesses, filled with colossal figures of dragons, infernal fiends, and other horrid forms." There is more in similar vein. But if these experiences do not suffice, the Chinese visitor is, "from time to time . . . surprized with repeated shocks of electrical impulse, with showers of artificial rain, or sudden violent gusts of wind, and instantaneous explosions of fire; the earth trembles under him."[9]

This interior of the "Stein" is reminiscent also of a passage from the Roman writer Spartian referring to the emperor Hadrian's vast garden at Tivoli, and which contemporaries saw Prince Franz as emulating. Hadrian had wished to re-create and commemorate famous scenes from all over the world—for example, the city of Canopus in Egypt, the vale of Tempe in Greece, the portico of the stoic philosophers in Athens—and, for completeness, "he even made a Hades"—"etiam inferos finxit."[10]

Hades below—like Dashwood's Hell-Fire Caves—built within a volcano. And, perched on the volcano's sides, as de Ligne observed, there was also "a fine roman amphitheatre," and then "a dwelling on another peak . . . inside, it is utterly magnificent, the whole of *Herculaneum*." In these two buildings, Prince Franz had recalled, *in parvo*, the essence of the Vesuvian scene. The "amphitheatre" brings to mind the Roman ruins of Pompeii and Herculaneum, buried by the eruption of Vesuvius and rediscovered in the eighteenth century, while the "dwelling" was named the "Villa Hamilton," no less, in memory of Sir William Hamilton, keen antiquarian among the Roman ruins, generous host at the Villa Angelica on the slopes of Vesuvius, and vulcanologist extraordinary.

A volcano, and a great deal more—the "Stein" was so packed with mysteries and marvels that it verged on the improbable. In his description written in 1797, Boetigger makes this clear, saying that, *seen in the bright light of day*, "am puren Sonnenschein betrachtet," the structure had the air of machinery behind the scenes at the opera—a dragon's chariot made of papier-mâché, a thunder-machine made from donkey's hide. But at night, says Boettiger, all would be different, and he states that the first "performance" of the "Stein" was in the presence of Frederick of Prussia— Frederick the Great—and the second, in July 1794, in the presence of the dukes of Weimar and of Meinungen. On this second occasion, "the Vesuvius spouted flames and destruction for the whole of three nights."[11]

Two footnotes to Boettiger's text deserve special attention. In one Dr. Erhard Hirsch, the editor of Boettiger's manuscript, comments that among the names in Prince Franz's visitors' book on this occasion (July 27, 1794) appears that of the Duke of Weimar's privy councillor, "Geheimrat v. Göthe." Dr. Hirsch adds that it is likely that Goethe made one or more sketches of the "Stein" as it "erupted," although these do not survive.[12] The second footnote, by Boettiger himself, states that the Duke of Meinungen was so impressed that he immediately had the "Vesuvius of Wörlitz" imitated "on a junior scale," and that *this* garden volcano served as background for a "rather unfortunate fire and water scene from the *Magic Flute*."[13] This was in June 1795. Dr. Hirsch adds (n. 180, p. 116) that there are no known pictures of this small and hastily constructed volcano at Meinungen, and that it must have been destroyed by the 1830s.[14]

No doubt the "Stein" at Wörlitz was best appreciated by night, when its artificiality could not be perceived, and when the spectacle, the excitement of the "fireworks," could be enjoyed most vividly. This was even more the case with two other much less solid and convincing volcanoes set up in pleasure parks at the turn of the century. One was in the Ruggieri gardens at Tivoli, in the Parisian suburb of Clichy. Ruggieri was a specialist in fireworks displays, and in his gardens the volcano was just one among many spectacles and amusements devised to attract the public. An anonymous engraving of ca. 1796-1800 shows the incongruously assorted features at Tivoli—a windmill, an Egyptian obelisk, a Chinese kiosk, a gothic tower, a Grecian temple, and, above all this, a hot-air balloon soaring into the sky. From behind the gothic tower separate flames and smoke shoot up—this is a reminder of the volcano.[15] The Tivoli volcano was visited by Prince Franz, creator of the "Stein" at Wörlitz, during a visit to Paris in 1807. His reactions are not recorded, although a companion, Friedrich von Rode, wrote that during their visit to the gardens "There was also a representation of a fire-spewing mountain, which was beautiful and natural."[16]

The Tivoli gardens declined rapidly after 1807. Such attractions did not last long—their novelty would soon wear off, and it is likely that the construction of the "volcano" was not especially robust. This was also the case with the "volcano" set up in the Cascine pleasure gardens on the outskirts of Florence, which flourished in the last decades of the eighteenth century. Today the level site is mainly occupied by a racecourse, and there is no trace of any volcano. But around 1800 the artist G. Maria Terreni (1739-1811) painted four views of the Cascine, two of which show the highly decorated gala rooms, the kiosks and promenades, and, in the background, a small conical mound with a trickle of smoke coming from the top. A third painting shows the main buildings, lit up at night with torches, and thronged with pleasure-seekers, and the fourth (*Plate 43*), again a night scene, looks out from these buildings at the volcano, in full and spectacular eruption. In a way, it is like Fabris's paintings of Vesuvius—both Fabris and Terreni have seized the excitement of the occasion. But Vesuvius remains, while the volcano in the Cascine gardens has gone—it may even have been destroyed in that one "eruption" recorded by Terreni.

Spectacular, expensive to make in a durable form, and, in daylight, at least a trifle improbable—such must be the conclusion that we draw from these three garden volcanoes created on the Continent. Yet seen in favorable conditions—related to the setting, as much as to the volcano itself—such a garden creation could nonetheless be *sublime*. At night, the erupting "Stein" at Wörlitz must have been so, and its craggy shape is still "am puren Sonnenschein betrachtet," far from ridiculous. But it is *not* sublime in the daylight, merely impressive, remarkable, bizarre.

In England, only one garden volcano was created, as far as I know. It was made by William Beckford (1760-1844), a man of immense wealth, in his garden domain of Fonthill, in Wiltshire. The nineteen hundred-odd acres of the enclosed part of the Fonthill estate were spacious enough to contain many elements, so widely separated that they did not clash or impinge on the main, gigantic landscape. The smaller features included a flower garden, a rosarium, a "thornery," an herb garden, and an "American plantation" containing flowering shrubs and exotics. This "American plantation" is the only one of these elements to survive, and this is merely in the form of a handful of huge and un-English conifers, around which surges a later Victorian tide of lurid rhododendrons. Beckford was to spend quite as much on Fonthill, on the gardens, grottoes, rides, plantations, and buildings, and, above all, on the abbey at their center, as did Prince Franz on his park at Wörlitz; but though Beckford's abbey collapsed, the volcano in his gardens was conceived with a sureness of touch which retained for it, at all times of day, and in all seasons, something genuinely sublime. And this—to avoid suspense—was because his volcano was *extinct*. No "eruptions" occurred at Fonthill, even if the abbey tower did fall down in dust and fragments—twice. Beckford's extinct volcano did not and could not erupt, as it was conceived and created as a lake—Bitham or Bittern Lake (*Plate 44*).[17]

Like Prince Franz from Wörlitz, Beckford had visited Naples, and had stayed at the Villa Angelica on the slopes of Vesuvius. This was understandable, as he was related to Hamilton, whose first wife became a confidante, almost a second mother to him. His second visit to Italy, and to Naples, was made in 1782; and with him he took the artist John Robert Cozens (1752-1797), who made many sketches and watercolors of the scenes they visited. Among these are a number of views, in the southern part of Italy, of lakes that had formed in the deep, tree-lined craters of extinct volcanoes (*Plate 45*), and which had long been renowned for their associations with the fabled or historic past—Lake Averno, near Naples, with a cave at its edge supposed, in classical times, to lead down to the underworld; Lake Astroni, nearby; Lake Nemi, south of Rome, with the picturesque village of Genzano on the brim of the crater; and Lake Albano nearby, with the Pope's summer residence, the palace-castle of Castel Gandolfo, on its brim. While Cozens sketched these scenes, he, and Beckford, knew that they had often been admired and painted before. For example, Beckford had visited the Barberini palace in Rome on his first visit to Italy in 1780, and there he would have seen Claude Lorrain's *Pastoral Landscape with a View of Castel Gandolfo*.[18] Lesser Continental artists had depicted these lakes, imitating Claude's golden glow, and British painters earlier in the eighteenth century had both painted the Italian scenes and produced their "Italianate" visions of views in Britain which they thought similar—such as Richard Wilson, whose two circa 1765 paintings of Snowdon, with a crater-like lake in the foreground,[19] look more Italian than Welsh and in their mood resemble closely the dozen or more paintings that he made of real Italian scenes such as Lake Albano.

Cozens knew therefore that his subject matter was not original. But his views have a mood that is new. The glaucous tints of his watercolors have no trace of a Claudian warmth; his views suggest, not the expansion of midday or the glory of sunset, but the uncertainty of twilight, in which the distant, elevated buildings on the lip of the volcano offer no security, the forest trees on the slopes are dense and unwelcoming, and the lake, low down in the encircling crater, is dark and still.[20]

Cozens presents a restrained yet undeniable version of the sublime; and it is this effect that Beckford aimed at, and, I think, achieved with Bitham Lake at Fonthill.

He made the lake in the 1790s, damming up the water from a stream on the side of the wooded hillslope, at the top of which stood his huge gothic creation, Fonthill Abbey—like the Pope's palace above Lake Albano. The entire view was painted by Turner in 1799,[21] and is matched, feature by feature, in a later description: "As a combination of wood, water, irregularity of surface, and enormous altitude in building, it is a most extraordinary scene."[22] Another description of Bitham Lake, in 1812, is likely to have given pleasure to Beckford, since its terms match his volcanic conception exactly:

> A fine pellucid lake reflects the surrounding beauties of the place; in some parts of unfathomable depth, and having the appearance of the crater of an ancient volcano.[23]

In 1818, twenty-odd years after he had created the lake, Beckford himself refers to the surrounding "oakwoods which are so like Genzano," the village above Lake Nemi. This remark comes in a letter where he expresses rapturous delight at the beauty of the scene:

> Nothing I've ever seen in my life can equal this unique vision in grandeur of form or magic of colour. . . . They talk of the mirage in Egypt and in the great desert: I have now seen it, and seen it at Fonthill.[24]

Beckford's comments refer to the scene as a whole—as it were, to the vision recorded by Turner in 1799 in which Bitham Lake is only a part. But the perfection of the lake itself, and its sublime quality, is caught in another, earlier note. Beckford was ecstatic, observing the way in which his lake (artificial, created by himself) was coming to look like an age-old feature of the landscape: "Here everything is gradually lapsing into antiquity—grass up to the very doors, etc. The lake looks as if God had made it, it is so natural . . . the swans look as if they are in Paradise."[25]

Prince Leopold Friedrich Franz von Anhalt-Dessau died in 1817; William Beckford left Fonthill in 1822. Their garden volcanoes survive, the one at Wörlitz immense, yet so complex and pretentious that it strains the credulity of a daytime visitor. The other, at Fonthill, survives as a tranquil, rather gloomy lake, shaded by the trees that rise up the slopes toward the site of Beckford's gothic abbey. Only a small part of Fonthill Abbey remains, but Bitham Lake is still entire, and—if we know what we are meant to be looking at—a creation in which we may believe.

By the beginning of the nineteenth century, interest in the sublime aspects of nature had progressed so far that it could no longer be satisfied by artificial re-creations within the confines of a garden, however large or extravagant the garden might be. No more garden volcanoes were built. Instead, *real* volcanoes are described, and romantic figures—the hero of Hölderlin's *Empedokles*, or Chateaubriand's René—climb up the slopes of Vesuvius or Etna to brood over their ambitions, their inadequacies and uncertainties. I cannot imagine René lost in reverie, perched on the lip of the "Stein" at Wörlitz. Even if the romantic hero is defeated by nature's unfeeling immensity, nothing less than nature, wholly and genuinely sublime, can now be enough.

An afterword: Japanese garden designers faced up to this problem centuries ago. There, they make no attempt at "one-for-one" realism, and they would consider the "Stein" both crude and thoughtless. Instead, a Japanese garden may, if it is fortunately sited, include a "borrowed" glimpse, in the distance, of the cone of Mount Fuji, in the manner of a woodcut by Hokusai. Otherwise, with discretion and success, the Japanese garden may (but does not necessarily) contain a *symbolic* Mount Fuji, a cone of gravel or sand, and this may be no more than a foot in diameter and so pure in its outline that we could not, *should* not conclude that it represents a volcano at all.

University of Reading

NOTES

1. Christopher Thacker, *The History of Gardens* (Berkeley and Los Angeles, 1979), pp. 85, 134, 145. See the four mounts recommended in William Lawson's garden scheme of 1618. *Ibid.*, picture 89, p. 130. In the reconstructed gardens of the Governor's Palace in Colonial Williamsburg, the small mount overlooking the maze is not uncharacteristic. It is symmetrical, surmounted by a seat, and set where its—artificial—elevation may allow a superior view of the equally artificial intricacies of the maze.

2. Joseph Addison, *The Spectator,* no. 414 (June 25, 1712).

3. Joseph Addison, *Remarks on Several Parts of Italy* (1705) in *The Miscellaneous Works of Joseph Addison* (Oxford, 1830), IV, pp. 110-113.

4. Charles Burney, *Music, Men & Manners in France and Italy in 1770*, ed. H. Edmund Poole (London, 1969), pp. 176-177.

5. Several of Wright's best studies of Vesuvius are held in the Derby Art Gallery. His works are fully illustrated in Benedict Nicholson, *Joseph Wright of Derby*, 2 vols. (New York, 1968). For the pair, *Vesuvius* and the *Girandola*, see II, plates 166 and 168. Fabris and Wright are but two among many artists in the second half of the eighteenth century who painted views of Vesuvius.

6. Quoted in John Dixon Hunt and Peter Willis, eds., *The Genius of the Place: The English Landscape Garden 1620-1820* (New York, 1975), p. 321.

7. For Dashwood and West Wycombe, see Thacker, *History of Gardens*, pp. 203-205. For Painshill and its grottoes, see Alison Hodges, "Painshill Park, Cobham, Surrey (1700-1800)," *Garden History*, II (Autumn, 1973), pp. 39-68; Alison Hodges, "Painshill, Cobham, Surrey: the Grotto," *ibid.*, III (Spring, 1975), pp. 23-28; and Christopher Thacker, *Masters of the Grotto: Joseph and Josiah Lane* (Tisbury, 1976).

8. Charles-Joseph Emmanuel de Ligne, *Coup d'oeil sur Beloeil*, in *Mélanges militaires, littéraires, et sentimentaires* (Paris, 1975), IX, pp. 162-166. Translation mine.

9. Quoted in Hunt and Willis, eds., *Genius of the Place*, pp. 321-322.

10. Spartian, *De vita Hadriani*, xxvi, in D. Magie, trans., *The Scriptores Historiae Augustae* (London, 1921), I, pp. 78-79.

11. Boettiger, *Reise*, p. 81.

12. Quoted by Erhard Hirsch, *ibid.*, p. 116, n. 179.

13. *Ibid.*, p. 81.

14. *Ibid.*, p. 116, n. 180.

15. The engraving, held by the Musée Carnavalet, Paris, is reproduced as picture no. 319, p. 163, in Monique Mosser et al., *Jardins en France 1760-1820: pays d'illusion, terre d'experiences* (Paris, 1977), catalog of an exhibition at the Hôtel de Sully, Paris, May 18-September 11, 1977.

16. Quoted by Hirsch in Boettiger, *Reise*, p. 116, n. 181.

17. For a description of Beckford's gardens, see Christopher Thacker, "England's Kubla Khan," in *William Beckford Exhibition 1976* (Tisbury, 1976), pp. 63-76.

18. Since 1963 in the Fitzwilliam Museum, Cambridge.

19. Now in the Walker Art Gallery, Liverpool, and the City Art Gallery, Nottingham.

20. C. F. Bell and Thomas Girtin, *The Drawings and Sketches of John Robert Cozens*, Walpole Society, XXIII (1935), plates xi, xii, and xiii (six views of Lake Nemi), plates xiv and xv (four views of Lake Albano).

21. Now in the British Museum, Prints and Drawings, no. LXX-P. It appears in Thacker, *History of Gardens*, plate xxxviii, p. 214.

22. John Rutter, *Delineations of Fonthill and Its Abbey* (London, 1823), p. 77.

23. James Storer, *A Description of Fonthill Abbey* (n.p., 1812), p. 28.

24. William Beckford to Chevalier G. F. Franchi, Dec. 18, 1818, in Boyd Alexander, trans. and ed., *Life at Fonthill 1807-1822 . . . From the Correspondence of William Beckford* (London, 1957), p. 260.

25. Beckford to Franchi, June 16, 1811, *ibid.*, pp. 97-98. Cf. the letter of Nov. 8, 1817, p. 234.

The American Garden at Millburn Tower

A. A. Tait

The American garden was a common feature of the larger British landscapes in the early nineteenth century. By and large it was planted to show the floral wealth of North America and justified its existence as a piece of botanical geography. Like the flower garden or rosary in the composition of Humphry Repton, it played a strategic role in the transition of plant to tree and hence from near to middle distance in the landscape perspective. But the American garden at Millburn Tower, near Edinburgh, had a more distinct message and one of greater significance for the later nineteenth century. It was for its creator Sir Robert and, especially, Lady Liston a kind of *mémoire du temps perdu*, a happy recollection of a diplomatic past in the New World, at Philadelphia in the 1800s.

Three figures were directly involved with the garden at Millburn and another, more distantly, with the landscape. The conversion of mill cottage to small castle, and the landscaping and agricultural improvement of the small village of Ratho, were Sir Robert Liston's world; that of his wife, the Jamaican-born Lady Liston, was the American garden, the conservatory, and the formation of a plant collection.[1] Professional advice, initially anyhow, came from the n'er-do-well landscape gardener George Isham Parkyns who was at Millburn early in 1805.[2] The continuing source of exhortation was Thomas Johnes whose great picturesque landscape at Hafod in Wales was a constant example[3] (*Plate 46*). The Johneses were friends and admirers of both the Listons, and all four corresponded, visited, and exchanged plants and designs throughout their lifetimes with remarkable sympathy and tact.

Sir Robert Liston retired, for the first time, from the diplomatic service in 1804 with the arrival of the Peace of Amiens. From then until his taking up post again as ambassador at Consantinople in 1811, he lived at Millburn and in rented houses in London. It is during this period, 1804 to 1811, that the new gardens and landscape at Millburn were established and the cottage rebuilt and castellated[4] (*Plate 47*). Although there was much later improvement, which ended only when Liston returned for the second time in 1821, the pattern followed that of the earlier period. This was essentially a picturesque castle-style house, classical lodge and stables, pretty village around a green at Ratho, and well-wooded domain, all set out in a small if not miniature scale, as a diminutive echo of the vast valley of Hafod and Baldwin's castle there.

The architect of Millburn Tower, for the first phase at least, was William Atkinson, who had an extensive Scottish practice and shared with the Listons an enthusiasm for gardening.[5] He was presumably responsible for the new tower and linking it to the existing cottage, though this was later altered and expanded by Liston's nephew, Captain Ramage, before 1820.[6] In 1821 Liston wrote of "having pulled down our old accommodation and not completed the new," and hopefully anticipated being finished in no distant time: "It is already so far advanced as to put it in your power to judge the stile of the Fabriks."[7] The pattern was the same for the landscape; whatever Parkyns had recommended in 1805 was now being refined by Liston as "smoothing the face of nature and embellishing the landscape."[8]

Parkyns's role at Millburn is almost as obscure as the rest of his professional career. He had met the Listons in Philadelphia when he had gone to the United States, ostensibly to look after a land investment that had gone sour, but in reality to try and establish a career there.[9] As James Kornwolf notes in his essay in this volume, he probably designed four or five important gardens in Philadelphia and Virginia, including some undetermined aspects of Monticello at Thomas Jefferson's request. He was not successful enough, however, and returned to England before 1804. In many ways his career and social standing—he was almost a gentleman—parallels that of Humphry Repton himself, although Parkyns never achieved Repton's success. But like him, Parkyns was an agreeable and cultivated person with an ability to draw who sought to improve his reputation by publication. He wrote *Six Designs for Improving Grounds* in 1792, and *Monastic and Baronial Remains* in 1796, with a second edition in 1816.[10] It was the *Six Designs* that Loudon had seen and noted in the library at Millburn. But unlike the successful and uxorious Repton, he was constantly short of money—borrowing from Liston in 1805, separating from his wife by 1810, and leaving his family in near destitution.[11] Apart from Millburn and those American gardens, Parkyns's other documented works were Dryburgh Abbey for the Earl of Buchan, and, possibly, work at The Grange for Lord Henry Stuart.[12] What is known of his theoretical opinions is contained in the *Six Designs* and this is very little. Of the six stereotypes, those of Fair Field and Rose Cottages offered a sort of cottage *orné* garden that could be compared with Lady Liston's American garden, although Parkyns offered no reference or discussion of that type. The other four examples show larger houses set in park landscapes very much according to the principles of the beautiful as exemplified by Capability Brown or Shenstone's The Leasowes. It was such motifs as the serpentine driveway, the lake, and the periphery belts and clumps that reappear at Millburn on an almost diminutive scale (*Plate 48*). To adapt those to Millburn required little imagination, and perhaps all the Listons sought from Parkyns was reassurance.

Of the six designs, ranging from Fair Field cottage with six acres to The Grange with 120, Laurel Hill offered the best approximation to Millburn. It contained sixteen acres with its buildings grouped close to the house and served by short driveways.[13] But neither it nor any of the others contained an American garden, or any other type of specialized area. They were all given a Leasowes-like setting with contrived walks linking a rich series of garden buildings. The small Laurel Hill contained nonetheless a gothic building, Temple of Concord, Temple of Friendship, hermitage, and rustic lodge, as well as the usual offices.[14] Unlike Millburn too, all Parkyns's case studies were classical houses that, for all the platitudes of the purely descriptive text, revealed little appreciation of the picturesque. As a book, *Six Designs* presented little challenge, either aesthetically or intellectually, to Repton's *Sketches and Hints,* which had appeared in 1795. Its characteristic banality is well shown in Parkyns's remarks about the rural poor—"A labourer would, doubtless, be permitted by a humane master to feed his cow: this might enable his little family, in some respect, to partake of the bounties he sees lavished around him and induce a daily return to toil with cheerfulness and content."[15]

Parkyns arrived at Millburn during a critical time when little had been settled and building only just begun. It is reasonable to assume that his visit—"to devote the slender abilities I possess, wholly, and for as long a time as you judge necessary"—influenced the proposed landscape, although nothing is known of any of his suggestions.[16] Millburn, at about this time, was given two driveways, north and south, a lake, an American garden, and the allied conservatory. The south approach that led directly to the house had at its head a circular lodge designed by Benjamin Latrobe for Liston probably when they and Parkyns were together in Philadelphia in 1800.[17] It had originated as a small "round house," forty feet in diameter with a library in the attic, which was recast, probably by the Edinburgh architect Thomas Hamilton, and survives as a remarkably austere piece of neoclassicism[18] (*Plate 49*). Its companion drive to the north was longer and more impressive, although without gatelodge. It crossed the Gogar burn by a simple bridge and ran to the house along a straight avenue of beech trees. The small lake with its island for the ducks, made from one of the mill streams, lay on the east side of this driveway. The dredging of this lake was in hand in 1805, following Parkyns's departure for Glasgow in January of that year. Lady Liston wrote then of "deepening and almost forming the piece of water in front," and in 1828 Sir Walter Scott noted in his journal that "the artificial piece of water is a failure like most things of the kind."[19] All of these—driveways, lake, and their planting—were thoroughly conventional and can easily be seen in most of Parkyns's *Six Designs.* They were the bread and butter of the landscape gardener and at Millburn were probably devised with Parkyns's professional help. The American garden and its conservatory, however, which were less familiar and more important, seem to have been the work of the Listons themselves.

The American garden at Millburn was a combination of botanic zeal and nostalgia; in fact, the nostalgia might even be regarded as a theme—happiness in Philadelphia remembered by the Listons, and happiness in the West Indies as a child remembered by Lady Liston. The garden itself had been started immediately after they came to Millburn in 1804, and at the end of the year, "all had been trenched and the gravel walks partly made ready for the complete *forming* in spring."[20] The idea of such a garden seems to have developed early. When traveling in the West Indies in 1801, Lady Liston noted in her journal, after visiting the botanical garden of Dr. Anderson on St. Vincent, that she found him "very liberal in giving his plants and very kind in his offers to supply me on my return to Scotland."[21] It was an offer taken up, and in 1805 she wrote that her "American Garden has received a great accession of Plants, some for *love*, some for *money*."[22] In the same year, and again later, Sir Robert Liston had a list of plants sent him from Philadelphia with the additional and obliging note that "whatever we can do for you in this way or any other pray command as freely."[23] Such plants usually came from North America and the West Indies to Greenock, the port for Glasgow, and were then collected from the customs house there and sent on to Edinburgh. As a diplomat—even a retired one on £2,000 a year—Liston was in an enviable position to solicit plants and seeds as such favors were almost routine. His collecting and correspondents extended to China and India.[24]

At home in Millburn, there was a similar pattern of exchange, although it seems that the Listons also dealt commercially with the distinguished London nurserymen Lee and Kennedy. There was a constant barter system with the Johneses of Hafod, the Douglasses at Douglas Castle, and their various Edinburgh neighbors, especially Lord Torphichen at Calder House. In 1808 he wrote to Lady Liston, saying that "my gardener has, very naturally, a great desire to see your collection of Plants, and I therefore take the liberty of sending him to Millburn"; and in 1810 in return he sent to Millburn a small collection of plants that included "Sumachs, Viburnum, Cheliones, Jessmaines, Broad-leafed Spirea, Nappea, Rudbeckia Nitida, Diervilla, Bladder Nut, dwarf horsechesnut, tall Phlox, Persimon, Fringe tree, Caster oil nut" and so on.[25] In a covering letter, he flattered Lady Liston, saying that he thought her American garden was unquestionably without rival in the country. Such an achievement was a very real one, for Lady Liston, although deeply interested in plants, was no botanist and went as far as to disclaim "the patience to learn the first Elements of that Science."[26] So much so that a Nottinghamshire correspondent, A. C. Smith, set about giving her a reading course starting with "Rousseau's letters in Botany, Dr Martyns, Botanical Dialogues by a Lady, Dr Smith's Flora Britannica and Hill's British Flora."[27] He gave as well a particular and informed account of the American garden. "I fancy myself at this moment," he wrote "in the midst of your Magnolias, Kalmias, Azaleas, Andromedas, Melastosmas, Clethras, Madias, and Dionquas, whose structure and character are quite familiar to me, but most of which, alas, I have only seen in dried specimens and in Plates."[28]

For all the attention paid to it, the American garden has now disappeared without trace. It probably lay on the garden side of the house, adjoining the conservatory to the north and with the lake to the east. Such a position accorded with the situation advised by J. C. Loudon in his *Encyclopaedia of Gardening.* "The American garden," he wrote, "may have a northern or eastern exposure, and if it slopes considerably it will be still less affected by the warm dry weather of summer."[29] Loudon also recom-

mended that the American shrubs should be "planted in beds or compart-
ments of peat earth; or entire gardens or shrubberies should be devoted
exclusively to them," and such was probably the case at Millburn Tower.[30]
However, whether the planting itself was in what Loudon termed "the
mingled manner or grouped or classified according to some system" is not
known. So ardently amateur a botanist as Lady Liston probably preferred
a casual, informal effect rather than that of the gardenesque. It was for
her essentially a garden of memories rather than an excursion into the
rarified groves of academe. In this way, it was closer to its predecessors, the
flower gardens of the eighteenth century, than the contemporary American gardens of Ashridge or Dropmore.[31]

The important, even essential, part of this garden was the conservatory.
The Listons seem to have had some sort of conservatory before 1808
when Mrs. Johnes of Hafod longed "to see both you [Lady Liston] and
your conservatory,"[32] and in 1807 an Edinburgh visitor noted in her diary
that Sir Robert Liston had "built a most curious Ho [use] but a remarkably
neat one, a green house at the top which answers for his study."[33] But this
was replaced in 1810 by one designed by John Hay of Edinburgh, the
hothouse specialist of his day, made from glass and Carron cast iron that is
shown in a rough sectional drawing[34] (*Plate 50*). Its position was adjoining
Liston's library, as the existing plan shows, and at the extreme south end
of the house. Before the later rebuilding it connected to the main building
only by a vaulted passage cloaked in jasmine and ivy (*Plate 51*).

Millburn's picturesque mood was sustained—even encouraged—by the
Listons' close friends the Johneses of Hafod. The correspondence between the two families was especially lively during the Listons's creation of
the garden at Millburn, although it continued into the 1820s and Mrs.
Johnes's widowhood. In this way, it repeated the experience of the
Johneses themselves who had built Hafod in 1786 and in the following
decades converted a barren Welsh landscape into a picturesque domain
much like that of their kinsman Richard Payne Knight at Downton.[35] Such
material is contained in Johnes's letters to Liston and those of Mrs. Johnes
to Lady Liston, the former largely concerned with building and improvement, the latter with gardening matters. It was to Liston that Johnes
described his intended rebuilding of Hafod, his new farm houses, and the
erection of his new chain bridge.[36] In return he received a discussion of
farming methods, a model of a gate for Hafod in 1810, and the following
year the suggestion of a suitable agricultural overseer for the estate.[37] The
correspondence culminated in the visit of the Johneses to Millburn in
1809.[38] In her turn, Lady Liston swapped seeds and plants. In 1808 she
received seeds from Sicily, "a beautiful convolulous which will not do out
of doors," and in 1807 Mrs. Johnes wrote in return that "I shall be able to
raise some beautiful plants from them and you will see them in a
flourishing state at Hafod."[39] Both discussed their conservatories; that at
Hafod was ingeniously formed as a glazed colonnade in 1807 to make "a
sort of conservatory for hardy plants," and in emulation John Hay's was
erected at Millburn Tower in 1810.[40] But the relationship between the two
families went deeper, wider, and embraced many matters. It showed a

similar modest patronage of the arts. David Wilkie as a family friend painted a small portrait of Liston that was finished in 1810, and Johnes also tried, unsuccessfully, to persuade Wilkie to come to Hafod and work for him.[41] Lady Liston recommended to them the watercolorist Hugh Williams, who stayed at Hafod in 1805.[42] The visit was not a success and the stumbling block seems to have been a conflicting interpretation of the picturesque. Johnes wrote to Liston that "Williams's ideas of landscape and mine are somewhat different for he complained of *too much* wood in Glamorganshire. I only saw two slight sketches of the Devil's bridge and part of Chepstow Castle and to judge from them I do not think he will make a great figure."[43] He tactlessly failed to find Johnes's new chain bridge a suitable subject for his pencil.

It must seem ironic that after so much effort and such enthusiasm, Liston departed for Constantinople in 1811, leaving new house and garden in another's care. It must seem perverse, too, that their American garden became a sort of institution on its own terms rather than Lady Liston's original nostalgic dream. For it succeeded not only in reminding the Listons of their Philadelphia days but in encouraging a taste and interest in North America. In this fashion, the Listons continued to serve as ambassadors to the very end.

University of Glasgow

NOTES

1. For an account of the career of Sir Robert Liston (1742-1836), see *Dictionary of National Biography*. A short account of Lady Liston (Henrietta Marchant, died 1828) is given in the introduction to Clare Taylor, *Journeys through the Caribbean* (Aberystwyth, 1976), pp. 1-2.

2. What little is known of the career of Parkyns is given in A. A. Tait, *The Landscape Garden in Scotland 1735-1835* (Edinburgh, 1980), pp. 200-202.

3. An account of Thomas Johnes (1748-1816) and his picturesque taste is given in Leslie Parris, *Landscape in Britain c 1750-1850* (London, 1973), pp. 69-71. For Hafod itself, see George Cumberland, *An Attempt to describe Hafod* (London, 1796).

4. Liston had been born in the vicinity of Ratho and had acquired the mill and cottage at Millburn sometime before 1803. Part of these early buildings existed until 1821. For an account of Millburn, see John Small, *The Castles and Mansions of the Lothians*, II (Edinburgh, 1883), unpaginated.

5. For an account of Atkinson's practice, see Howard Colvin, *Biographical Dictionary of British Architects, 1600-1840* (London, 1978), pp. 75-77. For the identification of Atkinson with Millburn, see *Farmers' Magazine*, VI (1805), p. 361.

6. Among the Liston manuscripts there are apparently only building accounts for 1806-1808, those for the mason John Anderson: MS 5609, fol. 177, National Library of Scotland, Edinburgh. There are additional but scattered references to the building and furnishing of the house—a red granite chimneypiece from the scholar-architect James Byres in 1810; furniture from the Edinburgh firm of Trotter in 1805: *Ibid.*, fol. 73. There is also a small

collection of architectural drawings for the expansion of the house between 1811 and 1821. MSS 5715-5716.

7. MS 5681, fol. 20.

8. *Ibid.* However, planting was on a sizable scale and in 1820-1821 he planted almost 45,000 trees of which 17,000 were Scotch pines. *Ibid.*, fol. 13.

9. Tait, *Landscape Garden*, p. 200.

10. *Ibid.*

11. MSS 5609, fol. 1; 5616, fol. 62.

12. For Parkyns's probable work at Dryburgh, see Tait, *Landscape Garden*, p. 201; for The Grange, see MS 5610, fol. 62. Parkyns's son appealed for help from what is likely to have been a group of his father's clients who included the trustees of Lord Henry Stuart, a tenant of The Grange before 1803. J. Mordaunt Crook, "Grange Park transformed," in Howard Colvin and John Harris, eds., *The Country Seat: Studies in the History of the British Country House* (London, 1970), p. 220.

13. Parkyns, *Six Designs*, p. 8.

14. *Ibid.*

15. *Ibid.*, p. 15.

16. MS 5608, fol. 112.

17. The Latrobe designs are dated 1800 and are at his home, Cloverhill, in Philadelphia. For Latrobe's career and his time in Philadelphia, see Talbot Hamlin, *Benjamin Henry Latrobe* (New York, 1955), pp. 146-167. There is no mention of either Parkyns or Liston in Latrobe's journals for that period. Edward C. Carter II, ed., *The Journals of Benjamin Henry Latrobe, 1799-1820*, III (New Haven, 1980).

18. For Thomas Hamilton's career, see Colvin, *Biographical Dictionary*, pp. 383-386.

19. MS 5608, fol. 132.

20. *Ibid.*

21. Taylor, *Journeys*, p. 36. See also MSS 5617, fol. 58; 5614, fol. 58.

22. MS 5608, fol. 132.

23. Liston's Philadelphia correspondent was T. Bond: MS 5609, fol. 124. Bond was a wealthy merchant at Front Street, Newcastle, near Philadelphia. Carter, ed., *Journals of Latrobe*, III, p. 39.

24. A relation of Liston's, Patrick Ramage, evidently regularly brought seeds and plants home from India and China: MS 5610, fol. 48.

25. MSS 5612, fol. 16; 5617, fol. 116.

26. MS 5617, fol. 44.

27. *Ibid.* These works all appear in Blanche Henry, *British Botanical and Horticultural Literature before 1800*, II (London, 1975).

28. MS 5617, fol. 44.

29. J. C. Loudon, *An Encyclopaedia of Gardening: Comprising the Theory and Practice of Horticulture, Floriculture, and Landscape-Gardening* (London, 1822), p. 1021.

30. *Ibid.*

31. For the development of the flower garden in the late eighteenth century, see John Harris, "Some Imperfect Ideas on the Genesis of the Loudonesque Flower Garden," in E. B. MacDougall, ed., *J. C. Loudon and the early nineteenth century in Great Britain* (Washington, D.C., 1980), pp. 45-49.

32. MS 5612, fol. 26.

33. William Park, "Extracts from the Journal of Jessy Allan," *Old Edinburgh Club*, XIII (1959), pp. 108-109.

34. The conservatory was finished and ready for assembly in August 1810: MS 5617, fol. 23. In May of that year, references were made to a drawing of the cast iron supports from Carron and this sketch may be that one: *Ibid.*, fol. 190. For John Hay, see Tait, *Landscape Garden*, pp. 144-146, 225.

35. For Hafod, see Colvin, *Biographical Dictionary*, p. 86.

36. MSS 5611, fol. 82; 5609, fol. 105.

37. MSS 5615, fol. 118; 5618, fol. 66.

38. MS 5614, fols. 129, 174.

39. MS 5611, fol. 70.

40. *Ibid.*, fol. 82. However, there was an earlier conservatory at Hafod that was seen by Cumberland before 1796: *Attempt to describe Hafod*, p. 3.

41. MS 5611, fol. 70. Wilkie later painted a scene from *The Gentle Shepherd* for Liston in 1823. Allan Cunningham, *The Life of Sir David Wilkie* (London, 1843), III, p. 526. There are frequent references to Liston in Wilkie's early journals: *Ibid.*, I, pp. 177, 201.

42. MS 5609, fol. 82. For some account of Hugh Williams, see David and Francina Irwin, *Scottish Painters at Home and Abroad, 1700-1900* (London, 1975), pp. 228-231. Williams probably came in contact with Lady Liston when in Edinburgh in the 1790s.

43. MS 5609, fol. 82.

1. Capability Brown, *the lake at Bowood.*

2. *Les Buttes-Chaumont*, Paris.

Veue en Perspective de la Grotte de Roccaille du Jardin de Ruel.

Israel Siluestre delin.

Perelle sculp.

3. Perelle after Silvestre, picturesque view (1661) of the so-called *Grotte de Roccaille* or *Grotte de la Baleine*, in Cardinal Richelieu's garden at Reuil. Engraving.

4. Antoine Richard, project for *Petit Trianon* (1774). G. L. LeRouge, *Nouveaux Jardins à la mode* (1774).

A View to the Grotto of the Serpentine River in the Alder Grove. .... Vue vers la Riviere Serpentine du Bosquet des Aunces prise de la Grotte.

Chatelain del.

G. Bickham sculp.

5. *Stowe: the alder grove*. Engraving by Bickham after Chatelain (1753).

6. William Kent, project for *Chatsworth* (1735-40). Pen-and-ink and wash drawing. (Courtesy of Trustees of the Chatsworth Settlement).

7. *Saint Leu Taverny: the rock, temple, and cascade*. LeRouge, *Nouveaux Jardins à la mode* (1774).

8. *Saint Leu Taverny: chateau and park.* A. de Laborde, *Nouveaux Jardins de la France* (1808), book XII, plate 8.

9. Jacques Blondel, *rococo trellis arbor and fountain. Maisons de Plaisance* (1737).

10. *Stourhead: the lake and Pantheon.*

11. *Stourhead: the bridge, cross, and village.*

12. Herman van Swanevelt, *Grotto of the Nymph Egeria*. Engraving (detail). (Courtesy of the National Gallery of Art, Washington, D.C., Ailsa Mellon Bruce Fund).

The inscription on the base reads:

HVIVS NYMPHA LOCI SACRI CVSTODIA FONTIS
DORMIO DVM BLANDAE SENTIO MVRMVR AQVAE
PARCE MEVM QVISQVIS TANGIS CAVA MARMORA SOMNVM
RVMPERE SIVE BIBAS SIVE LAVERE TACE

13. *Statue of sleeping nymph in garden of the Colocci family.* Engraving from Montfaucon, *L'Antiquité expliquée* (1719), I, 2, plate 220.

14. William Kent, *Pope in his grotto*. (Courtesy of Trustees of the Chatsworth Settlement. Photo: Peter Willis).

15. William Kent, *Pope's Shell Temple*. Drawing. (Courtesy of Trustees of the British Library).

16. Nathaniel Parr after Peter Rysbrack, *An Exact Draught and View of Mr. Pope's House at Twickenham* (1735).

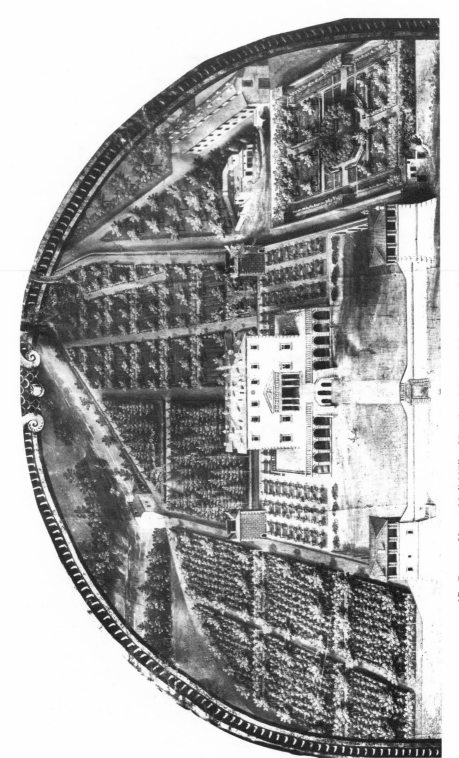

17. Gustave Utens, *Medici Villa of Poggio a Caiano* (1599). (Museo di Firenze com'era. Photo: Sopr. Gallerie, Florence).

18. Anon., *Pope's Villa at Twickenham.* Pen-and-ink and wash drawing.

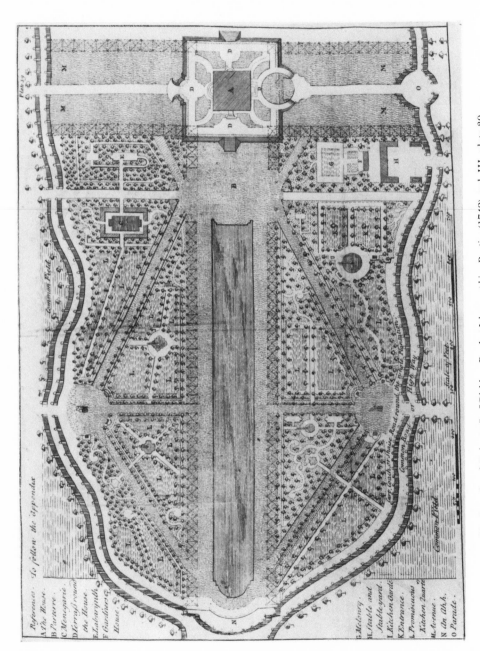

19. "regulated Epitome" of Riskins, Bucks. *Ichnographica Rustica* (1742), vol. III, plate 39. (Photo: R.G.I.T., Aberdeen).

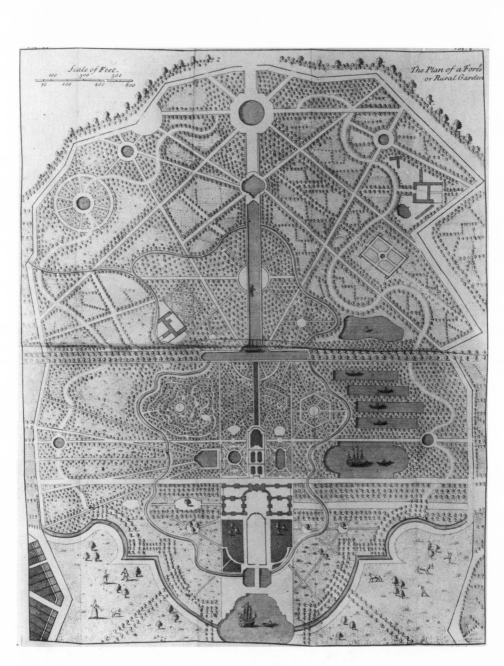

20. "The Plan of a Forest or Rural Garden" *Ichnographica Rustica* (1742), vol. III, p. 44. (Photo: R.G.I.T., Aberdeen).

21. *Woburn*, Surrey. Engraving by Luke Sullivan (1759). (Photo: Bodleian Library, Oxford).

22. and 23. *Bayham Abbey*, Kent. Humphry Repton, *Landscape Gardening* (1803), p. 208. Flap up: before Repton's improvements; flap down: after Repton's improvements. (Photo: Bodleian Library, Oxford).

24. Reverend William Gilpin, *The Wye Tour* (1782). Aquatint.

25. William Sawrey Gilpin, *Downton Castle*, Herefordshire, home of Richard Payne Knight. Water color.

26. *Scotney Castle*, Kent. Landscaped by William Sawrey Gilpin. (Courtesy of *Country Life*).

27. "Example of the Picturesque in Landscape Gardening," A. J. Downing, *Treatise on the Theory and Practice of Landscape Gardening* (1841), p. 417.

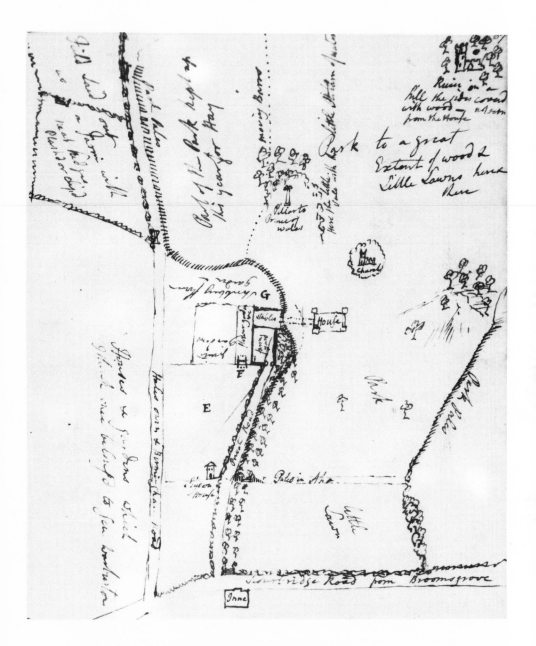

28. Parnell's garden tours. *Hagley: map.*

29. Parnell's garden tours. Hagley: Thomson's seat and plan of castle.

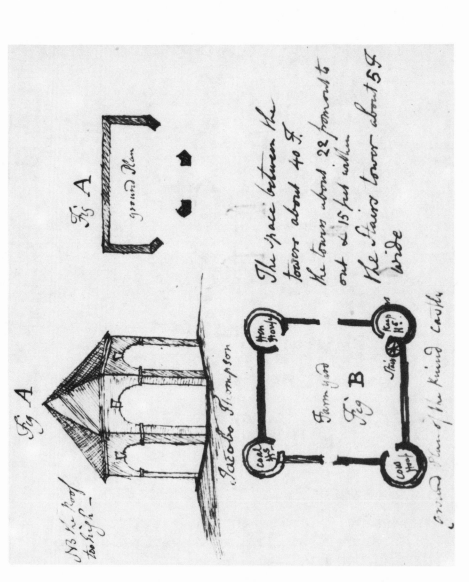

Fig A

Fig A

ground Plan

143 ft Roof too high —

Jacobs Thompson

The space between the towers about 40 ft.

the tower about 22 from out to out & 15 feet within

the Stairs tower about 5 ft wide

Farm yard
Fig B

Thom house

Coal Hs.

Cow Hs.

Keep Hs.

Stair

Ground Plan of the ruind castle.

View of the tower in approaching from the Cascade Valley —

The Best Tower on a larger scale

Battlement

Cornice fretwork, or sort of Gothic Dentices

30. Parnell's garden tours. *Hagley: elevations of castle.*

View of the most perfect front of the Ruind castle Mem^dm the towers I have Drawn too Small in proportion to the Body. by full a thurd of Each Diameter ——

Fig C

Seder Contemplationis

a simple semicircular wall Arch'd at Top. I think Built. of Brick

31. Parnell's garden tours. *Hagley: elevation of castle and seat of Contemplation.*

32. Parnell's garden tours. *Hagley: Hermitage and rustic alcove.*

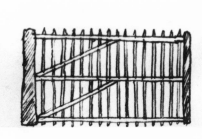

33. Parnell's garden tours. *Hagley: gate and doric portico.*

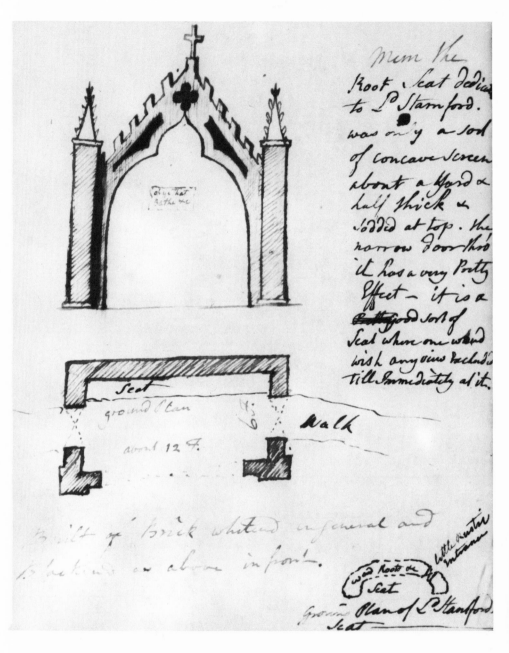

34. Parnell's garden tours: *The Leasowes: gothic seat and plan of root house.*

35a. Parnell's garden tours. *The Leasowes: gothic seat.*

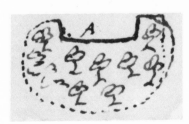

35b. *The Leasowes: plan of clump and seat.*

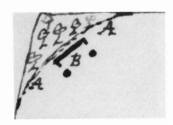

35c. *The Leasowes: corner of plantation.*

36. *Painshill ca. 1800*. Sketch by author.

37. William Woollett, *View from the west side of the grotto island* (1760). Engraving.

38. *Interior of gothic temple.* (Courtesy of the Architectural Press, Ltd.).

39. Reverend William Gilpin, *Temple of Bacchus* (1772). Sketch. (Courtesy of George Benson).

40. Pietro Fabris, *Vesuvius in eruption*. From Hamilton, *Campi Phlegraei*, vol. II. (Courtesy of Trustees of the British Library).

41. *The "Stein" at Wörlitz*, seen from the lake: grotto arches visible to the right. (Photo: Christopher Thacker).

42. *The "Stein" at Wörlitz,* with the "villa Hamilton" on its slopes. (Photo: Christopher Thacker).

43. G. M. Terreni. *The Volcano at the Cascine*, Florence. (Private collection).

44. *Bitham Lake*. Fonthill Abbey stood at the top of the slope. (Photo: Christopher Thacker).

45. J. R. Cozens, *Lake Albano and Castel Gandolfo.* (Dyce Bequest. Courtesy of the Victoria and Albert Museum).

46. Plan of the pleasure grounds at Hafod. From George Cumberland, *An Attempt to describe Hafod* (1796).

47. *Millburn Tower.*

48. Plan of the *grounds at Millburn Tower*, from the Ordnance Survey (ca. 1876).

49. *The circular lodge at Millburn, before alteration, after a design by Benjamin Latrobe.*

50. A section through the *conservatory at Millburn*, designed by John Hay.

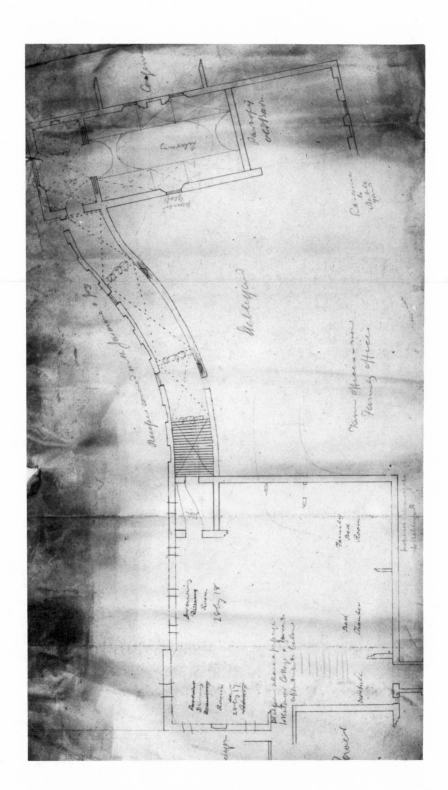

51. Plan of *additions at Millburn* (1813). Sketch. (National Library of Scotland).

The Picturesque in the
American Garden and Landscape before 1800

James D. Kornwolf

The stream from thence carried us gently down to Mr. Clemens' Milldam, through scenery in the highest degree Picturesque and delightful.

Benjamin Latrobe, *An Essay on Landscape* (1798)

The grounds which I destine to improve in the style of English gardens are in a form very difficult to be managed.

Thomas Jefferson to William Hamilton (1806)

The literature on the picturesque garden, *le jardin anglais*, which developed in England and France throughout the eighteenth century, is extensive, and the importance of the development well acknowledged. Yet there has been vitually no attempt since Fiske Kimball's half a century ago to trace its development in the United States before 1800 when Jefferson was planning his garden at Monticello.[1] American colonial and federal gardens are almost universally regarded to have been symmetrically formal—characterized by terraces, parterres, and allées of poplar or box—or quite naturally natural and pragmatically useful, free from the European passion for the pastorale à la Virgil. The effort here is to show that this was not entirely the case.

The mid-eighteenth-century political threat to Britain and America from France, when combined with a suspected Hanoverian "tyranny," has led Richard Quaintance, Leo Marx, and others to think that Americans as well as English saw the "political associations" of the picturesque garden. Quaintance believes that much theory underlying landscape design by Alexander Pope, Charles Bridgeman, William Kent, "Capability" Brown, and Horace Walpole was inspired by the Whig political milieu associated with Sir William Temple, Anthony Ashley Cooper (third Earl of Shaftesbury), Joseph Addison, Horace Walpole, and Thomas Whately.[2]

Leo Marx considered the political and artistic image of America as a garden in the minds of English poets and adventurers from the sixteenth century on, speculating that the American landscape nurtured ideas of political liberty and artistic freedom in both countries. Yet he was forced to conclude, as must this writer, that "the degree to which the idea of revolution was nurtured by the topographical awareness of the colonists cannot be established with any precision. It is the kind of link between feeling and action which the actors seldom make explicit."[3] John Locke, who went to the Carolinas in 1667 as the second Earl of Shaftesbury's secretary, considered "in the beginning . . . all the world was America." Marx thought Locke's belief in private property was woven into natural right theory, a view that apparently did not mature in America until the mid-eighteenth century and even then remained more "metaphoric" than "physical." This means that the land functions "*as a landscape*—an image in the mind that represents aesthetic, moral, political, and even religious values."[4] With Locke, William Penn, and others such a view of the landscape was posited in America before 1700; the political and economic ramifications of this view—Jefferson's agrarianism, for example—do not appear to emerge until after 1760. Manifestations of the picturesque before that date, therefore, must be ascribed mainly to aesthetic motivations, whether literary or artistic.

Other writers maintain either that the European picturesque aesthetic was not needed in America, for the sublime was already there, or that it did not appear until the end of the century with Jefferson. One writer maintained that American summerhouses were built not for Apollo but for breezes, that

> the only aspect of the new wave in English gardening [to come to America] was the emergence of that pretty excuse for combining utility and pleasure, the *ferme ornée*: . . . Only a few influential landowners . . . were torn between the long-accepted symmetrical plans . . . and the new free style. The standard American middle-of-the-road garden layout was fairly predictable, from New England to the Carolinas.[5]

There is some truth to this view, but it is also misleading because enough evidence exists to show an American awareness of the picturesque from at least 1740 onward by more than "a few influential landowners" who cannot be characterized as being "torn" between the two points of view.[6]

Yet it is also true that little documentary, and even less visual, evidence survives to prove that American gardeners followed picturesque principles on a large scale before 1786 when Jefferson and John Adams made their well-known tour of English (and, for Jefferson, of French) picturesque gardens. One must rely mainly upon isolated references or hints of them in correspondence, in diaries, and in published travels, particularly of foreign visitors like the Marquis de Chastellux and the Duc de la Rochefoucauld-Liancourt. Of course, American colonial garden literature abounds with references like those made by Robert Beverley in 1705 when he described the natural picturesqueness of Virginia and adjacent colonies, considering that "Paradice it self seem'd to be there," that all the colonies "are reckon'd the Gardens of the World."[7] Praise for the wildness of America continued well past 1791 when William Bartram published his *Travels*, but neither he nor his father made detailed reference to specific garden designs in any of their published travels or correspondence. Moreover, Beverley seemingly contradicted himself when he wrote that "they han't many Gardens in the Country, fit to bear that name," yet wrote elsewhere, "Have you pleasure in a Garden? . . . Colonel *Byrd*, in his Garden [at Westover], which is the finest in that Country, has a Summer-House set round with the *Indian* Honey-Suckle . . . A Garden is no where sooner made than there."[8] Marx viewed this more as a conflict of taste between the primitive and the pastoral, the latter extolled by Pope and Brown, the former by Whately and Richard Payne Knight. This "conflict" becomes less problematic if it is accepted that the picturesque landscape aesthetic evolved through several phases, each illustrating a different attitude to formal, informal, and "artificial" elements.[9] Marx held further that Jean-Jacques Rousseau had resolved the dichotomy, believing that "Mankind must depart from the state of nature—but not too far," a thought codified by Richard Price in his *Observations on the . . . American Revolution* (1785), a work Jefferson knew, wherein Price wrote, "The happiest state of man is the middle state between the *savage* and the *refined*."[10] This "middle landscape" corresponds nicely with the picturesque, which was viewed by a number of eighteenth-century critics as a happy "compromise" between landscapes associated with the beautiful or the sublime.

As the earliest and most populous of American colonies, Virginia is the natural place to begin looking for an awareness of the garden as a work of art. This requires a brief look at the emergence of the formal garden which appeared before those associated with the picturesque because the two types were interrelated in the earlier eighteenth century and involved some of the same people. The formal garden probably made its first monumental appearance in the British colonies at the College of William and Mary in 1694. The Reverend James Blair and Bishop Henry Compton, the college's first chancellor, were both much interested in botanical gardens; their interest helps explain why John Evelyn wrote John Walker of Virginia in the spring of 1694 that Mr. London, "his Majs Gardner here" at Hampton Court, "has an ingenious Servant of his, in *Virginia*, not unknown I presume to you by this time; being sent thither on purpose to make [?] and plant the Garden, designed for the new Colledge, newly built in yr Country." The college had not yet been built, for Daniel Parke II, Evelyn's cousin and connection with Walker, was still supervising the making of its bricks that year. One may speculate, however, that the gardener, one James Road, carried a design by "his Majs Gardner." Whether he or someone earlier carried the design for the building by his majesty's architect remains, unfortunately, unclear.[11] Evelyn was much interested in gardening, once observing that a well-designed garden was one that "agreed with the nature of the place."[12] Parke's daughters happened to marry talented and avid gardeners: John Custis of Williamsburg and William Byrd II of Westover. The English naturalist and gardener Mark Catesby contributed some ideas to both the Westover and Custis gardens before his departure from Virginia in 1719. Catesby's niece married Thomas Jones whose beautiful "English" gardens on the Pamunkey, like those of Custis and Byrd, attracted some attention later in the century.[13] Such familial interrelationships, when linked directly to garden designers in London or at Hampton Court, suggest how closely early formal gardens in Virginia were associated with the Wren-Hampton Court style. The Palladian movement of Lord Burlington and William Kent, associated as it was with the picturesque aesthetic, quickly brought an end to the Wren style in architecture and the Le Nôtre style in garden design throughout the 1720s and '30s. Surely, when plantations like Drayton Hall, Shirley, and Mount Airy were begun in the more Palladian manner after 1740, it is reasonable to believe their designers were also aware of, and inclined to follow, picturesque principles of garden design.

The emergence of the formal garden in America in the early eighteenth century is essential as a basis for understanding how a more esoteric, deliberately irregular picturesque garden could later come into vogue, especially given the overwhelming wildness of colonial America. Beverley's 1705 description of Byrd's summerhouse "set round with the *Indian Honey-Suckle*" does not conjure up a particularly formal image nor does Catesby's commentary on the same garden in 1712, for Byrd relates that Catesby "directed how I should mend my garden and put it in a better fashion than it is at present."[14] This observation brings into question Beverley's view of Byrd's garden as the "finest" in that country. Like so many observations that survive, neither makes clear which "fashion" is better and why Byrd's garden is the "finest." At Westover, however, one garden feature appears to have remained prolific throughout the eighteenth century. When the Marquis de Chastellux visited the plantation in 1782, he noted mainly that "the walls of the garden and the house were covered with honeysuckle."[15]

Governor Alexander Spotswood's gardens at the Governor's Palace in Williamsburg mark the initial maturing of the larger formal garden in America and, with some documentation, a drawing, and much archaeology, are the earliest clear evidence for such. Without doubt, these gardens were the model for many created in eighteenth-century Virginia. Specifications for the brick garden wall surrounding the parterres date to 1710; references to the "Falling Gardens," the terraces west of the Palace, to 1719. They appear to have been complete by 1723; a deep valley was dammed at the north end in order to create by that year a "fine canal," access to which was had from the east where the three terraces were afforded steps that led to the walk around the canal. As reconstructed, the canal is partly irregular. It may well have been so originally because the site was irregular.[16] The terraces at the Governor's Palace are among the earliest in America; it is difficult to gauge their influence, though terraces became quite common in eighteenth-century Virginia.

The first feature clearly associated with the picturesque known to come to Virginia before 1740 was the ha-ha, a ditch that obviated the need for fences. It was useful because it restricted livestock movement and beautiful because it permitted the viewing of broad expanses of unbroken landscape. Thomas Lee, who built Stratford Hall around 1730, the design of which has long been associated with Vanbrugh's style, also included this landscape feature. Mann Page's garden at Rosewell is not known but an undated eighteenth-century garden plan that includes a ha-ha has recently been attributed to the Page family and Rosewell because of its great scale, 240 by 450 feet.[17] The 1730s has also been postulated the decade when a number of overmantel and panel paintings appeared in Maryland and Virginia interiors featuring quite picturesque pastoral landscapes.[18] After John Bartram visited John Custis's garden in Williamsburg in 1738, Peter Collinson reported back to Custis that Bartram "was much Delighted with thy Garden which is the best Furnish'd next John Claytons of any He Mett With—in all that Journey."[19] It was noted that Mark Catesby visited and advised Custis on his garden before 1719, but whether by "best Furnish'd" Bartram meant variety of plant material or fineness of design remains unclear. When John Lawson visited South Carolina in 1709, he found that "the Flower-Garden in *Carolina* is as yet arriv'd but to a very poor and jejune Perfection."[20] By 1741, however, that situation had very much changed.

Henry Middleton's Middleton Place, near Charleston, South Carolina, laid out in 1741, was praised by André Michaux in 1787 as a wonder of America. Although little survives, it inspired John Drayton's Magnolia Gardens nearby, begun around 1743, which Baedeker's first American guide isolated with Niagara Falls and the Grand Canyon as alone meriting double stars as sensations of landscape. Both were undoubtedly picturesque, given two of the most complete descriptions to survive of eighteenth-century American gardens—those of the Duc de la Rochefoucauld-Liancourt and Eliza Lucas. When Rochefoucauld visited Middleton Place in 1769, he found it unkempt:

> The property . . . is esteemed the most beautiful house in this part of the country . . . The ensemble of these buildings calls to recollection the ancient English country-seats [the house, inside and outside] . . . is badly kept . . . the river, which flows in a circuitous course, until it reaches this point, forms a wide, beautiful canal, pointing straight to the house. The garden is beautiful, but kept in the same manner as the house.[21]

When he visited Drayton Hall, he described the gardens as if they had been laid out concurrently with the house around 1738:

> The Garden is better laid out . . . than any I have hitherto seen. In order to have a fine garden, you have nothing to do but to let the trees remain standing here and there, or in clumps, to plant bushes in front of them, and arrange the trees according to their height. Dr. Drayton's father . . . began to lay out the garden on this principle; and his son, who is passionately fond of country life, has pursued the same plan.[22]

Rochefoucauld visited other plantations near Charleston, including Batavia, owned by Commodore Gillion. He found the house to be "tolerably handsome," but "the garden is laid out with a more refined taste, and cultivated with more care than gardens generally are in this country."[23]

Given Rochefoucauld's decided taste for *le jardin anglais* as well as its early fashionability in South Carolina, Batavia may also have had such a garden. That Middleton Place also had picturesque gardens is suggested by Eliza Lucas's description in the 1740s of another Middleton plantation, Crowfield. Its gardens and those at Drayton Hall appear the earliest known picturesque gardens in America, both probably dating from around 1740. The house at Crowfield was located a mile from the road but within sight of it. There was a spacious basin of water in the midst of a large green. The garden facade was flanked by walls running out away from the house for a thousand feet, on each side of which, nearest the house, was a grass plot ornamented in a serpentine manner with flowers. Next to that, on the right, was what "immediately struck my rural taste, a thicket of young, tall live oaks. . . . Opposite on the left . . . is a large square boling green, sunk a little below the level of the rest of the garden." Passing over the "Mounts wilderness, etc. [one comes] . . . to the bottom of this charming spott where is a large fish pond with a mount rising out of the middle the top of which is level with the dwelling House, and upon it is a roman temple."[24] These descriptions certainly elicit more images of gardens designed by William Kent or "Capability" Brown than they relate to what is seen today restored at Gunston Hall or Stratford Hall in Virginia.

In 1749 Joanna Livingston laid out her long walk at Van Cortlandt Manor in New York, a garden where formality was not the intent. It still survives, apparently without much alteration. Anne Grant described Albany's houses and gardens before the Revolution as "wildly picturesque, and richly productive." Flowers were "not set in 'curious knots,' were ranged in beds, the varieties of each kind by themselves. . . . To the Schuylers this description did not apply; they had gardeners, and their gardens were laid out in the European manner."[25] Elizabeth McLean, in this volume of essays, has discussed a number of gardens near Philadelphia laid out in an apparently irregular and natural manner. In 1762 Anne Grant visited Oswego, New York, a fort under the command of a Major Duncan, who appears to have amused himself by having his soldiers build a picturesque garden. She wrote:

> To see the sudden creation of this garden, one would think the genius of the place [ah Virgil! ah Pope!] obeyed the wand of an enchanter; but it is not every gardener who can employ some hundred men. A summer house in a tree, a fish-pond, and a gravel-walk, were finished before the end of May.[26]

The fashion, she noted, spread to all the forts. In 1766 Richard Stockton of Morven in Princeton, New Jersey, planned a visit to Pope's garden at Twickenham. In his letter home it sounds as if the visit would be a highlight of his trip; he wrote that he planned to "take with me a gentleman who draws well, to lay down the exact plan of the whole"[27]—a plan that very likely was fulfilled since Stockton returned to Princeton and laid out an approximation of Pope's garden in New Jersey. The 1760s was also the decade when advertisements began to appear in American newspapers for exotic garden buildings, whether Chinese, gothic, or classical, and when at least one English landscape gardener, Thomas Vallentine, advertised his services to gentlemen who lived within a dozen miles of New York City.[28]

By 1770, then, the picturesque garden had established itself from New York to South Carolina. Jefferson had clearly formed a taste for picturesque gardens by 1771 when he envisioned Monticello having a "Gothic temple of antique appearance" and another by a waterfall described as a temple to be roofed in the Chinese or Grecian manner. By 1773 he had developed a romantic taste for Ossianic lore.[29] In 1774, when David Meade moved to Maycox, a plantation he had acquired earlier in Prince George County, Virginia, he appears to have begun an elaborate garden in the picturesque manner. The Reverend John Spooner left this description in 1793:

> These grounds contain about twelve acres laid out on the banks of the James River in a most beautiful and enchanting manner. Forest and fruit trees are here arranged as if nature and art had conspired together to strike the eye most agreeably. Beautiful vistas, which open as many pleasing views of the river; the land thrown into many artificial hollows or gentle swellings with the pleasing vendure of the turf, and the complete order in which the whole is preserved altogether tend to form it one of the most delightful rural seats that is to be met with in the United States, and do honor to the taste and skill of the proprietor, who is the architect.[30]

Interestingly, when the Marquis de Chastellux visited Westover and Maycox in April 1782, he found the house at Maycox "by no means so handsome as Westover":

> Mr. Meade's garden, like the one at Westover, forms a terrace along the bank of the river. It can become still more beautiful if Mr. Meade keeps his house and gives some attention to it, for he is a philosopher of a very amiable but singular turn of mind.[31]

By 1779 picturesque elements had found their way into New England gardens; a bark-covered hermitage à la Rousseau was built in the otherwise formal Hasket Derby gardens near Salem, Massachusetts.[32] In the winter of 1780-1781, Chastellux, whose taste kept him alert for signs of the picturesque, found the houses and hamlets along the road between Hartford and Farmington, Connecticut, made a *"jardin anglais*, which art would have difficulty equaling." In other areas in the vicinity, roads, fields, parks, and houses were "by accident so prettily laid out that it was impossible to imagine a better model for walks in the English style (*promenades anglaises*)."[33] In 1782 he visited Spring Garden, the plantation on the Pamunkey River owned by Thomas Jones, whom Mark Catesby's niece had married, and found it possessed a fine house and

> what is more uncommon in America, that it was further embellished with a garden laid out in the English style. It is even said that this kind

of a park, which is bounded in part by the river, yields not in beauty to those English models which we [in France] are now imitating with much success.[34]

As important as Jefferson is to the history of American landscape design, he cannot be considered its founder; others share that distinction. But Jefferson did bring the picturesque taste to its height.[35] His well-known taste for the picturesque is best documented by the gardens he designed and by his comments when visiting English and French gardens in 1786. At Esher, he wrote, the "clumps of trees . . . balance finely—a most lovely mixture of concave and convex," and at The Leasowes he found fine prospects and beautiful cascades; but at Claremont there was "nothing remarkable." At Chiswick, "the garden shows still too much of art"; at Stowe, he found the "straight approach . . . very ill"; and at Blenheim also "art appears too much."[36] Jefferson's particular taste for the picturesque was the latest taste—that of the Whately-Rousseau-Knight variety. If his drawing and picturesque design for the garden of Chalgrin's Hôtel de Langeac in Paris (*Plate 1*) dates to 1786, which is also the year Charles Bulfinch visited him there, it appears to be the earliest surviving plan by an American for a *jardin anglais*. Jefferson had himself thought of designing garden buildings in various styles before visiting Europe. But John Adams was left unmoved by the "Temples to Bacchus and Venus," and admired most William Shenstone's The Leasowes because it "is the simplest and plainest, but the most rural of all."[37]

In 1786 Jefferson was twenty years away from realizing his picturesque garden at Monticello, but John Penn, Jr., had already established one at his Philadelphia estate, Solitude (*Plate 2*), between 1784 and 1789, where he had built a ha-ha on the south lot line and had not "wholly banished" formality "from the neighborhood of the house . . . the flower garden was distant from the house, reached by a circuitous path which took in as many as possible of the best points of view."[38] William Hamilton, "whom the English style fired . . . with enthusiasm" equal to Jefferson's, built Woodlands (*Plate 3*) near Philadelphia in 1787-1789 and developed a picturesque setting that Jefferson visited and pronounced to be "the chastest model of gardening . . . out of England."[39] Curiously, when Rochefoucauld visited it around 1795, he found it quite the opposite:

> Woodlands, the seat of William Hamilton: it stands high, and is seen upon an eminence from the opposite side of the river. It commands an excellent prospect, but is not to be admired for anything else. The house is small and ill-constructed, very much out of repair, and badly furnished. The garden, which is small, is neglected; but in an adjoining hot-house Mr. Hamilton rears plants procured at great expence from all parts of the world.[40]

In 1802, however, Michaux described it as a "magnificent garden," one that comprised some ten acres and many winding walks by 1830.[41] George Washington, as interested in gardening as Jefferson, cleared land for his "Wilderness" in 1785-1786, possibly laying out about the same time the rather rococo curved road shown in the Vaughan plan of Mount Vernon of 1787 (*Plate 4*). Mount Vernon's gardens may well have influenced others in Virginia, such as Castle Hill in Albemarle County around 1800. Washington was not easily pleased when visiting gardens; his were described in 1798 as "well cultivated, perfectly kept, and . . . quite in the English style," although Benjamin Latrobe, visiting them two years before, thought they were "extremely formal."[42] By 1789 John Adams's daughter Abigail had acquired her father's taste for very natural picturesque landscape. Praising the landscape around Richmond Hill in New York City, which she compared to Honiton in Devonshire, she found it "intercepted, here and there, by a rising ground, and an ancient oak. . . . The venerable oaks and broken ground, covered with wild shrubs, which surround me, give a natural beauty to the spot, which is truly enchanting."[43] She married Colonel William Smith who built Mount Vernon on the East River in New York City on lands still rural in 1796. House and garden were designed with the picturesque in mind.[44] In 1789, when he acquired some four hundred acres in Rhode Island, Samuel Elam began to create an elaborate house and garden, Vaucluse, on some seventeen acres. His agents purportedly "ransacked" England and France for suitable plantings along some "six miles of 'winding walks,' " embellished by a Roman temple and a Trojan maze. When Rochefoucauld visited Vaucluse in 1796, he mentioned mainly its high stone garden and farm fences, not the six miles of winding walks. When, in the same period, he visited Colonel Howard's plantation, Belvedere, outside Baltimore he remarked about the "handsome house, surrounded with lofty and venerable trees. The ground, indeed, is a kind of park formed by nature."[45] Moreau de St. Méry corroborated Rochefoucauld's impression of the Howard plantation. The hill to the north of Baltimore belongs

> to Colonel Howard, whose residence and out-buildings are situated on the front portion. The rear portion is beautified by a park. Its elevated situation; its groves of trees; the view from it, which brings back memories of European scenes: all these things together fill every true Frenchman with both pleasure and regret; his mind and heart alike rejoice in the vistas and the sensations they inspire.[46]

An Essay on Landscape, written and illustrated by Benjamin Latrobe during his journey up the Rappahannock River in 1798, is a rare document in eighteenth-century American landscape history, not least because it is illustrated. Latrobe designed at least two picturesque gardens before 1800, that of circa 1798 for Colonel John Tayloe's residence in Washington, a commission that went ultimately to William Thornton, and the better known Sedgeley (*Plate 5*) outside Philadelphia for William Grammond, built in 1799 and unfortunately destroyed—the latter appears to be the first American house with gothic-revival features. Its simple and direct natural garden is much like that which Latrobe designed about 1808 at Clifton, for the Harris family in Richmond.[47] Had George Hadfield had a more successful career as an architect in America, there

can be little doubt, on the basis of his earlier predilections and achievements, that he would have made a contribution to the American picturesque garden.[48] Equally problematic is the quite picturesque plan for a
garden at Duanesburgh, New York (*Plate 6*), which has been dated circa
1800 and may be related to Dr. David Hosack's Elgin Botanical Garden in
New York City which had incorporated picturesque elements by this
date.[49] The serpentine walks and irregularly placed flower beds with
broad expanses of lawn that Jefferson planned for Monticello and
sketched in a letter to Anne Randolph in 1807 show a garden that he may
have conceived as early as 1786 when in Paris. This design is a fitting
ending to this account of the picturesque in eighteenth-century American
gardens as well as a fitting beginning to that which came afterward.
Jefferson's involvement on so many fronts from 1770 to 1810 prevented
him from devoting the time he wished to the Monticello garden; still, he
devoted no small amount of time to it. Moreover, he became absorbed
with the design of the buildings and gardens of his "academical village,"
the University of Virginia. This is a romantic conception because each
building and garden was designed in a different style with a typically
picturesque "mixed" result. Yet all of them were thoroughly ordered,
original, idealistic, democratic, and natural.[50]

The difficulty in tracing American colonial garden design, whether
through documents or artifacts, was acknowledged by Audrey Noël
Hume: "To the archaeologists searching for the beauty of Virginia's
colonial gardens and finding, instead, that his paths lead only to the
smokehouse or the privy, there is solace in recalling the assurance of
Nicholas Cresswell, who in 1777 wrote that 'some of their gardens [were]
laid out with the greatest taste' of any he had seen in America."[51] But his
"assurance," like so many observations of the eighteenth-century gardener, does not make clear which "taste" is being referred to—the formal,
informal, or something in between. The evidence cited in these pages,
though, suggests that many American eighteenth-century gardens were as
informal and regular as the one laid out about 1803 at Eleutherian Mills,
Delaware, by E. I. du Pont. In 1925 Mrs. Victorine du Pont Foster drew
the plan of this 1803 garden as she remembered it in 1880; subsequent
archaeology has, apparently, confirmed her memory and the presumed
appearance of the 1803 garden.[52] The description of Middleton's Crowfield in the 1740s is only the most sparkling of numerous allusions to
consciously picturesque American gardens in the eighteenth century. It
suggests that the archaeologist ought to be on the lookout for more than
just allées, parterres, and clairvoyées. Middleton's design, like many
others executed in the eighteenth century, are sources for what A. J.
Downing wrote about a century later, in 1841: "The modern style of
landscape gardening . . . the *English* or *natural* style." Downing, like Sir
William Temple with his appreciation of Chinese gardens, preferred this
style and contrasted it with the "geometric or ancient style" which featured
mainly sculpture. Identifying this ancient style, as Addison had before
him with autocratic societies, Downing reasoned that such a style could
never prevail in the United States where "the rights of man are held to be

equal."[53] This thought is well grounded in the eighteenth-century American, as well as English and French, view of the garden and landscape.

College of William and Mary

—————————————NOTES—————————————

1. Kimball made Jefferson the focus of his article, "The Beginnings of Landscape Architecture in America," *Landscape Architecture,* XLII (July 1917), pp. 181-187. Frederick Doveton Nichols and Ralph E. Griswold consider Monticello "one of the earliest . . . English-type landscape gardens in America," which is not really true: *Thomas Jefferson, Landscape Architect* (Charlottesville, Va., 1978), p. 90. Two picturesque plans for Monticello's gardens survive; one is datable to June 7, 1807, and appears on the reverse of a letter Jefferson wrote Anne Cary Randolph. The other is undated, but has notes, presumably put in later, in 1808, when the gardens were being laid out. Frederick Nichols dates this plan to the period 1785-1789 on the basis that graph paper was used: William Howard Adams, ed., *The Eye of Thomas Jefferson* (Charlottesville, Va., 1981), pp. 331-332. I have located more than two dozen garden designs and descriptions that suggest a picturesque intention in American gardens dating from before 1806-1808. Most of these gardens date to before 1786 when Jefferson is known to have drawn the picturesque plan for the Hôtel de Langeac gardens in Paris. Curiously, the United States was not included in Nikolaus Pevsner, ed., *The Picturesque Garden and Its Influence Outside the British Isles* (Washington, D. C., 1974). I view the picturesque both as an aesthetic category distinct from the beautiful and the sublime and one that greatly influenced the course of architecture, landscape design, and city planning from the early eighteenth century on and does so still. Its various style phases are outlined briefly in n. 9. Here it may be simply defined as the aesthetic underlying *le jardin anglais,* that natural, irregular, and deliberately asymmetrical kind of planting.

2. See Richard E. Quaintance, "Walpole's Whig Interpretation of Landscaping History," *Studies in Eighteenth-Century Culture,* IX (Madison, Wis., 1979), pp. 285-300.

3. Leo Marx, *The American Revolution and the American Landscape* (Washington, D. C., 1974), p. 8.

4. Leo Marx, *The Machine in the Garden* (New York, 1964), pp. 120, 128.

5. Ann Leighton, *American Gardens in the Eighteenth Century: "For Use or for Delight"* (Boston, 1976), pp. 363-364.

6. The controversy suggested by the term "torn" belongs not to the eighteenth century but to the turn of this century when designers like William Robinson and Reginald Blomfield in England, in reacting mutually against Victorian gardens associated with Joseph Paxton, took nearly opposite positions with respect to the merit of informal versus formal gardens, respectively: W. Robinson, *The English Flower Garden and Home Grounds* (London, 1883); Reginald Blomfield, *The Formal Garden in England* (London, 1892). This controversy has left a still detectable legacy among garden historians today who often project it upon earlier periods and confuse colonial revival and "new" picturesque gardens around 1900 with those of the eighteenth century.

7. Robert Beverley, *The History and Present State of Virginia,* ed. Louis B. Wright (Chapel Hill, N. C., 1947), pp. 16, 297.

8. *Ibid.,* pp. 316, 298, 299.

9. Marx, *Machine in the Garden,* pp. 84-85. Briefly put, the English picturesque garden evolved through at least three distinct phases in the eighteenth century. The first, ca. 1720-1750, is associated with the generation of Pope and Kent; the second, ca. 1750-1780, with that of "Capability" Brown and Walpole; the third, ca. 1780-1810, with that of Whately,

Uvedale Price, Richard Payne Knight, and Humphry Repton. In general, the first phase emphasizes some formal features and a variety of garden buildings in numerous styles (Pope at Twickenham, Kent at Rousham Park); the second phase emphasizes clumps of trees, artificial knolls, and serpentine ponds or lakes often with islands (Brown at Blenheim); the third phase generally stresses very natural settings and sweeps of turf with a minimum of "artificial" features.

10. *Ibid.*, pp. 101-102, 104-105, quotation on p. 105.

11. Ruth Bourne, "John Evelyn, The Diarist, and His Cousin Daniel Parke II," *Virginia Magazine of History and Biography*, LXXVIII (January 1970), pp. 3-33. Pipe Roll 4 for Hampton Court, May 1, 1689-Mar. 25, 1696, records £234 11s. 9d. paid "James Road. Gardiner. for going to Virginia to make a collection of foreign Plants . . .": *Wren Society*, IV (1927), p. 34. Two French maps of 1781 and 1782 (see Plates 7 and 9 in Peter Martin's essay in this volume) show gardens to the west of the college; neither shows the canal at the Governor's Palace. See also John W. Reps, *The Making of Urban America* (Princeton, N. J., 1965), fig. 64, and Reps, *Tidewater Towns: City Planning in Colonial Virginia and Maryland* (Williamsburg, Va., 1972), fig. 121.

12. John Dixon Hunt and Peter Willis, eds., *The Genius of the Place: The English Landscape Garden 1620-1820* (New York, 1975), p. 57.

13. These familial interrelationships are set forth by E. G. Swem, ed., *Brothers of the Spade: Correspondence of Peter Collinson of London, and of John Custis, of Williamsburg, Virginia 1734-1746* (Barre, Mass., 1957), pp. 11ff.

14. Louis B. Wright and Marion Tinling, eds., *The Secret Diary of William Byrd of Westover, 1709-1712* (Richmond, Va., 1941), p. 540.

15. Marquis de Chastellux, *Travels in North America in the Years 1780, 1781 and 1782*, ed. and trans. Howard C. Rice, Jr. (Chapel Hill, N. C., 1963), II, p. 432.

16. For analyses of aspects of the gardens at the Governor's Palace, see Peter Martin, " 'Promised Fruites of Well Ordered Towns'—Gardens in 'Early 18th-Century Williamsburg," *Journal of Garden History*, II (October-December 1982), pp. 309-324, and Martin, "Williamsburg: The Role of the Garden in 'Making a Town,' " *Studies in Eighteenth-Century Culture*, XII (Madison, Wis., 1983), pp. 187-204.

17. The plan is at the Massachusetts Historical Society, Boston, and has been identified as Rosewell by John Bedenkapp: Adams, ed., *Eye of Jefferson*, p. 318.

18. The overmantel painting at Holly Hill in Anne Arundel County, Maryland, is particularly noteworthy. H. Chandlee Forman, *Maryland Architecture: A Short History from 1634 through the Civil War* (Cambridge, Md., 1968), dates it to ca. 1730. It is also illustrated in Thomas Tileston Waterman, *The Dwellings of Colonial America* (New York, 1922), p. 23.

19. Swem, ed., *Brothers of the Spade*, p. 64. Curiously, when Washington visited Bartram's garden in Philadelphia in 1787 he found it had "many curious plants . . . [but] not laid off with much taste": Leighton, *American Gardens*, p. 264.

20. John Lawson, *A New Voyage to Carolina*, ed. Hugh Talmage Lefler (Chapel Hill, N.C., 1967).

21. François de la Rochefouchald-Liancourt, *Travels Through the United States of North America . . .* (London, 1799), I, p. 591.

22. *Ibid.*, pp. 591-592.

23. *Ibid.*, p. 592.

24. Harriott Horry Ravenel, *Eliza Pinckney* (New York, 1896), p. 54. The description is from a letter to a Mrs. Bartlett in London, known to date between 1740 and 1742, part of which is reprinted in Alice G. B. Lockwood, *Gardens of Colony and State* (New York, 1931, 1934), II, p. 228.

25. Anne Grant, *Memoirs of an American Lady: with Sketches of Manners and Scenery in America, as They Existed Previous to the Revolution* (New York, 1809), pp. 26, 21-22. For Van Cortlandt Manor, Croton-on-Hudson, see Lockwood, *Gardens of Colony and State*, I, pp. 270-274.

26. Grant, *Memoirs*, p. 236.

27. Kimball, "Beginnings of Landscape Architecture," p. 181. An undocumented Morven garden plan of questionable authority is illustrated in Lockwood, *Gardens of Colony and State*, I, p. 310.

28. Benjamin Bucktrout advertised "all sorts of Chinese and Gothick paling for gardens

and summer houses" in the *Virginia Gazette*, Jan. 6, 1767; Vallentine's notice appeared in the *New York Journal*, Aug. 11, 1768.

29. Edwin Morris Betts, ed., *Thomas Jefferson's Garden Book, 1766-1824* (Philadelphia, 1944), pp. 25-26. See William Beiswanger's essay in this volume on Jefferson's designs for garden buildings at Monticello. For Jefferson's interest in Ossian, see Chastellux, *Travels*, II, pp. 575-576, n. 8.

30. Fiske Kimball, "A Landscape Garden on the James in 1793," *Landscape Architecture*, LV (January 1924), p. 123.

31. Chastellux, *Travels*, II, p. 431.

32. Eliza Southgate mentions the hermitage in a letter of 1802. Fiske Kimball, "An American Gardener of the Old School—George Heussler, Born 1751, Died 1817," *Landscape Architecture*, LVII (January 1925), pp. 71-75. Samuel McIntyre prepared three plans for the Derby garden at Danvers before 1794, two of which were not formal, one of which was entirely picturesque. Lockwood, *Gardens of Colony and State*, I, p. 67.

33. Chastellux, *Travels*, I, pp. 76, 228.

34. *Ibid.*, II, p. 380. Rice considered this to be "a very early example of the 'English garden' in America": p. 569, n. 14.

35. Governor of Virginia and a member of the board of visitors of the College of William and Mary in 1779, Jefferson was instrumental in the curricular reforms instituted that year when Robert Andrews was appointed "Professor of Moral Philosophy, the Laws of Nature and of Nations, and of the Fine Arts." Faculty Minutes (Dec. 29, 1779), p. 280. Jefferson defined the fine arts as consisting of "Sculpture, Painting, Gardening, Music, Architecture, Poetry, Oratory, Criticism." The tendency to consider Jefferson the "father" of American landscape architecture was cited in n. 1.

36. Betts, ed., *Jefferson's Garden Book*, pp. 111-114.

37. Lyman H. Butterfield, ed., *Diary and Autobiography of John Adams* (Cambridge, Mass., 1961), III, pp. 185-186.

38. William Birch, *The Country Seats of the United States* (Springfield, Pa., 1808), quoted in Lockwood, *Gardens of Colony and State*, I, pp. 345-346.

39. Adams, ed., *Eye of Jefferson*, p. 328. Jefferson's letter to Hamilton in July 1806 is usually viewed as indicating his intention to pattern the Monticello gardens on those at Woodlands: Betts, ed., *Jefferson's Garden Book*, pp. 320-323ff.

40. Rochefouchauld-Liancourt, *Travels*, II, p. 245. Chastellux visited Richard Peters's Belmont near Philadelphia in 1780 and is usually cited as describing "the variegated beauties of the rural banks of the Schuylkill" and the seat as "the most enchanting spot that nature can embellish," but the description is actually by George Grieve, the eighteenth-century translator of Chastellux's *Travels*. See I, p. 325, n. 100. According to Mary G. Kimball, "The Revival of the Colonial," *Architectural Record*, LXII (July 1927), its grounds contained a Chinese temple. According to William Birch in his *Autobiography*, George Isham Parkyns may have designed both Woodlands and Solitude; Jefferson sought his aid in designing the Monticello garden. Jefferson to Hamilton, July 1806, in Betts, ed., *Jefferson's Garden Book*, p. 323. Parkyns's quite picturesque plan for Belmont of 1793 is, apparently, unrelated to Peters's Belmont: Adams, ed., *Eye of Jefferson*, p. 320. Parkyns's work in Scotland is the subject of a discussion by A. A. Tait elsewhere in this volume.

41. Lockwood, *Gardens of Colony and State*, I, p. 348.

42. The first description is by "a Polish visitor" in June 1798, quoted in Leighton, *American Gardens*, p. 269. The full context of Latrobe's remark affirms his dislike of formal gardens (July 19, 1796): "The ground on the West front [of Mount Vernon] is laid out in a level lawn bounded on each side with a wide but extremely formal serpentine walk, shaded by weeping Willows, a tree which in this country grows very well upon high dry land. On one side of this lawn is a plain Kitchen Garden, on the other a neat flower garden laid out in squares, and boxed with great precission. . . . For the first time again since I left Germany, I saw here a parterre, chipped and trimmed with infinite care into the form of a richly flourished Fleur de Lis: The expiring groans I hope of our Grandfather's pedantry." Edward C. Carter II, ed., *The Virginia Journals of Benjamin Henry Latrobe, 1795-1798*, 3 vols. (New Haven, Conn., 1977), I, p. 165.

43. Leighton, *American Gardens*, p. 378.

44. Smith's Mount Vernon was built in the years 1796-1798; its partly picturesque

garden plan is illustrated in Lockwood, *Gardens of Colony and State,* I, p. 264.

45. Rochefouchauld-Liancourt, *Travels,* I, pp. 495-496, where he described the farm at Vaucluse rather than the gardens. They are described, without sources cited, in Lockwood, *Gardens of Colony and State,* I, pp. 230-232.

46. Kenneth Roberts and Anna M. Roberts, trans. and eds., *Moreau de St. Méry's American Journey* (Garden City, N.Y., 1947), p. 79.

47. Benjamin Latrobe, *An Essay on Landscape* (Richmond, Va., 1798); Talbot Hamlin, *Benjamin Henry Latrobe* (Oxford, 1955).

48. Hadfield won the gold medal of the Royal Academy in 1784, studied under the gothic revivalist James Wyatt from 1784 to 1790, and made numerous picturesque drawings of Roman ruins before coming to the United States in 1795. Michael Richman, "George Hadfield (1763-1826): His Contribution to the Greek Revival in America," *Journal of the Society of Architectural Historians,* XXXIII (October 1974), pp. 234-235.

49. The Duanesburgh plan is illustrated in the American Society of Landscape Architects, *Colonial Gardens: The Landscape Architecture of George Washington's Time* (Washington, D.C., n.d.), p. 37, where it is not discussed but is labeled "The 'naturalistic' English style—a place at Duanesburgh, New York, about 1800" and is credited to Charles W. Leavitt & Son. Hosack laid out some twenty acres, the Elgin Botanic Gardens, in 1801 between 47th and 51st streets and Fifth and Sixth avenues. Their picturesque character was captured in a drawing by Hugh Reinagle about 1812. Adams, ed., *Eye of Jefferson,* p. 345; Lockwood, *Gardens of Colony and State,* I, pp. 268-269.

50. I am using the term "romanticism" in the sense Fiske Kimball defined it in "Romantic Classicism in Architecture," *Gazette des Beaux-Arts,* XXV (1944), pp. 94-112. The romantic encompasses all the revivals, whether Greek, Roman, or gothic.

51. Audrey Noël Hume, *Archaeology and the Colonial Gardener* (Williamsburg, Va., 1974), p. 91; *The Journal of Nicholas Cresswell, 1774-1777* (New York, 1924), p. 206.

52. Norman B. Wilkinson, *E. I. du Pont, Botaniste: The Beginning of a Tradition* (Charlottesville, Va., 1972), pp. 71ff. The archaeological work undertaken by the Eleutherian Mills-Hagley Foundation from 1968 onward is discussed on pp. 128-131.

53. A. J. Downing. *A Treatise on the Theory and Practice of Landscape Gardening,* 6th ed. (New York, 1859), pp. 22, 23.

"Long and Assiduous Endeavours:" Gardening in Early Eighteenth-Century Virginia

Peter Martin

From the closing years of the seventeenth century, several of the more affluent Virginians at their plantations had begun to see ornamental possibilities as they arranged their grounds around practical plantation layouts. William Fitzhugh at Eagle's Nest, Robert Beverley at Beverley Park, Philip Ludwell at Green Spring, Robert "King" Carter at Corotoman, Dudley Digges at Bellefield, and William Byrd I of Westover, among others, showed signs of this impulse for the decorative vein before the turn of the century.[1] But this tendency, exhibited chiefly by the so-called oligarchs of Virginia society, and by the more imaginative ones at that, did not find much expression in the new capital before the second half of the eighteenth century. During the first quarter of the century, notwithstanding the Palace and college gardens and the example of John Custis about which there will be more below, Williamsburg was too much the dusty little village to inspire such moves. Before the second half of the century it was left to strong-minded, even eccentric, personalities who either had to or especially wanted to live in town to lay out gardens for pleasure—people like Custis, Governor Alexander Spotswood, James Blair (the founder of the College of William and Mary in 1693), and a handful of hired gardeners highly valued for their work at the college and Governor's Palace.

This did not mean, though, that there was no cooperation between plantation and town gardening in the first half of the century. In fact, the chartering of Williamsburg as the colonial capital in 1699 may be said to have created a center or focal point of gardening in the colony, a meeting place where as the century wore on the increasing urbanity and civilized gentility encouraged people to think and talk about landscape use and gardens, exchange ideas, and buy plants.[2] Planters like William Byrd II even contributed plants from their own demesnes to beautify the Palace, as well as gardeners to help their friends in town. And later in the century certain town gardens commanded considerable interest both inside and outside the colony. Travelers, politicians, botanists, and planters made a point of seeing them, although few of these visitors apparently took the trouble to write out descriptions. Scarcely any descriptions, at least, have survived. Emerging from a new consciousness, both in Williamsburg and at plantations, regarding the importance of gardens as emblems of grace and urbanity in colonial life, was a gardening tradition which, in retrospect, could be traced as far back as to the end of the preceding century when the college was founded.[3]

In addition to the college and Palace gardens, which are not the subject of this essay, the initial grid town plan conceived by Governor Francis Nicholson between 1700-1704 appears to have opened up possibilities for the landscaping by creating neighborhoods on the edge of town that were "retired" and "healthful," as the *Virginia Gazette* frequently claimed in its sale advertisements. It was in these areas that the wealthier town residents purchased parcels of lots enabling them to lay out their grounds without the constraints imposed upon most residents by a single, mere half-acre, lot. Nicholson's axial town plan, with the Duke of Gloucester Street establishing the principal axis (*Plate 7*),[4] also delineated what John Reps in his important study, *Tidewater Towns: City Planning in Colonial Virginia and Maryland*, has urged us to see as landscape gardening-style vistas and perspectives.[5] Many of Nicholson's decisions about Williamsburg's appearance, and their elaboration later by Governor Spotswood, were conceived to illuminate a sense of unity in the townscape through an interplay of pictorial images—images that were linked to each other by streets, buildings, green spaces, shapes, and a variety of elevations throughout the town. This technique, explained by Reps, and Nicholson's own knowledge of garden and town planning, suggest that he applied the perspective of a landscaper to the organization of space there. Reps has even suggested the possibility that Nicholson contrived oblique vistas across the blocks of lots in an effort to engrave upon the town two enormous ciphers, "W" and "M," alluding emblematically to William and Mary, of course.[6]

It is certain when Spotswood came upon the scene in 1710 and embarked upon various architectural projects, including the completion of the Palace and the designing of its famous gardens, he perpetuated Nicholson's scheme by strengthening the vistas. One such vista was the Palace Green (*Plate 8*), which served his pride and self-interest since as governor he lived at its northern end;[7] another set of perspectives were those he unfolded in the Market Square by designing an octagonal powder magazine and placing it in the center where it could be seen not only all around the perimeter of the square but also up and down North and South England streets. An element in the townscape, incidentally, that neither Nicholson nor Spotswood could do anything about was the maze of gullies and ravines that bedeviled the street-makers in town. While they certainly constituted an engineering nightmare for the founders of the town, they also introduced a variety of elevation in an otherwise flat landscape. Today these ravines are sources of beauty enhanced by modern landscape treatment by the Colonial Williamsburg Foundation; even in the first quarter of the eighteenth century, though, they must have been valued at least as much as cursed by people like Spotswood and Custis. Spotswood's "capital stroke" in the Palace gardens around 1716 was to carve terraces out of a deep ravine in the grounds west of the Palace and have them overlook a formal canal that he created at the bottom.[8] If he could make this kind of imaginative use of a ravine, others could have, too, in perhaps less grand fashion.

One of these in the first half of the century was John Custis. With Custis we shift from the realm of public gardening, which comprised the wellspring of the Williamsburg gardening tradition, to the world of the amateur private gardener who perpetuated the tradition until by the time of the Revolution the town was full of pleasure, as well as practical, gardens of considerably varying sizes (*Plate 9*). As a private and very personal gardener, Custis illustrated several themes and features that heightened early eighteenth-century English garden history but that have not been acknowledged sufficiently as part of Virginia's or any other colony's garden history at the same time. These included iconography, political gardening, the pictorial, the classical, and the "poetic." By "poetic" gardening I mean landscape deriving from deeply personal motives and associations, so that a garden becomes for its gardener a somewhat complex psychological expression as well as a multifarious portrait of ideas.[9] Custis was perhaps the best example of the "poetic" gardener in early eighteenth-century America. At least we know more about him than we do about most gardeners because his letterbook has survived to tell us the emotional and botanical story of his Williamsburg garden.[10] Unfortunately, nothing whatever of his garden remains today.

"I have lately got into the vein of gardening, and have made a handsome garden to my house," he wrote to his London agent, Micajah Perry, in 1717.[11] He had just moved into his Williamsburg town house, with eight lots or four acres around it, while at the same time he maintained his plantation, Queen's Creek, about a mile north of town. Beginning that year, Custis embarked on a lifetime of plant exchanges that was immensely gratifying to both him and the botanists in England who received his Virginia flora; in addition, he spent his energies on garden design, showing an intelligent interest in the pictorial: colors, shapes, and the arrangement of features.

Nonetheless, there is a current of pathos and disappointment that runs through Custis's gardening letters, made all the more acute by his intensely personal commitment to his garden. He could write in 1725 to Robert Cary, another London agent, that he "should be very glad of some layers of good flowers" since "I have a pretty little garden in which I take more satisfaction than in anything in this world and have a collection of tolerable good flowers and greens from England"; but in the same letter he could quickly lapse into a vein of bitter disappointment, even crankiness, as he contemplated what he regarded as the idiocy and ignorance of English gardeners and ship captains who packed his treasured plants carelessly and shipped them to Virginia with total indifference as to whether they would ever get there alive. I have "had great losses," he complained, "by their coming in partly by the carelessness and ignorance of the masters of the ships . . . coming in too late. I had 100 roots of fine double Dutch tulips sent me from one Jervis [?] a gardiner at Battersy, but the ship came in so late that most of them split themselves; 2 or 3 came up which are now fine flowers."[12] He urged again and again that flowers be put in wooden boxes and placed in the ballast of ships and watered, that double tulips be kept dry in cabins, and so on. Repeated failure wore down him and his vanity for gardening. "The garden truck were carelessly put in the steerage," he wrote to Cary later in 1726 with the understandable despair of a man who had opened a long-awaited package to find everything spoiled, "where as I am informed a dog tore all to bitts; the cornations and auriculas; so that they all perished; the box and gooseberry trees; some of them lived, but the gardener you mentioned, under whose care you put them I believe to be an ignorant knavish fellow."[13]

That special brand of misery preceded his discovery of Peter Collinson in 1734, with whom he then undertook a decade or so of skilled gardening dialogue and plant exchange; but there were still the disinterested captains, the vagaries of weather at sea and at home, and the changes in his health to conspire against his hopes. In 1734, after seventeen years of gardening in Williamsburg, he boasted to Collinson:

> I am very proud it is in my power to gratify any curious gentleman in this [gardening] way; being myself a great admirer of things of that nature; I have a garden inferiour to few if any in Virga in which and in good [painting] my whole delight is placed. . . . [I have] ews [philly-rea?] and [gilded?] hollys; come safe to me and thrive very well; indeed any tree may be transported if carefully put in dirt and carefully minded.[14]

On the other hand, his desolation could be quickened by a drought or frost. "The greatest pleasure I find is in my garden," he confided to Collinson in 1739, "and sometimes even that is insipid." He begins to sound like Alexander Pope who often compared his garden to his life, alternatively flourishing and languishing. "At present I have little taste for anything my garden is the chiefest pleasure I have besides reading," Custis wrote in 1741, "which if I did not delight in [I] should have run mad"; as for the winter, "it has made dreadful havock in my garden . . . if I were a young man I would never plant any trees that would not endure our winters because I would not make myself uneasy for the loss of them." In another letter in 1741 he was again philosophical for Collinson: "I confess your charming description of the trees and flowers raises great desire in me but they soon whither . . . tis all vanity."[15]

Custis's pictorial and iconographic approach to gardening is also evident from his letters, and it links his gardening with new concepts that were gaining currency in England at the time. Custis's example, as well as Byrd's at Westover between 1710 and 1740, makes nonsense of the old loosely held notion that garden design in the colonies lagged over fifty years behind English practice. Not as many people were designing decorative gardens in the colonies, but that was not for want of knowledge of what was going on in England, or lack of interest, or unavailability of the gardening manuals being published in England. There was simply not enough money, nor were there enough individuals with sufficient land and time to indulge in this sort of deliberate landscaping. Custis and Byrd, however, showed their fellow colonials what could be done.

In his first gardening of 1717, just before he lapses into the role of the gardenist, Custis orders from Perry, his agent, several "diverting prints to hang in the passage of my house"; he mentions in particular some of "Mars and Venus and Neptune and Amphitrite."[16] In isolation this order would not appear to have any gardening significance, except that it turns out he had lead statues of classical deities in his garden,[17] that he also began to order prints of flowers as he started on his garden, that in the letter to Collinson in 1734 he linked gardening and painting as his two chief delights, and in a 1735 letter he observed that "a curious painter may nicely delineate the features and air of a face, or the pleasant prospect of A Landscape. . . ."[18] It is also revealing that Custis had himself painted by Charles Bridges, an English portrait painter who lived in Williamsburg after 1735. Custis holds a book titled, "Of a Tulip," and a cut tulip conspicuously rests on a table (*Plate 10*).

The painting is but one item in the iconography of his gardening. Back in 1723 Custis wrote to Byrd, who was then in England, asking for "two pieces of as good painting as you can procure; it is to put in the summer before my Chimneys to hide the fireplace. Let them be some good flowers in pots of various kinds."[19] Then by 1736 he had decided to turn the picture into a reality as he requested "6 flower pots painted green to stand in a chimney to put flowers in the summer time with 2 handles to each pot."[20] Custis's interest in acquiring pictures of flowers invites the plausible conjecture that he saw his garden as a large composition that he was "painting." His letters to Collinson are brimming with images of color; he was careful to request a wide range of colors in flowers and flowering bushes. His disappointment was profound when spring arrived and he discovered a blossom was the wrong color. Shapes and shades of greens also fascinated him. He boasted to Collinson of "the balls or standards having heads as big as a peck and the pyramids [being] in full shape." "I had very fine yews balls and pyramids which were established for more than 20 years," he mourned in 1742 after a cruel frost had killed many of them.[21]

One final word concerning Custis's political gardening is relevant. Given his devotion to gardening and Spotswood's landscaping at the Palace, it may appear surprising that in none of his letters does he ever mention the Palace gardens. The fact is that by 1716 he was in league with Blair, Byrd, and Ludwell to get rid of Spotswood as governor. The closest he ever comes to mentioning the Palace in his extant letters is in the first letter of his letterbook, addressed to Byrd on March 30, 1717. He dismisses Byrd's jest about his being the governor's "Court favourite" and asserts, "I assure you, Sir, it is so far from that, that I have not been within the Governor's palace doors nor exchanged one word with the Governor this nine months." In this political context, it would be understandable if Custis had actively disliked Spotswood's gardening. If Spotswood's gardening was "Court" gardening, then Custis's scientific and empirical gardening may be judged as the antithesis. Their gardening standoff reflected the political antagonism between them. Custis's impatience and disdain over the governor's desire for a vista from the Palace in 1717, and his claim of the governor's insensitivity to cutting down any trees in the way, further suggest this. So does the probability that Custis was the spur behind the House of Burgesses's inquiry into what they felt was Spotswood's lavish gardening at the colony's expense.[22]

Although Byrd helped Spotswood with some of his initial planting and gardening in 1712, he, too, was quickly disillusioned by Spotswood's politics, if not also by his imperial approach to gardening, and he never again mentioned the Palace gardening in his surviving correspondence. It is also true that Byrd did not again become interested in Spotswood the gardener until many years after the latter had been removed from office. In that instance, when there were no longer any political undercurrents to perplex these gardeners, it was Spotswood's humbler private gardens at Germanna that evoked a response.[23] To anyone in Virginia at the time, like Byrd himself, who understood the political underpinnings of much of the new gardening going on in England, Williamsburg's gardening rivalries would have sounded familiar.

Byrd in other ways represented one of the important early links in eighteenth-century Virginia between English, Williamsburg, and Virginia plantation gardening. In addition to the political theme, he revealed in his writings an alertness to the pictorial and a deliberateness in showing how open landscape could be "read" as a succession of compositions. His accounts in the late 1720s and early 1730s of expeditions to determine the dividing line between North Carolina and Virginia are rich with such compositions.[24] Having spent his youth and most of his young adult life in England, he apparently had become accustomed to seeing both open landscape and gardens in terms of pictures because his letters while in England often cite the pictorial elements in gardens he visited—and he made a point of visiting many.[25] One brief example must suffice here to illustrate how he "framed" scenes for himself in the wilderness, most of them conceived amid the well-ordered comfort of his campsites:

> The tent was pitched up on an Eminence, which overlookt a wide Piece of low Grounds, cover'd with Reeds and watered by a Crystal Stream gliding thro' the Middle of it. On the Other Side of this delightful Valley, which was about half a Mile wide, rose a Hill that terminated the View, and in the figure of a Semicircle closed in upon the opposite Side of the Valley. This had a most agreeable Effect upon the Eye, and wanted nothing but Cattle grazing in the Meadow, and Sheep and Goats feeding on the Hill, to make it a Compleat Rural LANDSCAPE.[26]

Richard Beale Davis has said it was through Byrd and his wit that the "sprightly charm" of early eighteenth-century English literature entered colonial American writing;[27] it may also be said it was through Byrd that the consciously pictorial English approach to gardening of the same era entered colonial American gardening.

If we credit Robert Beverley with not being a mere flatterer or promoter in his *History*, by 1705 the Westover gardens were worthy of an Englishman's attention: "Colonel *Byrd*, in his Garden, which is the finest in that Country, has a Summer-House set round with the *Indian* Honey-Suckle, which all the Summer is continually full of sweet Flowers."[28] Byrd II remained in Virginia from 1705-1716, during which time he improved his garden in unknown ways. The naturalist Mark Catesby helped him with some of the improvements: "Mr. Catesby directed how I should mend my garden and put it into a better fashion than it is at present," he wrote in his diary for June 5, 1712.[29]

After about ten more years in England, Byrd returned to Virginia for good in 1726. He thereupon embarked upon major landscaping at Westover. Instead of describing what the evidence allows us to say about these gardens, I wish here only to suggest Byrd's pose as a *beatus ille* and patriarch—a pose he conceived to compensate himself for the loss of English gardens and society. To the Earl of Orrery in July 1726, he cast himself as "one of the patriarchs" with "my flocks and my herds, my bond-men, and bond-women. . . . We sit securely under our vines, and our fig-trees without any danger to our property."[30] For Anne Taylor Otway in 1736 he fancifully sketched Westover as a new version of paradise: "We jogg on soberly and peaceably in our state of innocence, enjoying all the blessings of a comfortable sun and fertile soil. Our comforts like those of the good patriarchs are mostly domestique, observing . . . the flowers of our own planting improve."[31] John Bartram, the Philadelphia naturalist, tantalized Collinson in 1740 with this brief description of what Byrd had achieved in his garden: "Colonel Byrd is very prodigalle . . . [with] new Gates, gravel Walks, hedges, and cedars finely twined and a little green house with two or three orange trees; . . . in short, he hath the finest seat in Virginia."[32]

It was fortuitous that when Byrd first arrived in Virginia in 1705 to take up his legacy at Westover, Williamsburg had recently been chartered as the new capital and Nicholson had already laid out the first stage of the town plan. It was true then, and it remained true, that Byrd, familiar with the pleasures of high English country and London society, placed great store in the town life he could find in Williamsburg, just half a day's journey down the James River from Westover. He admired the public buildings, and his diaries record the people he visited and gardens in which he made a habit of walking. The James River with its sparkling plantations (if not villas) later in the century was occasionally compared to the fashionable stretch of the Thames from Fulham to Twickenham, with all its Palladian gems; it is not unlikely that Byrd might have perceived his own posture at Westover, in relation to Williamsburg, somewhat as Pope esteemed his own Horatian, "semi-retired" pose at Twickenham. Byrd read the classical authors almost every day: the image of Horace at his Sabine Farm could easily have occurred to him as an apt analogy to his own demesne. We know the Horatian model occurred to Landon Carter in the 1750s, who even advertised his imaginative claim to it by calling his plantation on the Rappahannock River Sabine Hall.

I stress Byrd's relationship to Williamsburg by way of suggesting that as the century progressed, the plantations within a few hours' ride from the town, chiefly along the principal rivers of the colony, enjoyed a cultural reciprocity with the town. This was especially vital to the development of gardening, both ornamental and practical. The town, which never developed as a large and dense center like Charleston, Annapolis, Philadelphia, or Savannah, but maintained its village character with well-ordered streets, pleasant public buildings, and several carefully styled gardens, remained a pleasant place to meet and was valued for its quiet urbanity. It became culturally rich and helped generate social coherence in the colony. Its gardens played a part in this. For their part, the plantations served as nurseries and sources of garden tools and gardeners for the town. Kingsmill plantation on the James (whose gardens, according to recent archaeology, appear to have been influenced by the Palace gardens), Rosewell, Carter's Grove, Nomini Hall, Mt. Airy, Gunston Hall, Sabine Hall, Corotoman, Monticello, and a good many others shared with each other a gardening world that would not have evolved as quickly as it did without the civilizing influence of the capital and its gardens.

Plantation gardening as a fashionable amusement and art flourished well into the nineteenth century; but the decline of Williamsburg gardens set in swiftly during the Revolution and after Thomas Jefferson, who in 1779 had introduced landscape design into the William and Mary curriculum, saw to it that the capital of Virginia was moved to Richmond. Except for St. George Tucker, poet, lawyer, and devoted gardener, whose town garden is well documented from 1789 to 1826, Williamsburg died as a gardening town as history began to pass it by.

Colonial Williamsburg Foundation and *New England College, Sussex*

NOTES

1. Most of the evidence for pleasure gardening at seventeenth- and early eighteenth-century plantations is still available only in manuscripts of diaries, accounts, letters, inventories, and orders for plants from England. I have assessed this impulse to garden in a study of colonial Virginia gardening, "From Sufficiency to Elegance: Gardening in Eighteenth-Century Virginia," recently completed for the Colonial Williamsburg Foundation. For a background study of the growing affluence of planters in the seventeenth century and their expressions of culture, see Louis B. Wright, *The First Gentlemen of Virginia* (Charlottesville, Va., 1964). See also Richard Beale Davis, ed., *William Fitzhugh and His Chesapeake World, 1676-1701* (Chapel Hill, N. C., 1963). For a more modern and realistic account of the struggle for survival in Virginia during the century—a life that would appear to have left little scope, indeed, for pursuit of the arts, including gardening—see Edmund S. Morgan, *American Slavery, American Freedom: The Ordeal of Colonial Virginia* (New York, 1975).

2. In *The Transformation of Virginia, 1740-1790* (Chapel Hill, N. C., 1982), Rhys Isaac sensitively analyzes the evolution of attitudes toward and use of landscape in Virginia. On the growth of Williamsburg as a civilized and urbane reflection of the English Enlightenment on the western shores of the Atlantic, see Sylvia Doughty Fries, *The Urban Idea in Colonial America* (Philadelphia, 1977), chap. 4.

3. On May 12, 1694, no less a horticulturalist and garden designer than John Evelyn wrote to John Walker, a small planter in the wilderness along the Mattaponi River, informing him that "an ingenious Servant" of George London, King William's head gardener, had been sent to the college "on purpose to make and plant the Garden, designed for the new Colledge": Nicholson Papers, Archives, Colonial Williamsburg Foundation.

4. The Frenchman's Map is so-called because it was drawn anonymously by a French cartographer about 1782. It is the most accurate surviving eighteenth-century map of Williamsburg.

5. (Williamsburg, 1972), pp. 125ff. Nicholson had more than a passing interest in garden design and horticulture. His library, which he cataloged in 1695 and gave to the college before he left the colony in 1705, included Jean de La Quintinie's *The Compleat Gard'ner*, trans. John Evelyn (London, 1693), whom Nicholson very likely knew, as Reps suggests; Evelyn's *Sylva* (London, 1670); John Worlidge's *Systema Agricultura* (London, 1669); Leonard Meager's *English Gardener* (London, 1670); Moses Cook's *Manner of Raising, Ordering, and Improving Forrest-Trees* (London, 1676); and a handful of others. Also among his papers in the Archives, CWF, is a manuscript by the botanist John Banister, "Treatise on the Flora and Fauna of Virginia, 1680." As governor of South Carolina in the 1720s, he also facilitated Mark Catesby's botanical research in that colony.

6. Robert Beverley in 1705 ungenerously attacked Nicholson for having flattered himself "with the fond Imagination, of being the Founder of a new City," but was alert and sensitive enough to praise his stately design of Duke of Gloucester Street and his having "mark'd out the Streets in many Places, so as that they might represent the Figure of a W. . . . he procur'd a stately Fabrick [the Capitol] to be erected, which he placed opposite to the College": *The History and Present State of Virginia*, ed. Louis B. Wright (Chapel Hill, N. C., 1947), p. 105.

7. See my account of Spotswood's seemingly arrogant display of power in 1717 as he destroyed a number of Custis's trees in lengthening the vista down (most likely) the Palace Green in " 'Promised Fruites of Well Ordered Towns'—Gardens in Early 18th-Century Williamsburg," *Journal of Garden History*, II (October-December 1982), pp. 309-324.

8. The terraces show up on the Frenchman's Map (*Plate 1*). Spotswood himself mentioned the terraces or "Falling gardens" in an indignant letter to the House of Burgesses in 1719, justifying the money he spent on them. H. R. McIlwaine and John P. Kennedy, eds., *Journals of the House of Burgesses of Virginia*, V (Richmond, Va., 1915), pp. 283-284. Archaeologists discovered traces of the terraces in 1929-1930.

9. See Morris R. Brownell's review of writing on the "poetic" garden in this volume.

10. Custis's letterbook is in the Library of Congress, but a complete typescript by Maude Woodfin is at the Virginia Historical Society, Richmond. My citations are from the typescript or from E. G. Swem's edition of the letters Custis exchanged with Peter Collinson, *Brothers of the Spade: Correspondence of Peter Collinson of London, and of John Custis of Williamsburg, Virginia 1734-1746* (Barre, Mass., 1957). Because Custis's spelling and punctuation are sometimes eccentric, I have modernized them in my citations.

11. Custis Letter Book, p. 2.

12. Swem, ed., *Brothers of the Spade*, p. 21.

13. *Ibid.*, pp. 21-22.

14. *Ibid.*, pp. 23-24.

15. *Ibid.*, pp. 61, 73, 75. The plants exchanged between Custis and Collinson over a decade are too numerous to mention here, but Swem has indexed them: *ibid.*, pp. 179-183.

16. Custis Letter Book, p. 2.

17. According to Robert Bolling, in a note to his poem, "An Incitation to Vineplanting" (1772), Custis had statues of Venus, Apollo, and Bacchus in his garden: Brock Collection, BR 64, Huntington Library, San Marino, Calif.

18. Swem, ed., *Brothers of the Spade*, p. 27.

19. Marion Tinling, ed. *The Correspondence of the Three William Byrds of Westover, Virginia 1684-1776* (Charlottesville, Va., 1977), I, pp. 341-342.

20. Custis Letter Book, p. 56. Flowerpots were excavated in the Custis site by Colonial Williamsburg archaeologists. See Audrey Noël Hume, *Archaeology and the Colonial Gardener* (Williamsburg, Va., 1974), pp. 45-52.

21. Swem, ed., *Brothers of the Spade*, pp. 53, 80.

22. McIlwaine and Kennedy, eds., *Journals of Burgesses*, V, pp. 277ff.

23. Byrd's account of Spotswood's Germanna garden is in "A Progress to the Mines in the Year 1732" in Louis B. Wright, ed., *The Prose Works of William Byrd of Westover* (Cambridge, Mass., 1966), pp. 355-366.

24. Byrd, *Secret History of the Dividing Line*, pp. 41-153, and the revised *History of the Dividing Line*, pp. 157-336, *ibid.* Excerpts are from this edition.

116

25. A quick run through the index of Tinling, ed., *Correspondence of the Three William Byrds*, II, will reveal how numerous were Byrd's country house visits up until he returned to Virginia for good in 1726.

26. William K. Boyd, ed., *William Byrd's Histories of the Dividing Line Betwixt Virginia and North Carolina* (Raleigh, N. C., 1929), p. 296.

27. See Richard Beale Davis's discussion of Byrd's writings in *Intellectual Life in the Colonial South 1585-1763* (Knoxville, Tenn., 1978), III, pp. 1367ff.

28. Beverley, *History of Virginia*, p. 299.

29. Louis B. Wright and Marion Tinling, eds., *The Secret Diary of William Byrd of Westover 1709-1712* (Richmond, Va., 1941), p. 540. Catesby's magnum opus was the *Natural History of Carolina, Florida and the Bahama Islands*, 2 vols. (London, 1731, 1743).

30. Tinling, ed., *Correspondence of the Three William Byrds*, I, p. 355.

31. *Ibid.*, II, p. 483.

32. John Bartram to Peter Collinson, July 18, 1740, Bartram Papers, fol. 21, Historical Society of Pennsylvania, Philadelphia. Rhys Isaac in *The Transformation of Virginia* briefly considers this patriarchal and arcadian pose in the second half of the eighteenth century. See pp. 39-42.

People and Plants: North Carolina's Garden History Revisited

John Flowers

The garden history of colonial North Carolina generally has been ignored, and some garden historians have assumed that the Old North State did not contribute much to this aspect of American colonial life. Historical investigation will not bear this out. Indeed, not only was North Carolina in the mainstream of botanical and horticultural investigation in the eighteenth century, but it also was the scene of some ambitious ornamental gardening, especially in the Cape Fear region of the colony.

I Horticultural Beginnings in the Colony

John White, a traveler with a naturalist's eye who was also a talented artist, introduced many native plants to England when he first visited North Carolina in the late sixteenth century. His drawings, including fauna and flora of this region, were among the first to introduce the natural history of America to Europeans.[1] A century later, the Reverend John Banister, an Oxford-trained naturalist, was sent to Virginia in 1678 from England by Henry Compton, the Bishop of London, with instructions to save souls and collect plants. Banister lived for fourteen years with Colonel William Byrd I at Westover plantation and at his estate at The Falls (present-day Richmond, Virginia). He sent plants to both the Oxford Physick Garden and Compton's garden, including the sweet bay (*Magnolia virginiana*), huntsman's horn, a pitcher plant (*Sarracenia flava*), hop hornbeam (*Ostrya virginiana*), swamp azalea, and several irises among about 340 other species. That the Reverend Mr. Banister collected seeds and plant specimens from the Carolina region seems unquestionable,[2] especially since Colonel Byrd ran a brisk commercial trade with the interior of North Carolina, his traders traveling down the Indian trading path across Carolina to the Cherokee Nation in northern Georgia.

In the early years of the eighteenth century John Lawson, an English historian and surveyor-general of the province of North Carolina, described with some artistic enthusiasm the wonders of the Carolina flora to his countrymen. Even his account of vegetables and herbs in his *History of North Carolina* (1709) evokes his feeling of having discovered a paradise, one in which the Indians and the colonial settlers cooperated harmoniously to put food on the table. He noted that the Indians originally supplied the colonists with the most successful varieties of beans and peas, including several kinds of pole beans, bush beans, field peas, and kidney beans. Illustrating the high priority of practical gardening in the lives of the colonists at the start of the century, John Lawson also supplied a long list of other garden plants which they, for their part, cultivated for home use, including leek, carrot, turnip, parsnip, radish, potato, horseradish, beet, artichoke, onion, shallot, garlic, chive, lettuce, spinach, French and English cress, various native wild greens, wild purslane, cabbage, colewort, asparagus, watermelon, cucumber, muskmelon, pumpkin, and squashes of all kinds. The pot herbs he mentioned were angelica, bugloss, balm borage, burnet, clary, marigold, "pot-marjoram," tansy, savory, columbines, wormwort, "dredge," thyme, hyssop, sweet basil, rosemary, lavender, and lamb's quarters. He also added a long list of native plants used for medical purposes, including dill, cumin, snakeroot, rue, mint, and Jamestown weed, among others.[3] Lawson noted that two myrtle bushes were different in leaf and berry and that sweet-smelling candles, known for their durability in hot weather, were made from both of them.

Lawson, however, was not interested merely in recording the vegetable and medicinal plants, and he gave us this tantalizing glimpse of the evolving flower garden of the region:

> The Flower-Garden in Carolina is as yet arrived to a poor and jejune Perfection. We have only two sorts of Roses; the Clov-July-Flowers, Violets, Prince Feather and Tres Colores. There has been nothing more cultivated in the Flower-Garden, which at present occurs to my Memory; but as for the wild spontaneous Flowers of this Country, Nature has been so liberal that I cannot name one tenth of the valuable ones.[4]

Although Lawson perhaps included this description of the flower garden of Carolina because he knew these details about decorative gardening would fascinate the curious gentlemen at the London coffeehouses, it would appear from this remark that by 1709 little in that vein had as yet been achieved or even pursued in the colony. He did not find that surprising or dispiriting, however, inasmuch as part of his intention in the *Natural History*, to a great extent a promotional tract, was to generate on the part of his English readers an enthusiasm for the colony's glorious but as yet untapped fertility. One of his techniques was to contrast repeatedly the fullness of the colony's Edenic natural world with the colonists' indolence; in the face of great plenty and fecundity, he argued, even their laziness could not deprive them of beauty and abundance. He implied that with proper art and industry—such as may be forthcoming from new settlers and the desire for civilizing culture and grace—flower gardens, beautiful and productive orchards, and other features of neat gardens could enhance life in the colony. Notwithstanding the considerable progress of decorative and landscape gardening over the next half-century, Lawson's complaint was still being voiced in the colony late in the century.

Gardening for profit, as it were, instead of pleasure, remained most pervasive.

Three years after Lawson published his *Natural History*, Mark Catesby, a self-trained artist sent out from England by the great naturalist and collector Sir Hans Sloane, arrived in Virginia where he, like Banister, became the friend of the Byrd family at Westover, and like Banister collected plants along the Indian trading path in North Carolina. He returned to England in 1719, and when he came again across the Atlantic in the early 1720s, he settled for a time in Charleston. From Charleston as a base he traveled into the mountains of North Carolina where he studied the plants of the Appalachians, and in 1722 referred to "Carolina" (the Carolinas) as "a Country inferior to none in Fertility, and abounding in Variety of the Blessings of Nature."[5] He never remarked whether he had found any ornamental gardens of note, although we know from correspondence with John Custis of Williamsburg and William Byrd II that he was eager to help with ornamental garden design if asked.

Like Lawson, Catesby remarked more on practical matters than ornamental ones. He thought it worth mentioning several crops: Indian corn, bunched Guinea corn, spoked Indian corn, rice, wheat, barley, oat, kidney bean, potato, yam, eddo, martagon (only the root is eaten), crab apple, pear, plum, cherry, raspberry, strawberry, blackberry, English mulberry, red mulberry, silkworm mulberry, quince, fig, orange, lemon, pomegranate, and grapes. And he remarked in detail that the fields of Carolina were bounded by wooden fences, which were usually made of pine split into räils of about twelve or fourteen feet in length. He continued: "The frequent removing of these fences to fresh land, and the necessity of speedy erecting them are partly the reasons why hedges are not hitherto made use of, besides the facility of making wooden fences in a country abounding in trees."[6] Catesby said that when the soil of one field was worn out, the fences were removed and taken to a new field where trees were cut and burned, stumps left to rot, and crops of maize and rice sown about the stumps.[7] According to the account by Janet Schaw, a Scottish traveler in North Carolina, these split-rail fences were still the predominant fence type in the countryside on the eve of the Revolution.[8]

Another important botanical connection between North Carolina and Britain involved Peter Collinson and an Irishman named Arthur Dobbs. Collinson (1694-1768), an English Quaker and member of the Royal Society of London, had for years been busy exchanging plants with American friends like Custis and John Bartram: and his account book, recording "The first introductions of American seeds into Great Britain" (meaning seeds that he first introduced), mentions sending two boxes of seeds to "Dobbs of Ireland." In addition to his control of an extensive demesne in Ireland, Dobbs invested heavily in North Carolina land— some two hundred thousand acres. Not entirely unexpectedly, he became governor of North Carolina in 1754, whereupon he entered into active correspondence with Collinson, sending him numerous plants over the years. On April 2, 1759, for example, he wrote to Collinson: "We have a kind of Catch Fly Sensitive which closes upon anything that touches it."[9]

This became known as the Venus's-flytrap, until then completely un-known. We do not know how carefully Dobbs maintained his contacts with the Dublin Society, later incorporated as the Royal Dublin Society, of which he was a founding member, but almost certainly he did correspond with the botanists in the Society.[10] The influence of American flora on Irish gardens of the eighteenth century, as transmitted by Dobbs, remains to be explored.

Another chapter in the botanical history of North Carolina was opened by the famous Bartram family of Philadelphia. John Bartram had become in the 1730s and 1740s Peter Collinson's most scientific and prolific supplier of American plants. William, John Bartram's son by his second wife, was a celebrated botanist, traveler, and naturalist in his own right (*Plate 11*). He left his father's home on the Schuylkill River near Philadel-phia in 1759 and settled on the Cape Fear River near Wilmington, North Carolina, as an independent trader.[11] He may have come to the Cape Fear region at the urging of his uncle, Colonel William Bartram, who had settled there by 1731 and was a justice of the peace in Bladen County in 1740. It is not known exactly where William Bartram settled when he arrived in the Cape Fear area, or exactly how long he remained on his first sojourn. He referred to his North Carolina uncle's house as "open, and his table free, to his neighbor, the oppressed and the stranger."[12] By 1766 he was back in Phildelphia, returning to North Carolina in 1770 and remain-ing there until late 1772, during which time he supplied some drawings for Dr. John Fothergill.[13] In 1791 he published his magnum opus, *Travels through North and South Carolina, Georgia, East and West Florida*, a great fund of information about natural history in those regions of America; among others of its distinctions it sparked the imagination of a few of the English Romantic poets of the early nineteenth century. William Bartram's mind was fertile, and that he was influenced in his life's work by his stay in the Cape Fear region of North Carolina seems unquestionable, although the absence of a fuller record of his activities makes the job of determining exactly what influenced him very difficult.[14]

André Michaux, the botanist to the French king, Louis XVI, who arrived in Charleston to collect plant specimens for the French govern-ment, also visited North Carolina as early as 1787 and collected plant materials. Equally as important as the native plants he collected were the plants that he introduced into America: the gingko tree, candleberry tree, crape myrtle, mimosa, chinaberry, and the fragrant tea olive. By sustained tradition he is credited with the introduction of the *Camellia japonica* and the Indian azaleas, which have become hallmarks of the southern gar-den.[15] In 1787 he began his exploration of the mountains of North Carolina, and he continued this plant search in 1789. He was, like Byrd II, intensely interested in the distribution of ginseng, and during this period he introduced the idea of its commercial exploitations to the mountain people.[16]

One of Michaux's associates, John Fraser, a Scotsman, who had learned much of plants from visits to the Chelsea Physick Garden, was traveling

�ᵃ in 1808 when, after climbing all morning through a fog
n on the North Carolina-Tennessee border, they came
at the summit and were rewarded with the sight of "a
f *Rhododendron catawbiense* in full bloom. Fraser's most
bution to horticulture was the assistance he gave to the
n, Dr. Thomas Walter, in getting his *Flora Caroliniana*
7. Although Walter's book included much of Fraser's own
he plants of the highlands to the west in North Carolina,
best remembered for his introduction of the yellow
onicera flava).[17]

ists and naturalists all worked in North Carolina and
gnificantly to the introduction of American plants into
European and oriental plants into America, thus enriching
f both Europe and America.

Claude Joseph Sauthier, Landscape Gardener

nown, trained, landscape gardener to live and work in North
as Claude Joseph Sauthier. In an age of amateur garden
design, he was one of the earliest such professionals to live and work in
the British American colonies prior to the Revolution. The ten North
Carolina town plans, executed between 1767 and 1771, which Sauthier
drew for the colonial government are among the most interesting series of
maps produced in the American colonies and as such they form a body of
work that relates to several different disciplines: cartography, landscape
design, and town planning.

Until recently little has been known of Sauthier. What has been known is
that he came to North Carolina in 1767 to join Governor William Tryon,
that he mapped ten of the colony's towns, that he was at the Battle of
Alamance in 1771, and that he then left North Carolina with Tryon when
the latter became governor of New York that same year.[18] Recently, more
has come to light to illuminate this previously shadowy figure.

Sauthier was a native of Strasbourg, France, born there on November
10, 1736, the son of a saddler, Joseph Philippe Sauthier, and his wife,
Barbe Primat.[19] He studied architecture, surveying, and landscape gardening, and grew up during a period of cartographic activity in Alsace
where the precise system of triangulation for mapping all France was
established in 1744, and during which many local surveyors were needed
and employed. In 1759 de Luche, superintendent of Alsace, began a
comprehensive and detailed survey of that part of France through the
mapping of agriculture, pastures, forest cover, and other features.[20] We
have no direct evidence that Sauthier was a part of this great survey, but
William P. Cumming has stated that Sauthier's maps, preserved in the
Grand Seminaire, Strasbourg, France, definitely show the influence of this
survey and the Alsatian school of cartography.[21]

Most important for our purposes are the treatises that Sauthier completed in 1763—one a work on civil architecture and the other on landscape gardening, with beautiful colored designs and including, interestingly enough, plans for a governor's mansion.[22]

One can only speculate why Governor Tryon brought Sauthier to North Carolina. It is possible that Tryon brought him over to assist with the building of the new government house at New Bern, begun early in 1767. When Tryon was appointed governor of New York in 1771, Sauthier went along with him and was occupied for the next few years in extensive mapping projects of the province of New York and of New York City, with the result that in 1773 Tryon appointed Sauthier surveyor of the province of New York. In 1774 Sauthier accompanied Tryon to England, but soon returned with him to New York where he became acquainted with Lord Percy, who was forever after his patron and friend. In 1790 Sauthier removed from the Percy estates, where he had gone to live after the Revolution, to his native Strasbourg where he remained until his death on November 26, 1802. His works at the Grand Seminaire include his work on architecture, landscape gardening, and a few of his printed and manuscript maps of American and European subjects.[23]

Sauthier's contributions to North Carolina are singularly important. His twelve North Carolina town plans (there are two of both Edenton and New Bern) form an impressive map series of small towns that is unique in America for the years prior to the Revolution. The maps were carefully executed between the years 1767 and 1771, when the Assembly accepted them on Governor Tryon's express recommendation and paid Sauthier for them.

Some have suggested that the garden plots that appear in most of these towns plans were used merely to decorate the maps and that there is no topographical significance to their appearance on the maps. But Sauthier was too careful a draftsman and accurate surveyor to ornament his work so casually. The more intricate garden plots, where records are still available to check them, are all located on tracts owned by people well able to afford ornamental gardens and possessed with the education to know and care about such refinements. Also, the contours of the maps appear to follow the known land patterns in their respective locations, and in the case of the towns of which he drew two maps apiece—Edenton and New Bern—one notes in the more polished versions of the maps the exact same attention to accuracy and detail, even down to the same number of trees in any given orchard and the same number of buildings, as in the working version of the map. Tryon placed a great deal of trust in Sauthier; so did Lord Percy and the crusty old Lord Howe.

In 1767, when Sauthier arrived in North Carolina, Governor and Mrs. Tryon were residing at Castle Tryon at Brunswick Town on the Lower Cape Fear River, which had formerly been the residence of Governor Arthur Dobbs, and still earlier the residence of Captain John Russell, who had called the fifty-five-acre estate Russellborough. This estate held great interest for Tryon, who from 1765 when Dobbs died, until 1767 when he finally was able to purchase it, made plans for its improvement.[24] Fortunately, he described the existing gardens and plants in a letter to his uncle, the Hon. Sewallis Shirley, comptroller to Queen Caroline's household, in 1765, though his description pertains mostly to the culture of fruit and vegetables, not to garden design. In the following passage, however, he repeats Lawson's theme about the need for industry and skill to collaborate with the luxuriance of nature in achieving a "greater perfection" in this and other North Carolina gardens:

> The garden has nothing to Boast of except Fruit Trees. Peaches, Nectrs Figgs and Plumbs are in perfection and of good Sorts. I cut a Musk Melon this week which weighed 17½ Pounds. Apples grow extremely well here I have tasted excellent Cyder the Produce of this Province. Most if not all kinds of garden greens and Pot herbs grow luxuriant with us. We are in want of nothing but Industry & skill, to bring every Vegetable to a greater perfection in this Province. Indian Corn, Rice, and American Beans (Species of the Kidney Bean) are the grain that is Cultivated within a hundred and fifty Miles of the Sea Board at which distance to the Westward you begin to perceive you are approaching high ground, and fifty Miles farther you may get on tolerable high Hills.[25]

When archaeological excavations were begun in 1966 at Russellborough, the large kitchen (30' × 40') mentioned by Tryon[26] was discovered to have been sited on the exact location of the building that Sauthier had drawn on his map of Brunswick Town, dated 1769. Also shown on this 1769 map was a garden area south of the mansion house (*Plate 12*) which included a series of garden squares as well as a shaded area interspersed with walkways and centered on a circle, though Tryon did not mention this park-like area in the letter to Sewallis Shirley in 1765, nor the series of well-designed canals throughout the low-lying areas of the estate where rice was grown. Sauthier's role in all this is unknown, but with his training in landscape gardening and civil engineering, it would have been natural for Tryon to employ him for these landscape projects. The archaeological evidence to date, incidentally, confirms the accuracy of the Sauthier map of 1769.

Sauthier's map of New Bern, also dated 1769, shows the same sort of garden squares on either side of the land entrance to the governor's palace then under construction. In 1777 Governor Richard Caswell was empowered by the Assembly to "make necessary repairs of the State House [Palace], offices, buildings, fences, and Gardens appendent thereto,"[27] which confirms that gardens of some description were laid out at the Palace prior to 1777. Whether these gardens were actually laid out by Governor Tryon or his successor, Josiah Martin, as they appear on the Sauthier map, or were simply planned by Sauthier in anticipation of the official move of the capital to New Bern in 1770, is not known. What is known is their contribution to the elegant appearance of the Palace. Don Francisco de Miranda, the South American patriot who toured America during 1783-1784, in his journal for June 10-17 recorded seeing New Bern. He speaks in glowing terms of the "Palace" and states that it was built eighteen years prior to this time by an "able English architect" who came for this purpose with Governor Tryon, and who still resided in New Bern. He went on to add that "he [John Hawks] furnished me with an exact plan of said edifice and gardens which gives a clear idea of the whole."[28] Luigi Castiglione, an Italian traveler, wrote in May 1786 of his visit to New Bern, stating that the most worthy public building in the town was "the governor's house which was provided with large grounds formerly surrounded by a wall."[29] The entire town, in fact, had taken on an attractive grace, owing to the gardens perhaps as much as to anything else; in 1778 Ebenezer Hazard, a northern traveler, recorded that New Bern was "more Grand than any Town I have met with since I left Annapolis, but the Houses are scattered, and each of them has a Garden Spot belonging to it."[30] This further substantiates the evidence on the Sauthier map of New Bern, which shows garden plots adjacent to most of the house lots.

Sauthier's existing garden plans are French in style and, at first glance at least, are similar to those of all the French landscape gardeners of the period that were dominated by the work of André Le Nôtre at Versailles. The plans to be found in his personal papers at the University of Strasbourg are for gardens that are extremely elaborate in both design and plantings. The gardens found on the North Carolina town plans are geometric in design, but of so simple a composition as to be only faintly similar to anything in Sauthier's papers. Only in a few gardens in Edenton and New Bern is there any evidence that Sauthier might have planted or upgraded existing gardens. The garden at Pembroke plantation near Edenton (*Plate 13*) is a case in point. In the first survey of the area that Sauthier did, the garden at Pembroke was composed of a large number of garden squares focused on three small decorative elements—two rectangles and a circle interspersed throughout the entire configuration. In the final version of the Edenton map, the Pembroke garden is more harmoniously laid out with one large rectangle with elliptical ends at the center of the garden. In Sauthier's treatise on landscape garden design, he advocates making a design large enough to be useful and convenient, with large sections rather than many small ones. This is certainly what can be seen on the Edenton map in relation to both Pembroke and Hayes (*Plate 14*), the estate of Samuel Johnston.

III   The Hermitage Garden

One of the truly lovely gardens of North Carolina in the late eighteenth century was at the Hermitage, the plantation on the Northeast Cape Fear River belonging to John Burgwin. Burgwin was a native of Hertford, England, the son of John Burgwin (1682-1751), who left his estate in South Wales to an elder son, forcing John to seek his own fortune elsewhere. Early in 1750-1751, in Charleston, South Carolina, John Burgwin worked as a merchant with the firm of Hooper, Alexander and Company, but by 1752 had moved to Wilmington. In 1753 he married an heiress, Margaret Haynes, became interested in politics, and by 1760 was clerk of the governor's council. In 1762 he served as private secretary to Governor Dobbs, and in 1769 Governor Tryon commissioned him clerk of the high court of chancery for North Carolina. About the year 1767 he was appointed treasurer of the colony and held this office under both Governor William Tryon and Governor Josiah Martin.[31]

Although we know almost nothing of Burgwin's garden in town,[32] a good deal of information about his garden at the Hermitage plantation has come down to us. Eliza Caroline Burgwin Clitherall (Caroline Elizabeth Burgwin), Burgwin's daughter, remembered the Hermitage plantation well in the last years of the eighteenth century and beginning of the nineteenth; in an autobiography she wrote in her later years she has left us the following picture of the home she came to as a small child. She wrote first of arriving in the colony:

> When sufficiently recover'd from the fatigue and anxiety of the voyage, the family proceeded to their new home, "The Hermitage," the great contrast, between this, and the country they had left [England]; the Piney Woods, the narrow road, scarcely as wide as the English lanes, and total absence of travellers, were subjects of astonishment, their very novelty was a theme of conversation, and drew their minds from less cheerful recollections.[33]

She continued with an account of the house:

> You have seen the picture representing the Hermitage, Tho' in appearance it fell far behind Alveston or Ashley [English estates belonging to Burgwin relatives]. Yet it was larger in the number of rooms, and had a more imposing aspect from the avenue to its approach—the Center building was considerably higher than the wings; of two stories high and a garret the lower story contain'd the drawing room; a large handsomely finish'd room the middle door opening to a porch, leading to the front garden, on either side of this room, were glass doors opening upon the Piazza to each wing—and t[w]o other doors led to the Entry—communicating with the wings, and the stair case, leading to the rooms above, and another stair case to the rooms below.[34]

After describing the south and north wings of the house and their piazzas that led to the garden, she then proceeded to describe the gardens:

> The Gardens were large, and laid out in the English style—a Creek wound thro' the largest, upon its banks grew native shrubbery; in this Garden were several Alcoves, Summer Houses, a hot-house—an Octagon summer house high and a Gardener's tool house beneath—a fishpond, communicating with the Creek, both producing abundance of fish—The Second Garden was ornamental, and in front—The "Cook's Garden," was on the opposite side to the large. Upon a mound of considerable height was erected a Brick room containing shelves and a large number of books—chairs and table and this was call'd the family chapel, for in those days there was no regular worship in

Wilmington—and My Father was of opinion, that family worship, was a duty, and a building thus consecrated, and used only for that purpose, wou'd stamp upon the performance, a greater reverence. It was in this little building years after that Brothers, servants and Myself assembled to regular Sunday Service—a bridge at the back of the house, over the Creek, made a short walk to Castle Haynes, where we often walk'd after Church.[35]

This was a garden laid out according to the spirit and style of the English landscape garden. Several of the fashionable elements of contemporary garden design were present in this large garden complex: the formal flower beds, the long allées with their summerhouses, the fish pond, the bosquets whose naturalism fooled no one, and the little pavilion on the mound. This mound or mount, incidentally, is one of the few garden mounts of which any record has survived in eighteenth-century America.

Eliza Caroline Burgwin had been sent to England to be educated, and when she returned in 1801 at the age of seventeen she recorded even more impressions of the vast garden:

These were extensive and beautifully laid out. There was [sic] alcoves and summer houses at the termination of each walk, seats under trees in the more shady recesses of the Big Garden, as it was called, in distinction from the flower garden in front of the house. There were many evergreens and a creek winding its way through the grounds.[36]

She continued with a brief description of the most charming aspect of the garden, the study on the mound:

In a small brick building called the study, on a high mound in the Big Garden, was a fine collection of books, writing desk and tables.[37]

This must have been a remarkably sophisticated garden feature, bringing to mind a similar pavilion-study in the 1730s on the summit of the Third Earl of Peterborough's mount in his gardens at Bevis Mount, near Southampton, England. Peterborough's study was quite comfortable and had classical associations as a place of meditation and retreat. Regardless of whether Burgwin actually used his mount-study or valued it as a garden ornament commanding distant views, it seems to have been an unprecedented garden feature in the colonial South.

A drawing of the Hermitage house with a small portion of its garden about it,[38] and another painting[39] of the house and flower garden bordering on Prince George's Creek, and similar to the earlier drawing (*Plate 15*), have survived. Pictured in both is a large frame house with several additions. The scene is sylvan with large trees and shrubs; a sundial in the center of the walk is bordered with low shrubs of flowers. A picket fence encloses the garden area and house. Though not polished, sophisticated renderings, their overall effect is one of peace, plenty, and charm—qualities that characterize the setting in Eliza Caroline Clitherall's recollections. We do not have to rely only on Mrs. Clitherall's description of her father's estate; for James G. Burr, an early historian of the Cape Fear region, has left us an equally interesting verbal picture of this estate as it existed in 1885. Although he described it in a fairly forlorn state, as the house had burned on Easter Sunday, 1881, his account matches Eliza Clitherall's. He is describing the house, its approach, and the garden setting:

> It was about one hundred and twenty feet long, the north front faced a sloping lawn extending about one hundred and fifty yards to Prince George's Creek, and the south front faced a large flower garden from which extended a broad avenue about a half mile along, with a double row of elms on each side, continued by a carriage way of more than a mile in length, under ditch and banks, through the pines, until it entered the country road leading to Wilmington. . . . Other additions were made from time to time, the workmen being his own slaves directed by an English architect. Alcoves, bowers, a hothouse and fish-pond adorned the six acres laid off for pleasure grounds; a large vegetable, or as it was called cook's garden yielded plentifully for the table.[40]

These descriptions are further supported by the remaining garden features there today, which include a few of the giant trees from the avenue and the small fish pond noted in all the descriptions. A variety of flowering bulbs have spread into the deep thicket that was once the garden and testify to a few of the flowering varieties that once grew there. Except for the tabby foundations of a part of the manor house, little else remains today.

At the death of John Burgwin on May 21, 1803, it was decided to offer the estate for sale. The enticing advertisement in the *Wilmington Gazette* for September 27, 1803, notes, among other things, the fashionable classical allusion to the Hermitage as a "villa":

> That elegant and highly improved Villa called the Hermitage, situated eight miles from town, on which is a Range of Buildings handsomely finished, upwards of one hundred feet in length, with offices and a number of convenient out Buildings in good repair. The Gardens and Pleasure Grounds of about two acres, are disposed with much taste, and in point of beauty and improvement equal to any in the United States. There are about eight hundred acres of Land annexed to the premises, with good Barns, Stables and Buildings requisite for farm-ing. Also a good Mill Seat contiguous to Navigation.

Burgwin had wished to sell the estate as early as 1797 because he described it to a friend in Bristol, England, on May 9 of that year as containing "The mansion-house is large, elegant, and commodious for a large family, with barn, stabling for twenty horses, cowhouses, pigeonhouse, and every other outhouse convenient or necessary."[41] The English-style natural landscape that he created there was the most fashionable landscape of the period in North Carolina, and perhaps in all of America, of which we have a record today.

The evidence of North Carolina's involvement in the eighteenth-century gardening world presented here is only part of a much larger picture that developed from John Lawson's 1709 description of the Carolina flower garden as having reached only a "poor and jejune Perfection," to John Burgwin's elegant and highly sophisticated Hermitage garden at the turn of the century, exhibiting the most fashionable elements of the English landscape garden. What evolved between 1709 and 1800 resulted from the constant efforts on the part of Carolinians to have and enjoy gardens and plants about them as they worked to develop the society that had a European base with a strong and distinctive American flavor. Much of this cultural achievement occurred in the Cape Fear region which Josiah Martin, North Carolina's last royal governor, described as "the region of politeness and hospitality!"[42]

Stagville Preservation Center, Durham

NOTES

1. Paul Hope Hulton and David Beers Quinn, *The American Drawings of John White, 1577-1590* (Chapel Hill, 1964), p. 35; Bruce Cotten, "Thomas Hariot and his 'Briefe and true report of the new found land of Virginia,'" manuscript, North Carolina Collection, University of North Carolina, Chapel Hill.

2. Joseph Ewan and Nesta Ewan, "John Banister and His Natural History of Virginia, 1678-1692," *Proceedings, Tenth International Congress of the History of Science* (Ithaca, N.Y., 1962), pp. 927-929.

3. John Lawson, *History of North Carolina* (London, 1709), pp. 77-79.

4. *Ibid.*, p. 80.

5. Mark Catesby, *The Natural History of Carolina, Florida, and the Bahama Islands* (London, 1731, 1743), I, p. vi. The definitive biographical study of Catesby is George Frederick Frick and Raymond Phineas Stearns, *Mark Catesby: The Colonial Audubon* (Urbana, Ill., 1961). See also David Scofield Wilson, *In the Presence of Nature* (Amherst, Mass., 1978).

6. Catesby, *Natural History*, II, p. xvi.

7. *Ibid.*, I, p. xvi.

8. Janet Schaw, *Journal of a Lady of Quality; Being the Narrative of a Journey from Scotland to the West Indies, North Carolina, and Portugal, in the years 1774 to 1776*, ed. Evangeline Walker Andrews and Charles M. Andrews (New Haven, Conn., 1923), p. 163.

9. Arthur Dobbs to Peter Collinson, Apr. 2, 1759, quoted by Frank A. Montgomery, Jr., "Venus Fly Trap Native of Carolina," *The News and Observer* (Raleigh, N.C.), Apr. 2, 1967.

10. Beth G. Crabtreem, *North Carolina Governors, 1585-1958* (Raleigh, N.C., 1958), pp. 39, 40. For a more complete biographical sketch, see Desmond Clarke, *Arthur Dobbs Esquire, 1689-1765, Surveyor-General of Ireland, Prospector and Governor of North Carolina* (Chapel Hill, N.C., 1957).

11. *Dictionary of American Biography*, s.v. "Bartram, William."

12. Donald R. Lennon and Ida Brooks Kellam, eds., *The Wilmington Town Book 1743-1778* (Raleigh, N.C., 1973), p. 95n.

13. Joseph Ewan, ed., *William Bartram, Botanical and Zoological Drawings, 1756-1778* (Philadelphia, 1968), p. 6; Francis Harper, ed., *The Travels of William Bartram* (New Haven, Conn., 1958), p. xvii.

14. Ernest Earnest, *John and William Bartram, Botanists and Explorers, 1699-1777, 1739-1823* (Philadelphia, 1940), p. 104.

15. Evangeline Davis, *Charleston: Houses and Gardens* (Charleston, 1975), n.p., located on p. 10 of text.

16. *Dictionary of American Biography*, s.v. "Michaux, André"; Harper, ed., *Travels of Bartram*, pp. xviii-xix.

17. Ewan, ed., *William Bartram*, pp. 22-23.

18. William P. Cumming, *British Maps of Colonial America* (Chicago, 1974), pp. 72-74.

19. *Ibid.*

20. *Ibid.*

21. William P. Cumming is an authority on colonial cartography and is the author of *North Carolina in Maps* (Raleigh, N. C., 1966) and *The Southeast in Early Maps* (Princeton, N. J., 1958). He is professor emeritus at Davidson College, Davidson, N. C. I am indebted to Dr. Cumming for direction with research on Claude Joseph Sauthier.

22. See the transcript of the Sauthier manuscript material from the Grand Seminaire, Strasbourg, France, in the Research Branch, Archaeology and Historic Preservation Section, Division of Archives and History, Raleigh, N. C. The drawings of Sauthier's buildings, garden plans, and short course on architecture are also with the transcript.

23. Cumming, *British Maps*, pp. 72-74.

24. For a description of the Russellborough estate, see Stanley A. South, "Russellborough: Two Royal Governors' Mansion at Brunswick Town," *North Carolina Historical Review*, XLIV (October 1967), pp. 360-372.

25. William S. Powell, ed., *The Correspondence of William Tryon and Other Selected Papers* (Raleigh, N. C., 1980), I, p. 139.

26. *Ibid.*

27. A. T. Dill, Jr., "A Documentary History of the Governor's House at New Bern, North Carolina," p. 202, research report, Research Branch, Div. of Archives and History.

28. *Ibid.*, p. 245.

29. *Ibid.*, p. 257.

30. *Ibid.*, p. 214.

31. William S. Powell, ed., *Dictionary of North Carolina Biography*, s.v., "Burgwin, John."

32. *Ibid.* See also the Burgwin-Wright House nomination to the National Register of Historic Places, Div. of Archives and History.

33. "Autobiography and Diary of Mrs. Eliza Clitherall," II, p. 1, Archives, Lower Cape Fear Historical Society, Wilmington, N. C.

34. *Ibid.*, p. 2.

35. *Ibid.*, p. 3.

36. James G. Burr, *The Hermitage* (Wilmington, N. C., 1885), p. 12.

37. *Ibid.*

38. Archives, Lower Cape Fear Hist. Soc.

39. The photograph of this painting is in the Photographic Collection, Div. of Archives and History. The painting from which the photograph was taken appears to be the one executed in the nineteenth century by Eliza Inglis Clitherall, daughter of Mrs. Eliza Clitherall the diarist, and appears to have been painted from the earlier drawing with the addition of the gateway and carriage house to the right of the picture, which may have come from the senior Mrs. Clitherall's memory of the Hermitage site.

40. Burr, *The Hermitage*, pp. 6, 8, 9.

41. James Green Burr, "Historic Homes: The Hermitage, Burgwin's Seat," *Magazine of American History*, XVI (November 1886), pp. 433-442.

42. Henry Jay MacMillan, "Colonial Plantations of the Lower Cape Fear," *Bulletin of the Lower Cape Fear Historical Society, Inc.*, XII (February 1969), p. 6.

Eighteenth-Century New England Garden Design: The Pictorial Evidence

Abbott Lowell Cummings

There is no scarcity of contemporary written information about eighteenth-century gardens in New England. Word pictures abound in diaries, travel accounts, and even in such official documents as deeds and probate records. One thinks at once of Thomas Hancock's written request from Boston on December 20, 1736, to a London seedsman for the price of "100 small Yew Trees in the rough which I'd Frame up here to my own fancy."[1] Visual documentation, on the other hand, is exceptionally sparse, and as a consequence, the few pictures which have survived are of critical importance. Happily, the contemporary graphics, although severely limited in quantitative terms, nevertheless portray a range from modest rural situations to imposing urban and semi-urban estates, a geographic spread from Connecticut to the Piscataqua region of Maine and New Hampshire, and a time span from mid- to late-eighteenth century.

The illustrations shown here, which are characteristic of the restricted data, share in common an emphasis upon formality in landscape design and the layout of gardens. Such seems to have been the prevailing taste in America during much of the eighteenth century. Not until the 1790s, and then especially in the planning of country estates, are there important excursions into the long-popular cult of English naturalism. Indeed, Fiske Kimball, in his discussion of the Elias Hasket Derby House in Salem, Massachusetts, built between 1795 and 1797, has published contemporary designs showing that naturalism had by then affected even the planning of an in-town site.[2]

The evidence in terms of pictures and documents, however, confirms my earlier statement that formality in garden design seems to have been the ruling concern for much of the century. Whereas the limited number of views available to us do not happen to show terraces, their almost universal popularity is revealed over and over again in the written documents. "My Gardens all Lye on the South Side of a hill with the most beautifull Assent to the top," wrote Thomas Hancock of his Beacon Hill estate in Boston in 1736. The gardener whom he engaged that same year contracted on October 4 "to layout the upper garden allys. Trim the Beds and fill up all the allies with such Stuff as Sd Hancock shall order and Gravel the Walks and prepare and Sodd the Terras . . . [and] to layout the next Garden or flatt from the Terras below."[3] At about the same time, Isaac Royall erected upon the flat terrain of his country seat in Medford,

Massachusetts, a double mounded terrace in concentric circles upon which he placed his summerhouse.[4] And later, on July 6, 1774, Elihu Ashley of Deerfield, Massachusetts, recording a visit to Timothy Ruggles of nearby Hardwick, noted that his "land descends to the South, and he designs to make three Squares one about four feet above the other, which will make a most agreable Graduation, and if ever finished will be the grandest thing in the Province of its kind."[5]

Nor can these pictorial sources distinguish readily between old and new design motifs. Presumably, for the most part we are dealing with images of single building campaigns, and that is clearly the case with the Moses Gill estate in Princeton, Massachusetts (*Plate 18*). One detects occasionally in contemporary writings, however, a concern with those elements of the landscape rendered more effective by the passage of time. The Reverend William Bentley of Salem, passing through Haverhill, Massachusetts, for example, recorded on September 22, 1790, concerning the "elegant Seat" of the Saltonstall family that "it has about 30 acres of land, an ancient row of Elms, and Buttons, and most engaging Prospect of the River and adjacent country."[6] Such long-evolved features, inherited from an earlier generation, must have stood in sharp contrast to the innovational introduction of eighteenth-century European aquatic features in landscaping. Francis Goelet, traveling from New York to Boston in 1750, was impressed with Edmund Quincy's country seat with its "Beautyfull Pleasure Garden Adjoyning" in what is now the city of Quincy, Massachusetts: "About Ten Yards from the House," he wrote, "is a Beautifull, Cannal, which is Supply'd by a Brook, which is well Stockt with Fine Silver Eels."[7] There is an early nineteenth-century watercolor view of the house and its canal[8] and some later photographic evidence as well, but our attention here is centered upon contemporary or near-contemporary pictorial sources; and with annotations these will be allowed to speak for themselves.

 Detail of map showing Brattle Street, Cambridge, Massachusetts, by Henry Pelham, 1775 (*Plate 16*).

The road leading from the center of Cambridge to Watertown, Massachusetts, is of very early origin, and portions of at least two late seventeenth-century houses survive here in an otherwise eighteenth-century appearing structure. By the middle of the eighteenth century a number of the most distinguished and influential men in the province, for the most part related by blood or through marriage, had established themselves here apart from the hubbub of Boston along what is known today as Brattle Street in Cambridge. Their presence and character would eventually give to this short thoroughfare the popular designation of Tory Row.

Four of the estates pictured still survive: that of "Col. Vassel" is the Craigie-Longfellow House, erected by John Vassall, Jamaica planter and loyalist, in 1759, which later became the home of the poet, Henry Wadsworth Longfellow, and is now administered by the National Park Service; Judge Lee's, as noted, represents the transformation and enlargement by Judge Joseph Lee about 1760 of two seventeenth-century frames brought together, and the structure as a whole is now the headquarters of the Cambridge Historical Society; the house of "Mr. Fairwather" was built probably in the mid-1760s by another Jamaica planter, Colonel George Ruggles, who conveyed the property to patriot Thomas Fayerweather in 1774; finally, at the upper end of the street is the house erected by loyalist Lieutenant Governor Thomas Oliver in 1767, later birthplace and life-long home of the poet, James Russell Lowell, and now the residence of Harvard presidents.

The map itself, engraved by John Singleton Copley's half-brother, Henry Pelham, is of importance for its close attention to detail and for its careful delineation of natural features and gardens. Stippled in a darker gray than the background, the several formal garden schemes associated with each of these celebrated mansions are individually distinguished and each in certain respects is distinctive. Lieutenant Governor Oliver's is perhaps the most elaborate and reveals a parterre garden on axis with the rear or garden facade of the existing house and four additional "squares" to the north.

 "South West Prospect of the Seat of Colonel George Boyd at Portsmouth, New Hampshire," 1774, by an unidentified artist (*Plate 17*).

George Boyd, Portsmouth shipbuilder, purchased this property in 1771. The site, near the outlet of Islington Creek (later called the North Mill Pond), had originally been acquired in 1744 by another shipbuilder, Nathaniel Meserve, and a house erected here passed at his death in 1758 to a son, George Meserve. A room-by-room inventory taken in 1759 would suggest some correspondence with the mansion house of the painting, although alterations before the period of Boyd's ownership are hinted at in the contemporary record. Nevertheless, the division of Meserve's estate in 1760 refers to "the broad Ally" and the "Barn standing upon the East Side of said Garden,"[9] and a letter written in 1764 that discusses "the house that belong'd to Colln. Meserve" mentions "two good warehouses close to the water, a very good Garden, [and] good deal of wharf."[10] These references suggest that much of what we see in the painting of 1774 at the front and to the right of the house may have been accomplished before Nathaniel Meserve's death in 1758.

An almost identical garden plan with radial paths existed apparently at the Governor Benning Wentworth country seat in Little Harbor, just south of Portsmouth. Governor Wentworth took up his residence here about 1753, and the garden was presumably laid out then or during the years immediately following. Although somewhat sketchily executed and miniscule in scale, the Wentworth garden was included by James Grant in his "Plan of Piscataqua Harbor . . ." rendered the year of the Boyd painting, 1774.[11]

In terms of general position, another very similar layout can be found in a watercolor painted about the time of the Revolution with the contemporary caption: "A View of the house and part of the Farm of the Hon.[1b] Benjamin Pickman Esq."[12] Located in South Salem, Massachusetts, the property had been developed beginning in 1754. As a Salem gentleman's "farm," the pastures and fields for tillage are prominent, but a fenced garden directly in front of the house lines up with the left-hand elevation and projects appreciably further to the right, beyond which are located the barns—precisely the arrangement found in the Boyd view. Like the Boyd view also, there is a single broad alley on axis with the front entrance of the house and one or two trees at casual intervals. The Boyd and Wentworth gardens are distinguished for their central motif from which all paths radiate as spokes in a wheel. The original painting would suggest that the central motif of the Boyd garden is an aquatic feature.

 "View of the Seat of the Hon. Moses Gill Esq. at Princeton, in the County of Worcester, Massa[ts]," 1792 (*Plate 18*).

"Foreigners," declares the accompanying text, "must have an high idea of the rapid progress of improvement in America, when they are told that the ground which these buildings now cover . . . [was], in the year 1766, as perfectly wild as the deepest forest of our country. The honourable proprietor must have great satisfaction in seeing improvements so extensive, made under his own eye, under his own direction, and by his own active industry."[13]

Mowing fields, stable, and barnyard form an integral part of the complex, but are separated from the carefully planned foreyard set off with ornamental fences. The garden statuary on either side of the path find a documentary counterpart in the Reverend William Bentley's description on June 12, 1791, of the grounds of Joseph Barrell's well-developed in-town Summer Street estate in Boston: "The Squares are decorated with Marble figures as large as life."[14] The functions of the minor buildings between the foreyard and the formal garden with its barely visible latticework summerhouse (at far right) are uncertain.

 Thomas Banister House, Brookfield, Massachusetts, by an unidentified artist, late eighteenth century (*Plate 19*).

This "portrait" of a house and its environs was painted directly upon the large overmantel panel above the ballroom fireplace of the Banister House. Located on the old road between Brookfield and Fiskedale, the structure itself (no longer standing) could be dated to the 1780s or very early 1790s on grounds of style.[15] The painting is presumably contemporary with the building of the house or was executed soon thereafter. Costumed figures (not visible in the detail) which form a decorative part of the composition are decked out in late eighteenth-century finery and are probably taken from a printed source. In other respects, the artist is clearly responding to the subject according to his own perceptions and inspiration.

Emphasis here, in the neatly fenced foreyard, lies in the use of plant materials to heighten the formal setting of the house. A line of trees replaces on either side the ornamental fence at the front that is characteristic of late eighteenth-century fences in the use of two differing lengths of pickets. Traveling from Boston to New York in 1794, Henry Wansey, the English textile manufacturer, noted as he passed through nearby Worcester: "Most of the houses have a large court before them, full of lilacs and other shrubs, with a seat under them, and a paved walk up the middle,"[16]—a contemporary description of houses within the vicinity of Brookfield that has much in common with the painting of the Banister House.

 Unidentified formal garden plan, late eighteenth century (*Plate 20*).

Samuel McIntire was born in 1757 and trained by his carpenter father to follow that craft. Known particularly for his carving skills, McIntire's earliest works show unusual proficiency, and by 1792 he had sought out and sketched some of the more progressive architectural ideas introduced into New England by Charles Bulfinch. This elaborate garden scheme, which survives among an extensive number of McIntire's drawings, bears a watermark that can be assigned to the 1790s. Although otherwise unidentified, it clearly suggests an urban site, and if from McIntire's own hand may reflect something of the young architect's exposure to the ambitious plans for landscaping the Elias Hasket Derby House, built in Salem between 1795 and 1797.

For his projected mansion house, erected on the site of what is now Salem's Old Town Hall, Elias Hasket Derby solicited plans and elevations from Bulfinch and McIntire, and procured at least two other sets of drawings by unidentified architects, perhaps from the mid-Atlantic area. McIntire's was the scheme adopted, with modifications based largely on Bulfinch's ideas. McIntire was also involved extensively in the construction of the house. Of two additional drawings for the landscaping of the site, also of unknown authorship, one is fairly crude, the other, by a different hand, quite polished. Both show naturalistic elements combined with a formal, walled "Kitchen Garden."[17]

 Formal garden plan for Jonathan Leavitt House, Greenfield, Massachusetts, by Asher Benjamin, 1797 (*Plate 21*).

Jonathan Leavitt of Greenfield, Massachusetts, judge of common pleas and later judge of probate, married Emelia, daughter of President Ezra Stiles of Yale, in the spring of 1796, and the house was designed and erected soon thereafter by Asher Benjamin (1773-1845). Benjamin, a native of Hartland, Connecticut, was locally trained as a carpenter and early distinguished himself in Suffield and Hartford, Connecticut, as a master builder of exceptional promise. During the same year that the Leavitt House was being built, Benjamin published in Greenfield *The Country Builder's Assistant,* the first native American builder's guide and the first in a series of seven architectural books produced during his subsequent career as a successful Boston architect.

This garden design is among those working drawings from Benjamin's Greenfield period that can be identified with the Leavitt House (shown in outline form at the top of the illustration). The building still stands (with its wings enlarged) as the Greenfield Public Library.

Yale University

NOTES

1. Walter Kendall Watkins, "The Hancock House and Its Builder," *Old-Time New England,* XVII (July 1926), p. 7.

2. Sidney Fiske Kimball, *Mr. Samuel McIntire, Carver, The Architect of Salem* (Portland, Me., 1940), pp. 77-90.

3. Watkins, "The Hancock House," p. 7.

4. Abbott Lowell Cummings, "History in Houses: The Royall House in Medford, Massachusetts," *Antiques,* LXXXVIII (October 1965), pp. 506-510.

5. Elihu Ashley Diary, Mar. 1, 1773—Nov. 5, 1775, MS, Pocumtuck Valley Memorial Association Library, Deerfield, Mass.

6. *The Diary of William Bentley, D.D.* (1905; reprint ed., Gloucester, Mass., 1962), I, p. 198.

7. "Extracts from Capt. Francis Goelet's Journal . . . ," *New-England Historical & Genealogical Register,* XXIV (January 1870), p. 55.

8. *A Pride of Quincys,* A Massachusetts Historical Society Picture Book (Boston, 1969), second illustration.

9. New Hampshire Probate Records, XXI, p. 527, New Hampshire State Archives, Concord.

10. Peter Livius Copy Book, Peter Livius Papers, p. 29, New Hampshire Historical Society.

11. Collections, New Hampshire Historical Society. I am indebted for information concerning the Boyd and Gov. Benning Wentworth gardens to James L. Garvin, curator, New Hampshire Historical Society. These estates will be more fully discussed in his forthcoming doctoral dissertation on the early architecture of the Piscataqua region of New Hampshire and Maine.

12. George Francis Dow, ed., *The Diary and Letters of Benjamin Pickman (1740-1819)* . . . (Newport, R.I., 1928), opp. p. 64.

13. *The Massachusetts Magazine,* IV (November 1792), p. 651.

14. Bentley, *Diary,* I, p. 264.

15. For photographs taken before the house was demolished, see Historic American Buildings Survey, Library of Congress, Washington, D.C.

16. Henry Wansey, *An Excursion to the United States of North America, in the Summer of 1794,* 2nd ed. (Salisbury, Eng., 1798), p. 34.

17. Kimball, *Samuel McIntire.*

Town and Country Gardens in Eighteenth-Century Philadelphia

Elizabeth McLean

The first English settlers in the colony of Pennsylvania during the 1680s brought over with them not only seeds and cuttings of familiar plants to cultivate in their intended gardens, but also certain concepts of late seventeenth-century garden design that were to prevail, especially in and around Philadephia, well into the eighteenth century. William Penn's plan for the city, which he projected as a "greene Country Towne," made particular provision for small gardens throughout the townscape that would both please the eye and produce vegetables, fruits, and herbs for the economy of the households.[1] The frontispiece of *Systema Agriculturae* by John Worlidge[2] illustrates the sort of garden as very likely was laid out in Philadelphia in the early years, enclosed, rectilinear in design, practical in use, and informal in planting; it also exists in relation to a total scene that includes orchard and pasture.[3] It was not really until the mid-eighteenth century that larger landscape gardens began to be laid out around elegant country houses picturesquely positioned along river scenery near the city, especially along the Schyulkill River. Perhaps because he saw only the smaller town gardens and did not have an entrée to the larger estates, the German traveler, David Schoepf, visiting the colonies in 1783-1784, judged that "the taste for gardening is, at Philadelphia as well as throughout America, still in its infancy. There are not yet to be found many orderly and interesting gardens. Mr. Hamilton's near the city [Woodlands] is the only one deserving special mention." Schoepf was plainly wrong in that there were at least ten in the area by then that represented conspicuous artistic achievements in landscape gardening. To his credit, though, Schoepf did note that behind each house in the city "is a little court or garden, where usually are the necessaries, and so this often evil-smelling convenience of our European houses is missed here, but space and better arrangement are gained. The kitchen, stable etc., are all placed in buildings at the side or behind, kitchens often underground." He then added, "I remember once reading in some book of travels that Philadelphia was a city of Quakers and beautiful gardens. Brief enough, and . . . probably true."[4] Andrew Burnaby, an earlier traveler in 1759, seems to have had a wider and more revealing perspective when he described the city as well endowed with "villas, gardens, and luxuriant orchards."[5]

In colonial gardens of the late seventeenth and early eighteenth centuries there was little difference between a pleasure or ornamental and a practical or useful garden. These two elements tended to cohabit a garden. William Penn, a sophisticated gardener himself, instructed his gardener at Pennsbury on the Delaware to "sett out the garden by the house, plant sweet herbs, sparragrass, carrets, parsnups, hartechokes, salatin, and all flowers and kitchen herbs there";[6] others of Penn's letters described terraces in front of the house, an allée of poplars, orchards, and meadows. In 1698 Edward Shippen owned a house in the newly established city of Philadelphia with "an Orchard and Gardens adjoyning to his Great House . . . having a very famous and pleasant Summer-House erected in the middle of his extraordinary fine and large Garden abounding with *Tulips, Pinks, Carnations, Roses,* (of several sorts) *Lilies,* not to mention those that grow wild in the Fields."[7] Even Mayor Shippen's flower garden had practical aspects; pinks were used to spice wine, and the rose had culinary, medicinal, and fragrant uses. Virtually every description of eighteenth-century Philadelphia gardens, and not just those of large gardens like Penn's and Shippen's, mentions fruit trees.

That was the predominant pattern, and the style of the English natural landscape school was to reach Philadelphia by slow degrees. Israel Pemberton's garden was described "as laid out in the old fashioned style of uniformity, with walks and allies nodding to their brothers, and decorated with a number of evergreens, carefully clipped into pyramidal and conical forms."[8] Although there is no sense of explicit indictment in that comment, the word "nodding" does echo Alexander Pope's poem, *Epistle to Burlington* (1731), which sharply criticized formal gardens where

> Grove nods at grove, each Alley has a brother,
> And half the platform just reflects the other.[9]

As for Charles Norris's city garden before 1767, it contained only a hint of wilderness. Although the main garden near his house was "laid out in square parterres and beds, regularly intersected by graveled and grasswalks and alleys," another part of the garden was "more irregular." It was later described by Norris's daughter, Deborah Norris Logan, as having a walk leading to the cottage of a retired servant "with a grass plot and trees in front, and roses intermixed with currant bushes, around its borders . . . completely a 'Rus in Urbe.' "[10]

"Rus in Urbe," however, was not to be sufficient for a good number of Philadelphians who wanted their "country" *in* the country. As early as 1698 Gabriel Thomas wrote of "many Curious and Spacious Buildings, which several of the *Gentry* have erected for their Country-Houses."[11] By 1752 one map shows over two hundred country houses within a ten-mile radius of Philadelphia.[12] Many of these represented the "Country Seat" of men like Israel Pemberton who already had a townhouse. Many Quakers, like Isaac Norris, preferred the country life, which he could pursue at Fairhill on the road to Germantown (*Plate 22*). There, in 1717, he wrote, "We are surrounded with woods and all nature in its rough dress."[13] His son, Isaac Norris II, retired to Fairhill upon inheriting the estate and there lived "downright in the country way." In 1743 he wrote of "opening my woods into groves, enlarging my fishponds and beautifying my springs." He quoted Virgil, as did contemporary English gentry, for whom the development of the "classic English landscape" was part of the self-image of a Roman senator retired to the country.[14]

The owners of these large estates that were being built clearly required accessible and reliable nurseries to provide them with plants for their gardens. It should be noted that John Bartram, farmer and self-taught botanist, decided to establish just that: a large nursery on the banks of the Schuylkill. Bartram quickly became part of the transatlantic network of Quakers interested in natural science and may thus be said to have contributed to the development of the English landscape. Through Peter Collinson, London draper and fellow Quaker, Bartram sold boxes of seeds and plants of American trees and shrubs to over one hundred British patrons and clients.[15] One patron, the eighth Lord Petre, planted ten thousand American trees before he died at the age of twenty-nine.[16] Peter Collinson also had an influence upon American horticulture; he introduced his American clients to one another, creating opportunities for plant exchanges between gardeners and botanists like John Bartram, John Custis of Williamsburg, Dr. Alexander Garden of Charleston, and others. As the English agent for the Library Company of Philadelphia, Collinson also saw to it that John Bartram had copies of such important works as Philip Miller's *Gardener's Dictionary*,[17] the standard reference, in its successive editions, for the Anglo-American gardener. Even the great urbanite, Benjamin Franklin, had a copy.[18] Peter Collinson was also busy sending seeds of interesting plants to his American friends. Although John Bartram did not seem particularly appreciative of Collinson's "Common" double daffodils, he was, however, enthusiastic about such rarities as the "pretty blue aster from the cape ye sent me."[19] A drawing of his garden indicates a very practical design, with vegetable and flower garden separated from one another and the nursery.[20] In 1787 Washington was to describe it as "stored with many curious Trees, Shrubs and Flowers, [but] was neither large nor laid out in much taste."[21]

Peter Collinson and John Bartram may have been the most significant figures in the Anglo-American exchange of seeds and plants, but they were not alone. A sophisticated gardener like William Logan could order "exotics" from a variety of sources in England and America for his garden at Stenton, which was begun in 1728 by his father, James Logan. The senior Logan, Penn's provincial secretary, had an international reputation as a botanist because of his experiments on maize (or Indian corn) that were to help establish the sexual nature of plants,[22] a novel concept in the eighteenth century. There are no descriptions of the gardens at Stenton as it appeared in the time of either James Logan or his son William—even from the indefatigable pen of the latter's daughter-in-law, Deborah Norris Logan. William Logan's order lists cover pages, and include several hundred varieties of trees, shrubs, and flowers ("the very best"). Except for vegetables and bulbs, Logan's lists run to only one or two of everything; one suspects that except for spring bulbs and carnations, there was a rather casual mix of plants.[23] They ran the eighteenth-century gamut, from striped hollies and "gold stripe rosemary" to "horse-shoe leaved geranium" and yucca.[24] Certainly William Logan had a "collector's garden," reflecting the increasing wealth of plant material from Africa and other foreign countries that was reaching avid Philadelphia gardeners by way of England.

Although country estates such as Fairhill and Stenton in the Germantown area were important, the country house gardens most associated with Philadelphia were those along the banks of the Schuylkill River. A number of river landscape gardens laid out at mid-century turned the Schuylkill into an elegant stretch of landscape. Francis Baily, eventually president of the Royal Astronomical Society in London, remarked in 1796 that the Schuylkill was a "pleasant stream running along the back of the city, on the banks of which there are innumerable number of little country seats."[25] These gardens unquestionably document the widespread practice of landscape gardening near Philadelphia around mid-century.

William Penn's estate, Springettsbury, which encompassed an area known as "Faire Mount" just outside Philadelphia, was one of the earliest and most beautifully varied landscapes to be laid out along the river. Penn's son, John, inherited this estate, then known as the "Proprietor's Garden," and proceeded to employ a professional gardener, James Alexander, to maintain it.[26] There is no surviving evidence that Alexander actually did any designing of the garden, though he certainly did take control of the estate's large vineyards and regularly sent seeds from the garden to John Penn upon the latter's return to England in 1741. The two Penns were themselves likely the designers since the pattern in the colonial period was generally for owners of large houses to lay out their own grounds while hiring competent gardeners like Alexander to see to the day-to-day planting and maintenance. In any case, by 1754 the gardens of Springettsbury were worthy of Ezra Stiles's enthusiastic attention. A visitor from New England who kept a careful journal of his visits to gardens, Stiles commented on these gardens with language that imparts a sense of the romantic. He wrote of

> passing a long spacious walk, set on each side with trees, on the summit of a gradual ascent . . . besides the beautiful walk, ornamented with evergreens, we saw fruit trees with plenty of fruit, . . . oranges, limes, limons, and citrons . . . Spruce hedges cut into beautiful figures, etc., all forming the most agreeable variety, and even regular confusion and disorder . . . the whole scene most happily accommodated for solitude and rural contemplation.[27]

According to Stiles's description this was a good example of what may be called a "transitional" garden, one possessing "an agreeable variety" comprised of both traditional regular and suggestive irregular features: a "small wilderness," topiary work, a "neat little park," and sundry "groves." The phrase, "solitude and rural contemplation," suggests that for Stiles, at least, the garden layout evoked a sense of the private and encouraged an indulgence in personal reveries. In order to do that it had to be full of variety and surprise.

Part of the estate of Springettsbury was bought in 1770 by Robert Morris, financier of the American Revolution. There he built The Hills as his country house. After the devastation caused by the British occupation of Philadelphia during the Revolution, Morris evidently had to rebuild it. The Reverend Manasseh Cutler, a visiting botanist from New England, reported that "his country-seat is not yet completed but it will be superb. It is planned on a large scale, the gardens and walks are extensive, and the villa, situated on an eminence, has a commanding prospect down the Schuylkill."[28] Despite its "unfinished" state, George Washington went out to see it several times during that same summer of the Constitutional Convention.[29] A special character of the Philadelphia country houses was their proximity to the city—within an easy ride from town for the fashionable afternoon tea—unlike the relationship of either southern plantations or the Hudson River estates to the city.

Unfortunately, Morris, who did everything "on a large scale," speculated heavily in real estate and went bankrupt. At a sheriff's sale in 1799 The Hills was bought by Henry Pratt, who renamed it Lemon Hill for the lemon trees in the greenhouse, and developed an extensive garden. Morris has been credited as the first to grow lemon trees in Philadelphia. However, Deborah Norris Logan wrote that "[William] Logan had a Green house in town, as well as a good one [at Stenton]. He had many rare and beautiful plants: indeed the large and fine orange and lemon trees which now ornament Pratt's greenhouses at Lemon Hill were originally of his raising . . . I know this to be so."[30]

Bush Hill, near The Hills, was also originally part of Springettsbury. It had been awarded to the Philadelphia lawyer, Andrew Hamilton, by the Proprietors, and he built a house there in 1740. His son James, subsequently governor of Pennsylvania, lived there when Ezra Stiles visited in 1754 and "took a walk in his very elegant garden, in which are 7 statues in fine Italian marble curiously wrot."[31] The malcontent Daniel Fisher, a year later, was less enthusiastic. "It [did not] contain anything that was curious . . . a few very ordinary statues. A shady walk of high trees leading from the further end of the Garden looked well enough; but the Grass above knee high, thin and spoiling for the want of the Sythe."[32] Abigail Adams spent some time at Bush Hill in 1790 and had some mixed feelings about what she called the "appearance of uniformity" in the distant landscape, but she was a believer in the variety and irregular charm of the gardens themselves: "A beautiful grove behind the house, through which there is a spacious gravel walk, guarded by a number of marble statues [they were still there almost forty years after Stiles saw them], whose genealogy I have not yet studied . . . A variety of fine fields of wheat and grass are in front of the house, and, on the right hand, a pretty view of the Schuylkill presents itself."[33]

Further upstream, a Scottish sea captain, John Macpherson, built the charming Georgian house of Mount Pleasant in 1761. Although the garden was "restored" in 1927 with terraces of formal gardens and a Chinese Chippendale gazebo, and in spite of John Adams's remark that Mount Pleasant was "the most elegant seat in Pennsylvania," there is no indication that Mount Pleasant in the eighteenth century was ever more than a working farm with a fine orchard and kitchen garden. An advertisement in the *Pennsylvania Gazette* in 1769 described

> A great number and variety of the best inoculated and grafted fruit-trees, viz. apples, apricots, cherries, peaches, pears, plumbs, quinces and a number of chestnut and shell-bark trees. The kitchen garden is large, and within a stone wall. It contains a variety of the fine fruit trees, above 50 beds of asparagus, as many of strawberries, and one of artichokes. . . . The situation is remarkably healthy and beautiful.[34]

Across the river stood Belmont, the home of William Peters who purchased the land in 1742. Hannah Callender, who seems to have enjoyed social visits as much as any of Jane Austen's heroines, described it in 1762:

> A broad walk of English cherry trees leads down to the river. The doors of the house opening opposite admit a prospect of the length of the garden over a broad gravel walk to a large handsome summer house on a green. From the windows a vista is terminated by an obelisk. On the right you enter a labyrinth of hedge of low cedar and spruce. In the middle stands a statue of Apollo. In the garden are statues of Diana, Fame and Mercury with urns. We left the garden for a wood cut into vistas. In the midst is a Chinese temple for a summer house. One avenue gives a fine prospect of the City. . . .Another avenue looks to the obelisk.[35]

Although choosing woods and "vistas," Philadelphians were not yet ready to give up their hedges of spruce, cedar, or "quickset." Boxwood, the ubiquitous hedge in twentieth-century colonial revival gardens, was not mentioned at all.

Another impressive garden near Philadelphia already mentioned, with a view of the Delaware River, was Fairhill, owned and landscaped by Isaac Norris and owned later in the century by John Dickinson. Josiah Quincy found enough there in the way of a landscape garden in the 1770s to call it a "show place": "Greenhouse, bathing house, grotto, study [in the gardens], fishpond, fields, meadows, vista through which is a distant prospect of Delaware River."[36] John Adams, who lived at Bush Hill for a time courtesy of William Hamilton, noted the following about Fairhill in his diary on September 12, 1774: "Mr. Dickinson has a fine Seat, a beautyfull Prospect of the City, the River and the Country—fine Gardens."[37] R. T. Paine, who was with Adams on this visit to Fairhill, found the place "a convenient, decent, elegant Philosophical Rural Retreat."[38]

The number of well-known houses along the Schuylkill increased dramatically after the Revolution. Lansdowne was built by John Penn, a grandson of William Penn, before the Revolution. It became a showplace when purchased by the extremely wealthy William Bingham in 1796. In 1785 another John Penn, also a grandson of the founder, built The Solitude on the grounds of what is now the Philadelphia zoo. Raised in England and arriving in Philadelphia in 1784 with a good understanding of the latest English gardening, he proceeded immediately to landscape the grounds around his newly built house. The result is preserved in a good contemporary plan (*Plate 23*) showing a bowling green surrounded by thick groves threaded by paths, a "Wilderness," a vista with a ha-ha at the end of it, and kitchen and flower gardens removed some distance from the house. There is even a clump of trees shown between the house and river, placed there for perspective, and an oblique allée offering a view of the river from the house. The point was to "banish" formality from near the house and unfold a multiplicity of natural effects throughout the grounds, as along a circuitous path from the house to the flower garden which took as many as possible of the best picturesque points of view.

Further down the river, Gray's garden was one of the first public gardens in Philadelphia. It was designed by Samuel Vaughan, who had also designed the garden on State House (Independence Hall) Square.[39] Not only was there the requisite greenhouse, with its orange and lemon trees, but the gardens "seemed to be in a number of detached areas, all different in size and form. The alleys were none of them straight, nor were there any two alike. At every end, side, and corner, there were *summer-houses*, arbors covered with vines or flowers or shady bowers encircled with trees and flowering shrubs, each of which was formed in a different taste."[40] Manasseh Cutler on his 1787 visit walked on unending winding paths through groves, past grottoes and hermitages, to vistas complete with Chinese bridges. "There is every variety that imagination can conceive," he wrote, "but the whole improved and embellished by art, and yet the art so blended with *nature* as hardly to be distinguished, and seems to be only a handmaid to her operations."[41]

Near neighbor to Gray's garden, and to Bartram's gardens, Woodlands was the greatest garden in Philadelphia at the end of the eighteenth century, and one of the greatest in the United States. William Hamilton, a grandson of Andrew Hamilton, inherited Woodlands as well as Bush Hill. A friend of Thomas Jefferson, the Bartrams, and the principal botanists of his time, Hamilton was one of the most interesting personalities in American garden history.

In 1779 Hamilton wrote of the necessity of "repairing in some degree the damage my estate has sustained"[42] (presumably from the war) and proceeded to spend the next decade doing just this. From the letters it emerges that he enjoyed the good life and had a "refined taste"[43] as well as an eye for details and a streak of perfectionism. He wanted to "make a small park," and felt that the "Hill'n'Dale" terrain of Woodlands lent itself to this.[44] Later, from England in 1785, he wrote, "The verdure of England is its greatest beauty and my endeavors shall not be wanting to give the Woodland some resemblance of it."[45] His contemporaries certainly felt that he succeeded. Thomas Jefferson, who himself traveled to England to visit the great landscape gardens like Stowe to get ideas for landscaping

Monticello, wrote to Hamilton about the problems he encountered since "the disposition of the ground [at Monticello] takes from me the first beauty in gardening, the variety of hill and dale."[46]

Jefferson then hinted for a visit by Hamilton to Monticello so that the latter might share with him his genius; Jefferson spoke of "indulging on a new field some of the taste which has made the Woodlands the only rival I have known in America to what may be seen in England."[47]

Hamilton planned ahead. From England he wrote, "The first thing to be set about is a good nursery for trees, shrubs, flowers, fruits etc. of every kind."[48] He then advised the sowing of seeds of a variety of American trees, from dogwood to magnolia, as well as the "collecting" (he didn't say where) of "handsome small plants" of other native trees and shrubs. Hamilton sent great numbers of plants from England before his return, and inquired constantly (not without reason) as to their health. When George Smith had evidently written to report that certain plants in a large shipment were dead, Hamilton erupted, "Pray am I to infer that all [those] plants are dead—pray are none of the eastern plane, the Portugal Laurels . . . the evergreen sweet Briar, Singleton's Rose, the evergreen Rose [etc. etc.] . . . now living? Did not any of the seeds vegetate of a Bushel of Horsechestnuts, a peck of Spanish chestnuts, 3 pounds of pistichia [etc. etc.] . . . or have they gone to the Dogs too?"[49] One wishes that some of Smith's replies were extant.

Hamilton is credited with introducing the Lombardy poplar and the gingko; they appear in his letters.[50] He was certainly one of the first to use English ivy. "I have been frequently pleased [in England] with the effect of Ivy in certain situations especially when growing over Buildings and Arches. Suppose you were to plant half a dozen young ones on the east side of the new Bridge over the mill creek? I dare say no objection would be made by the owner of the ground."[51] Hamilton seemed to have a passion for "double" flowers; he was constantly concerned that his gardener mark the "double-convolvulus," and the double "thorns" (hawthorn); double cleander was one of his "exotics," and he even liked the "common" double daffodil.

Hamilton's energy was particularly evident in his concern over his "exotic"; he was constantly fussing over his large greenhouse, hothouse, and "exotic yard." He had to be out of town a great deal, seeing to family property in Lancaster, and his letters are full of concern about placement of plants in the greenhouse, how often to water, how long to open the greenhouse windows, and so on. Jefferson coveted his *Albizzia julibrissin* (and had to ask for it more than once).[52] It would appear that at times, however, he was less than forthcoming in sharing his acquisitions. He not only instructed Smith to seek out the "pike's tooth aloe," but also to make sure that no one else got one; he was furious when his secretary failed.[53] There was an element of the secretive in his pursuit of exotic plants. He asked Smith to go down to the dock when ships from India were in and ask passengers if they had seeds.[54] He coveted William Bartram's "cape plants."[55]

Bernard M'Mahon, Philadelphia seedsman and fine horticulturist, com-

plained to Jefferson about Hamilton's horticultural parsimony and cov-
etousness.[56] It was to M'Mahon and Hamilton that Jefferson entrusted the
seeds from the Lewis and Clark explorations to be grown in great
secrecy.[57] M'Mahon was successful, but we hear no more about the seeds
entrusted to Hamilton. Perhaps he could not bear to share these either,
even though they were not his.

Probably the best description of Hamilton and his garden comes from
the pen of Manasseh Cutler, who paid a visit to Hamilton in November
1803:

> We then walked over the pleasure grounds, in front, and a little back
> of the house. It is formed into walks, in every direction, with borders
> of flowering shrubs and trees. Between are lawns of green grass,
> frequently mowed, and at different distances numerous copse of the
> native trees, interspersed with artificial groves, which are of trees
> collected from all parts of the world. . . . We then took a turn to the
> garden and green houses. . . . The garden . . . [is] ornamented with
> almost all the flowers and vegetables the earth affords. . . . The green
> houses which occupy a large space of ground, I cannot pretend to
> describe. Every part was crowded with trees and plants, from the hot
> climates, and such as I had never seen. . . . He assured us, there was
> not a rare plant in Europe, Asia, Africa, from China and the islands in
> the South Sea, of which he had any account, which he had not
> procured.[58]

Cutler, who had had a fall and was not feeling well, was permitted to retire
to the house only when it was too dark to see outdoors. However, the
botanical excursion continued with books. "When we turned to rare and
superb plants, one of the gardeners would be called, and sent with a
lantern to the green house to fetch me a specimen to compare with it. This
was done perhaps twenty times."[59] After ten o'clock at night, poor Dr.
Cutler finally had an elaborate dinner followed by more botany until the
early hours of the morning. Only the legitimate plea of having to catch the
next stage got him away after breakfast.

A garden of the quality of Woodlands was possible because of, among
other reasons, the firm horticultural base in eighteenth-century Philadelphia. The siting of the "greene Country Towne" and the early relationship
of garden and "country" were a background to the development of the
landscape gardens along the Schuylkill. The substantial economic base of
the second largest city in the English-speaking world made possible the
wealth behind the creation of the great country estates. Even though by
the third generation many Quakers had become fashionable Anglicans,
they had by then left their stamp on the horticultural development of
Philadelphia. Their early inquiring interest in natural science and the
close international network of botanists abetted the development of both
plant interchange and botanical knowledge. At the same time, the emphasis on the practical kept the mix of "pleasure garden" and "edibles" a
strong part of the eighteenth-century tradition (even Hamilton was
growing hundreds of cabbages). By the time Hamilton was planning his

"park," there had been a hundred years of sophisticated gardening in temperate Philadelphia conditions.

Wynnewood, Pennsylvania

NOTES

1. In his "Instructions to his Commissioners for settling the Colony of Pennsylvania," October 1681, William Penn wrote: "Let every House be placed, if the Person pleases in the middle of its platt . . . so there may be ground on each side, for Gardens or Orchards or Fields, that it may be a greene Country Towne, which will never be burnt, and always be wholesome": Pennsylvania Miscellaneous Papers, Penn and Baltimore, 1653-1754, large folio, pp. 5, 6, Historical Society of Pennsylvania, Philadelphia.

Pennsylvania's first colonists were mainly English fellow Quakers, attracted to his "Holy Experiment." "Three-quarters of the so-called First Purchasers who bought tracts of Pennsylvania land, were merchants, shopkeepers, and artisans from London, Bristol, Dublin, and other British towns . . . who shared his hopes for peace and prosperity but wanted their new home on the Delaware to be essentially like the other towns they had come from in England and America": Mary Maples Dunn and Richard S. Dunn, "The Founding 1681-1701," in *Philadelphia A 300 Year History* (New York, 1982), p. 2. The first wave of settlers included Quaker merchants "of substance" such as Isaac Norris from Jamaica, Samuel Carpenter from Barbados, and Edward Shippen from Boston. A useful collection of original early accounts has been edited by Albert Cook Myers in *Narratives of Early Pennsylvania, West New Jersey, and Delaware, 1630-1707*, in J. Franklin Jameson, ed., *Original Narratives of Early American History*, (New York, 1912).

Except for Pennsbury, there seems to be no detailed description of the *design* of a seventeenth-century Philadelphia garden; one assumes current English practice because everything which *is* described follows this. The plants used are often repeated in various letters and tracts, such as Thomas Budd's *Good Order Established in Pennsilvania & New Jersey* (Philadelphia, 1685), p. 7, where he listed "Garden Fruits which groweth well, *Cabbage, Colwarts, Colliflowers, Sparagrass, Carrats, Parsneps, Turnups, Oynions, Cow-cumbers, Pumkins, Water-Mellons, Musk-Mellons, Squashes, Potatoes, Currants, Goosberries, Roses, Carnations, Tulips,* Garden-Herbs."

In 1683 another group of Dutch Quakers, Mennonites, and German pietists founded Germantown, in rural Philadelphia County. Francis Daniel Pastorius, an agent of the Frankfort Company, quickly became its leading citizen. His "Vineyard, and Orchard and Garden" included "Flags, Tulips, Marjoram, Pinks, Burnet, Columbines, Sage, Poppies, white Lillies, Daffodils, etc. etc.," but obviously his main concern was practicality. Francis Daniel Pastorius, *Deliciae Hortenses or Garden-Recreations and Voluptates Apianae*, ed. Christoph E. Schweitzer (Columbia, S. C., 1982), pp. 73, 50.

2. John Worlidge, *Systema Agriculturae; The Mystery of Husbandry Discovered* (London, 1669). William Penn had a copy at Pennsbury, as indicated in Hubertis M. Cummings, "An Account of Goods at Pennsbury Manor, 1687," *Pennsylvania Magazine of History and Biography*, LXXXVI (October 1962), p. 404. Another copy, which belonged to Samuel Carpenter and was given to Isaac Norris, is at the Library Company of Philadelphia.

3. One must remember that as a horse was essential for transportation, so a pasture was essential for a horse.

4. Johann David Schoepf, *Travels in the Confederation . . .*, Alfred J. Morrison, trans. and ed. (Philadelphia, 1911), I, pp. 93, 60.

5. Andrew Burnaby, *Travels Through the Middle Settlements in North America, in the Years 1759 and 1760*, 2nd ed. (London, 1775), p. 75.

6. William Penn to Ralph Smith, n.d. (late 1684?), transcript of Penn Papers, Richard and Mary Dunn, eds., Hist. Soc. Pa.

7. Gabriel Thomas, *An Historical and Geographical Account of the Province and Country of Pennsylvania . . .* (London, 1698), p. 43.

8. Alexander Graydon, *Memoirs of a Life Chiefly Passed in Pennsylvania Within the Last Sixty Years* (Harrisburg, Pa., 1811), pp. 34-35. Graydon, who was born in 1752, felt that his memory went back to 1758 or 1759.

9. Alexander Pope, *Epistle To Burlington*, lines 117-118, in F. W. Bateson, ed., *Epistles to Several Persons*, John Butt, gen. ed., *The Poems of Alexander Pope*, Twickenham Edition, III, ii (London, 1951).

10. Although Deborah Norris Logan wrote her description of the garden in 1827, it represents her childhood memory of a garden created by her aunt, Deborah Norris, who died in 1767: Deborah Logan, *The Norris House* (Philadelphia, 1867), pp. 5-6.

11. Thomas, *Historical and Geographical Account*, p. 42.

12. N. Scull and G. Heap, "A Map of Philadelphia and Parts Adjacent" (Philadelphia, 1742).

13. Isaac Norris I to Benjamin Coole, Mar. 11, 1716, Norris Letter Book, 1716-1730, p. 60, Hist. Soc. Pa.

14. "Rura Gelu cum claudit Hyems." Isaac Norris II to Robert Charles, June 22, 1743, Norris Letter Book, 1719, 1756, p. 14, Hist. Soc. Pa.

15. Edmund Berkeley and Dorothy Smith Berkeley, *The Life & Travels of John Bartram* (Tallahassee, Fla., 1982), pp. 311-318. Through the eighteenth century most plants for large estates in Philadelphia were imported from nurseries in England or South Carolina. In fact, John Bartram's American trade was relatively small; it was not until the time of William Bartram that the nursery sold foreign exotics in any quantity.

16. Peter Collinson to John Bartram, Sept. 1, 1741, in William Darlington, *Memorials of John Bartram and Humphry Marshall* (1849; reprint ed., Philadelphia, 1967), p. 145.

17. Collinson to Bartram, May 20, 1739, Bartram Papers, II, 48, Hist. Soc. Pa.

18. Benjamin Franklin to Deborah Read Franklin, May 27, 1757, in Leonard W. Labaree et al., eds., *The Papers of Benjamin Franklin*, VII (New Haven, Conn., 1963), p. 219. In an unpublished manuscript on gardening books in eighteenth-century Philadelphia, Edwin Wolf 2nd has written: "Throughout the eighteenth century Miller's *Gardener's Dictionary* and *Gardener's Kalender* were almost as ubiquitous on colonial bookshelves as the contemporaneous essays of Addison and Steele, known as the *Spectator*, and that was very ubiquitous indeed."

19. Bartram to Collinson, Nov. 1761, Bartram Papers, I, 55, Hist. Soc. Pa.

20. A drawing of John Bartram's practical garden/nursery is in the library of the Earl of Derby, Knowsley, Prescot, Lancashire, England.

21. "Extracts from Washington's Diary, Kept While Attending the Constitutional Convention of 1787," *PMHB*, XI (1887), p. 300.

22. *Philosophical Transactions*, XXXVI (1737), p. 192. These experiments were undertaken in Logan's town garden ("in hortuli mei urbani"), which was about forty feet wide and eighty long.

23. The variety of gardening going on in Philadelphia in the second half of the century is suggested by a few details about planting that have come down to us. William Allen grew only "edibles" at his country house in Mount Airy ("Extracts from the Diary of Daniel Foster, 1755," *PMHB*, XVII [1893], p. 296), while John Smith, who married William Logan's sister Hannah, had a terraced garden on the Delaware above "town" with an orchard and hedges (Albert Cook Myers, ed., *Hannah Logan's Courtship* [Philadelphia, 1904], pp. 74, 93). Perhaps the most unusual garden was that of Daniel Wister in Germantown. His garden book of the 1770s records "best tulip bed," "best hyacinth bed," and dozens of varieties of "carnations," also planted in their own round bed ("Daniel Wister Garden Book 1771-76," Wister Notebooks, American Philosophical Society, Philadelphia).

24. The American sources included Thomas Young of "Charles Town" (S.C.) and John Watson of "Carolina." The English sources included James Gordon, Elias Bland, Thomas Bincks, and botanist John Blackburne. See Letitia Ellicott Wright, *The Colonial Garden at*

Stenton Described in Old Letters (Philadelphia, 1911). A typescript of all known Logan correspondence pertaining to Stenton is in the possession of the Pennsylvania Society of the Colonial Dames of America, Philadelphia.

25. For Francis Baily's description of the city, see *Journal of a Tour in Unsettled Parts of North America in 1796 and 1797*, ed. Jack D. L. Holmes (Carbondale and Edwardsville, Ill., 1969), p. 29.

26. James Alexander to Thomas Penn, Nov. 20, 1775, Penn MSS, Official Correspondence, VII, 159, Hist. Soc. Pa.

27. "Ezra Stiles in Philadelphia, 1754," *PMHB*, XVI (1892), p. 375.

28. William Parker Cutler and Julia Perkins Cutler, *Life, Journals, and Correspondence of the Rev. Manasseh Cutler, LL.D.*, I (Cincinnati, 1888), p. 257.

29. "Washington's Diary," pp. 301, 306, 307.

30. "Deborah Logan's Journal," XIII, 168, Hist. Soc. Pa.

31. "Ezra Stiles," p. 375.

32. "Diary of Fisher," p. 267.

33. See *The Adams Papers*, ed. L. H. Butterfield, Ser. 1, II (Cambridge, Mass., 1961), p. 32.

34. *Pennsylvania Gazette* (Philadelphia), Jan. 12, 1769. I am indebted to the extensive and as yet unpublished research of Beatrice Garvan on Mount Pleasant, its history, and its relationship to similar Scottish estates in the eighteenth century.

35. "Extracts from the Diary of Hannah Callender," *PMHB*, XII (1888), pp. 454-455.

36. Quincy's account of Fairhill is in the *Proceedings* of the Massachusetts Historical Society, 2nd Ser. (June 1916), pp. 471-473.

37. *Adams Papers*, Ser. 1, II, p. 133.

38. *Diary*, Sept. 12, 1774, Maryland Historical Society, Baltimore.

39. Samuel Vaughan also drew a fine plan of Mount Vernon for Washington in 1787.

40. *Life of Cutler*, I, p. 275.

41. *Ibid.*, pp. 274-275.

42. William Hamilton to William Tilghman, Jr., Apr. 1779, Hamilton Papers, Society Collection, Hist. Soc. Pa.

43. A. J. Downing, *A Treatise on the Theory and Practice of Landscape Gardening*, 6th ed. (New York, 1859), p. 26.

44. Hamilton to Tilghman, Apr. 1779, Hamilton Papers.

45. Hamilton to Dr. Thomas Parker, Sept. 24, 1785, Hamilton Papers.

46. Thomas Jefferson to Hamilton, July 1806, in Edwin Morris Betts, ed., *Thomas Jefferson's Garden Book, 1766-1824* (Philadelphia, 1944), p. 323.

47. *Ibid.*

48. Hamilton to George Smith, Sept. 30, 1785, George Smith Collection, Hist. Soc. Pa.

49. Hamilton to Smith, Nov. 2, 1785, Ferdinand Dreer Collection, *ibid.*

50. Hamilton to Smith, June 1790, Smith Collection, *ibid.*

51. Hamilton to Smith, Sept. 30, 1785, *ibid.*

52. Jefferson to Hamilton, July 1806, in Betts, ed., *Jefferson's Garden Book*, p. 323.

53. Hamilton to Smith, Aug. 3, 1792, Smith Collection, Hist. Soc. Pa.

54. Hamilton to Smith, June 12, 1790, *ibid.*

55. *Ibid.*

56. Bernard M'Mahon to Jefferson, July 3, 1809, in Betts, ed., *Jefferson's Garden Book*, p. 401.

57. Jefferson to M'Mahon, Mar. 22, 1807, *ibid.*

58. Cutler to Mrs. Torrey, Nov. 22, 1803, *PMHB*, VII (1894), pp. 109-110.

59. *Ibid.*, p. 110.

Gardens and Landscapes in Eighteenth-Century South Carolina

George C. Rogers, Jr.

David Ramsay in 1808 devoted three pages of his *History of South Carolina* to "some observations on horticulture as a branch of agriculture." He mentioned the gardens of Mrs. Elizabeth Lamboll, Mrs. Martha Logan, Mrs. Sarah Hopton, Henry Laurens, John Watson, Robert Squibb, André Michaux, Charles Drayton, and William Williamson. These town and plantation gardens were among the exceptions to his statement that the planters of South Carolina "have always too much neglected the culture of gardens." Yet he emphasized that when Carolinians did garden, they did so "both for use and pleasure."[1] In the first half of the eighteenth century the colony's gardens conformed to the prevailing pattern of formality and practicality that characterized both town and plantation gardens in other colonies. Essentially rectangular or square in shape, divided into sections by straight paths, enclosed with fences of sundry types, and combining vegetables and fruit with flowers and decorative bushes, these gardens reflected the prevailing late seventeenth- and early eighteenth-century English and European taste for balanced and symmetrical layouts. What especially distinguished South Carolina gardening throughout the century was the flourishing of numerous nurseries or botanical gardens, in Charleston for the most part.[2] Also, as in other colonies like Virginia, North Carolina, and Pennsylvania, by mid-century there was clear evidence of a growing taste in more naturalized garden treatment, in large-scale landscape gardening, and in gardens that would more evocatively generate moods and associations. In particular, at the end of the century the colony was fortunate to have as one of its citizens Charles Fraser, a painter with an eye for picturesque natural landscape, who sketched or painted a number of established country seats or landscape gardens near Charleston. With perhaps less virtuosity but more feeling than Benjamin Latrobe in Virginia at about the same time, Fraser has left us a record of the fulfillment of the landscape garden in eighteenth-century South Carolina.

It was not so much ideas and trends that differentiated gardening from one colony to another, but rather individual gardening personalities. At mid-century, two such South Carolina personalities were Henry Laurens and Dr. Alexander Garden. Both had gardens in Charleston and at their country seats not too far away. John Bartram, who visited Laurens's town garden in 1765 when Laurens was "making great improvements," noted that it was a garden walled with brick—200 yards long and 150 yards wide.[3] According to David Ramsay, Laurens's son-in-law, the latter began to lay it out in 1755; apparently it was well endowed both botanically and ornamentally,

> enriched with everything useful and ornamental that Carolina produced or his extensive mercantile connections enabled him to procure from remote parts of the world. Among a variety of other curious productions, he introduced olives, capers, limes, ginger, guinea grass, the alpine strawberry, bearing nine months in the year, red raspberrys, blue grapes; and also directly from the south of France, apples, pears, and plums of fine kinds, and vines which bore abundantly of the choice white eating grape called Chasselates blancs.[4]

It is interesting, too, that it was Laurens's wife, Elinor, who appears to have tended it much of the time, supervising its productiveness perhaps as well as its decorativeness with "ardor." As Ramsay noted, "The whole was superintended with maternal care by Mrs. Elinor Laurens with the assistance of John Watson, a complete English gardener"[5]—which was no small distinction, incidentally, considering the scarcity of competent English gardeners in any of the colonies for much of the century. The mere fact of an English gardener on the scene indicates the seriousness of the Laurenses as a gardening family. The mistress of a family frequently was the chief source of gardening enthusiasm in the eighteenth century, as in the case of Robert Carter's wife at Nomini Hall in Virginia,[6] but in December 1763 Laurens thought his wife was actually going too far with this activity. He wrote to Thomas Mears thanking him for roots and seeds brought from Liverpool:

> That lady has a wonderful inclination and some taste for Gardening but I am forced to check her Ardor a little now and then as I am not quite weary of her company nor satisfied with her services. If I was not to interpose I believe she wou'd soon become the Sextons property for Gardening in this moist uncertain Climate is often injurious and sometimes destructive to our good Women.[7]

Perhaps Laurens brought John Watson over from England to ease the burden upon his wife.[8]

Laurens knew well the gardens of the great English horticulturists of his day—those of Thomas Pennant, of John Blackburne at Orford near Warrington, of John Fothergill at Upton in Essex, and of John Coakley Lettsom at Camberwell. When he toured Europe in 1772-1774, he made a point of visiting the famous gardens.[9] Clearly he brought to his town garden a botanist's curiosity about plants; it may well be that he looked upon it not only as a useful source of produce but also as a nursery for plants he wished to cultivate in the gardens of his country estate, Mepkin.

More is known about Dr. Garden, whose professionalism and competence as a botanist was widely recognized throughout the southern colonies and in England. He and Laurens were intimate friends over the years and doubtless carried on a fruitful dialogue concerning matters botanical.[10] Always eager for new garden plants, Garden was in touch with botanists on both sides of the Atlantic and as far away as China. Laurens, for example, may have helped Garden acquire some plants from China by introducing him to John Ellis of London and through him to John Bradby Blake who had gone out to Canton in 1766. In a letter that year to Ellis, Garden wrote that he had just received from Blake

> seeds of two sorts of China indigo, the one of a deep, and the other of a sky blue; the lacquer tree, the oil tree, used to mix up the lacquer for cabinets; the alcea, described in Kempher's history of Japan, which is an article of vegetable food, and many other seeds from Pekin, and other more northerly provinces of China, and particularly several from Corea, a country between China and Tartary, above 300 leagues from Canton.[11]

In their biography of Dr. Garden, Edmund and Dorothy Smith Berkeley have noted that Dr. Garden planted the seeds of the tallow tree at his Otranto plantation.

Two other naturalists who gardened in Charleston and helped make that city known for its gardens in the second half of the century were Robert Squibb and John Watson. Identified as "Nursery and Seedsman of Charleston," Squibb published in Charleston his *Gardener's Calendar for South Carolina, Georgia and North Carolina* (1787), a work ambitiously intended to be a guide to two other colonies besides South Carolina—two colonies which in climate and topography he thought resembled South Carolina.[12] By the time of his death in Georgia in 1806, he was superintendent of the botanical garden near Savannah.[13] His *Calendar* is a practical monthly guide to garden duties, a genre which became not uncommon in the colonies in the late eighteenth century but examples of which for the most part remained unpublished; Squibb's was one of the few exceptions. As for Watson, after initially assisting Laurens with his botanical garden in some undefined capacity, he established his own nursery in town between Meeting and King streets. He has been called Charleston's most respected gardener in the middle of the century, selling at his nursery a wide assortment of plants and seeds, and a good range of garden tools as well. It was through his and others' efforts before the Revolution that Carolina gardeners did not have to depend upon seedsmen of the northern colonies for plants.[14] Dr. John Farquharson testified to this in June 1789 when he wrote:

> I lately went to Islington where is a Nursery of fruit trees and bushes kept by a relation of Mr. Watson, who has a Nursery near Charleston and corresponds with him; if he is properly encouraged with a small douceur from your Assembly every Gentleman may have at an easy rate all the fruits and vegetables that this Country produces.[15]

In 1808 Ramsay recorded that Watson's garden had "gone to ruin"; but Charles Fraser, with his eye for the ornamental picturesque, remembered that "those who preferred riding" had gone "to Watson's garden, a beautiful cultivated piece of ground, between Meeting and King-streets, about a mile from the city, adorned with shrubbery and hedges, and fine umbrageous trees, some of which either now, or lately, served to indicate its situation."[16]

Outside Charleston, in 1786 another botanist and nurseryman, André Michaux, purchased 222 acres near the ten-mile house up Charleston Neck which he transformed into the French Botanic Garden inasmuch as he had been sent by the French government to acquire trees, shrubs, and plants to be sent back to the king's garden in Paris. Michaux traveled extensively in the eastern half of America. Not only did he export examples of what he had found, but he also imported plants from around the world. He reputedly introduced the *Camellia japonica* to Middleton Place on the Ashley River. It is known that he and Dr. Charles Drayton of Drayton Hall exchanged frequent visits, plants, and horticultural information. Being situated between the Ashley and Cooper rivers, he could with ease supply the Charleston country retreats with plants necessary for their landscaping needs.[17]

Around mid-century there were clear signs that the abundance of nurseries and botanic gardens in and near Charleston was encouraging that area of the southern colonies to become a significant venue for ambitious and talented garden design. Alicia Hopton, for example, the daughter of William and Sarah Hopton whose gardens were later mentioned by Ramsay in his survey of the colony's gardens, had become aware of Alexander Pope's imaginative, innovative, and expressive garden not far from London along the Thames in Twickenham and wanted to transform her father's Wando River plantation into a "Rural retreat" worthy of Pope's new gardening ideas. The fact that John Laurens had promised to send her a sketch of Twickenham, on one of his visits to England, thrilled her immensely. "Its being the Sweet Retreat of my dear Mr. Pope will make me almost adore it," she purred.[18] Actually, there is no evidence that John Laurens and his father, Henry, visited Pope's garden, though we do know that they visited Lord Burlington's famous gardens at Chiswick, which Pope knew well and admired.[19] Alicia Hopton's desire to emulate Pope reveals that there existed in Charleston by mid-century an awareness of the more naturalized mode of gardening that Pope through his Twickenham example and his writings was promoting.

Another type of evidence of this increasing awareness emerges from the gardening enthusiasm and letters of Eliza Pinckney Lucas, who knew exactly what she preferred in the more natural and expressive mode and once even linked a garden she liked with the pastoral classical world of Virgil. In her 1743 detailed account of William Middleton's gardens at Crowfield along the Cooper River, she luxuriated in the artistic spectacle of gardens laid out with a highly developed pictorial and natural style; it is all here—serpentine walks, variety of elevation, prospects within and outside the garden, mounts, wildernesses or groves, and a classical flavor:

> The house stands a mile from, but in sight of the road, and makes a
> very hansoume appearance; as you draw nearer new beauties discover
> themselves, first the fruitful Vine mantleing up the wall loading with

delicious Clusters; next a spacious bason in the midst of a large green presents itself as you enter the gate that leads to the house, which is neatly finished; the rooms well contrived and elegantly furnished. From the back door is a spacious walk a thousand foot long; each side of which nearest the house is a grass plat ennamiled in a Serpentine manner with flowers. Next to that on the right hand is what imediately struck my rural taste, a thicket of young tall live oaks where a variety of Airry Chorristers pour forth their melody; and my darling, the mocking bird, joyned in the artless Concert and inchanted me with his harmony. Opposite on the left hand is a large square boleing green sunk a little below the level of the rest of the garden with a walk quite round composed of a double row of fine large flowering Laurel and Catulpas which form both shade and beauty.

My letter will be of an unreasonable length if I dont pass over the mounts, Wilderness, etc., and come to the bottom of this charming spott where is a large fish pond with a mount rising out of the middle—the top of which is level with the dwelling house and upon it is a roman temple. On each side of this are other large fish ponds properly disposed which form a fine prospect of water from the house. Beyond this are the smiling fields dressed in Vivid green. Here Ceres and Pomona joyn hand in hand to crown the hospitable board.[20]

Two places in England that represented the perfection of the new taste as well as the close association of landscaping and literature were Hagley Park in Worcestershire, laid out by George Lyttelton (created first baron Lyttelton in 1756), and The Leasowes, the small farm not far from Hagley, belonging to William Shenstone. Shenstone himself wrote an "Ode to Rural Elegance," which, according to his biographer, showed that he had developed "a Vergilian rusticity which was near to the heart of the eighteenth century, with its gentleman farmers and literate aristocracy."[21] The Leasowes was a consummate *ferme ornée*. These examples made an impact upon South Carolina. There was to be a Hagley on the Waccamaw River in South Carolina. It was the creation of Plowden Weston whose grandfather had come to Carolina from Warwickshire with Governor William Henry Lyttelton, the brother of Lord Lyttelton.[22] And Henry Laurens, who in 1769 used the word "elegant" to describe Shenstone as a writer, may well have had The Leasowes in mind as he molded Mepkin, his rural retreat, to his own taste. Mepkin, laid out about twenty miles above Charleston on the Cooper River,[23] was sketched by Charles Fraser, whose three views leave no doubt about its "Vergilian rusticity" (*Plate 24*).[24]

Without urging that he was influenced by either Hagley or Shenstone, we may be sure that Dr. Garden, too, was determined to lay out his own landscape garden at a country seat near Charleston. He began by purchasing in 1771 some land about fifteen miles from Charleston along Goose Creek, Berkeley County. He immediately christened it "Otranto," perhaps an allusion to Horace Walpole's gothic novel. Intent on enjoying beautiful views of landscape and water, he chose as a site for his house a lovely hill overlooking the river, beyond which lay the dense forest. The Berkeleys, Garden's biographers, quote a poem written by a friend who visited Garden at Otranto a few years after the gardens had been laid out. It is worth citing because of its expressed delight not only with pictorial

prospects and river scenes, but also with the mood of the gardens around
the house on the green hill:

> There midst the grove, with unassuming guise
> But rural neatness, see the mansion rise!
> . . . .
>
>   Nor are the Garden's beauties all conceal'd
> By night, tho' Cynthia veils her silver shield;
> Unnumber'd Fire-flies from their slumbers rise,
> Till earth's star'd surface emulates the skies;
> As their quick sparkles light the welkin round,
> Gleam on the leaves, or glow along the ground;
> And ev'ry flow'r its brightest tints displays
> Illumin'd by the transitory blaze.
> But eastward see where James's sacred Fane,
> Crowns the green hill that wide commands the plain,
> O'er lofty pines, that the horizon trace,
> The moon slow rising shews her ruddy face,
> And bright'ning gradual, as her orb ascends
> The azure vault, to which she radiance lends;
> Through yonder fork'd tree, her glories break
> In liquid silver, trembling on the lake.[25]

The fact that a visitor could respond thusly to a garden is almost as
significant in the garden history of South Carolina as the garden itself.

Such country seats or villas, as Charles Fraser's sketches so beautifully
illustrate at the end of the century (1796-1806), were studded around
Charleston on the banks of the Ashley, the Cooper, and the Stono rivers
and on adjacent islands. A visit to the most celebrated of these seats was a
must on many travelers' itinerary. The journal of the Duc de la Rochefoucauld-Liancourt provides a glimpse of such a circuit. When the duke
met Ralph Izard in Philadelphia in the winter of 1795, he promised that
he would visit Izard's "country-seat," The Elms, at Goose Creek, when he
went to South Carolina. He made his pilgrimage there in 1796 at a time
when the Izards were busy creating a garden. The Elms, a property of
1,400 acres of which only 300 were in cultivation, had "properly speaking,
only a country-house," which had been "built by his great grandfather."[26]
While Izard was abroad before the Revolution he had acquired William
Shenstone's *The Works in Verse and Prose* (published in Edinburgh in 1765)
and Thomas Whately's *Observations on Modern Gardening* (London, 1770),
both of which influenced him.[27] Shenstone's and Whately's ideas for the
landscape garden must surely have been in the minds of the Izards as they
set about improving the gardens at The Elms in the mid-1790s. On
December 11, 1794, Mrs. Alice Izard wrote her husband that Moses the
gardener, who had worked formerly for Mrs. Daniel Blake at Newington,
was hard at work to complete the walks, to merge the kitchen gardens with
the pleasure grounds, the useful with the ornamental. As for the former,
she wrote on January 1, 1795, that everything she served on the table
came out of the produce of The Elms except for the fruit. This she was
trying to correct by planting "hiccory" and chestnut trees, having taken

some buds from Mrs. Horry's trees. She had also set out the Antwerp raspberries that Ralph Izard had sent south by William Henry DeSaussure. On January 8 she reported on some olive trees that had come to the South Carolina Agricultural Society from their correspondent in France, "four of which Mr. P. Smith had sent to The Elms. They are planted out, and one of them is in leaf, or rather has put out leaves. The stocks are about four feet long."[28]

After Rochefoucald-Liancourt made one excursion to see the Izards, he set out on another with John Julius Pringle to view the country seats "which enjoy the greatest celebrity." On this tour the duke commented upon Dr. Alexander Baron's Fetteresso, Pringle's newly purchased Greenville (which Pringle had renamed Susan's Place in honor of his wife), Alexander Gillon's Batavia, Middleton Place, and Drayton Hall. Dr. Baron was trying to cope with the sameness of the landscape, the duke wrote, by transforming the land beyond the garden "into meadow ground." Although Middleton Place was "altogether undeserving the celebrity it enjoys," the duke was delighted with Drayton Hall: "The garden is better laid out, better cultivated and stocked with good trees, than any I have hitherto seen."[29] Dr. Charles Drayton apparently spent most of his lifetime improving the grounds of Drayton Hall. Dr. John Farquharson had been told in 1789 that "Doctor Drayton has a fine taste in laying out pleasure grounds, he assisted Dr. Garden in his Goose Creek plan."[30] The archaeological work now going on at Drayton Hall should reveal the scope and the plan of these gardens.[31] That all of them were in the naturalistic school seems plain from Rochefoucauld-Liancourt's concluding comment about Drayton Hall: "In order to have a fine garden, you have nothing to do but to let the trees remain standing here and there, or in clumps, to plant bushes in front of them, and arrange the trees according to their height." Dr. Drayton's father [John Drayton] began to lay out the garden "on this principle; and his son, who is passionately fond of a country life, has pursued the same plan."[32]

Fortunately, the sketches of Charles Fraser remain to provide us with a turn-of-the-century visual tour of these country seats. His brother James and his brother-in-law Joseph Winthrop happened to live on Goose Creek, and another brother, Frederick, had a place in Prince William parish. Through his aunt, Mrs. John Rutledge, Charles Fraser moved naturally in the Rutledge circle and thus would have had a chance to visit Richmond, the seat of Edward Rutledge on the Eastern Branch of the Cooper River. He also studied law in the office of John Julius Pringle, who had established himself on the Ashley. The country seats of all these gentlemen were sketched by Fraser between 1796 and 1806.[33]

The two places that most struck Fraser's fancy were Richmond, the seat of Edward Rutledge on the Eastern Branch of the Cooper River, and Sheldon, the seat of the Bull family in Prince William parish. That these two places were not as much in the family circle as others he sketched would suggest that he singled them out for certain characteristics that they exhibited. He sketched at least seven views of Richmond[34] and the same number of Sheldon[35] and only one or two of each of the other seats.

At Richmond he seems to have been struck with the rise of the land, of which there was little in the lowcountry. In fact, as Rochefoucauld-Liancourt ungenerously recorded, "it is hardly possible to meet with a pleasant landscape" in that flat terrain.[36] If Fraser was particularly disposed to savor and paint picturesquely rolling landscapes, it could on the face of it be said that he was living in the wrong region to satisfy his tastes. But Rochefoucauld-Liancourt clearly was thinking of open landscape, not landscape gardens such as Fraser knew well. Moreover, the rather greater rise and fall of the land along the Eastern Branch of the Cooper must have been interesting enough to engage his imaginative energies. His paintings of the landscapes around Richmond and Rice Hope reveal his enthusiasm for distant prospects opened up by some variety of elevation (*Plate 25*). But the most telling view is the one he drew from the front door of Richmond.[37] In this sketch it appears that the landscape beyond the nearby tranquil river had been created by the careful removal of trees rather than by any significant planting—the method that Rochefaucauld-Liancourt had described while looking at the grounds of Drayton Hall. The soft contours of the land gently frame the river as it glides into the pastoral distance. There is also a neat contrast between the straight, canalized-looking river in the foreground near the house and the winding river in the middle ground of the picture. Fraser may have felt an analogy here to the contrast in late eighteenth-century plantation gardens between regular or formal gardens adjacent to the house and the more distant landscape scenery created by the planned picturesque interplay of hills and field, well-placed trees, water, and forests.

Sheldon appealed to a slightly different interest of Fraser's. He would have known that estate from his frequent visits to his brother Frederick Fraser whose plantation was nearby in the same parish.[38] He pictured the approach to Sheldon rather romantically in a sketch of two horsemen crossing Horseshoe Bridge.[39] And nearer Sheldon House were some picturesque ruins (*Plate 26*) that Fraser apparently thought evocative and pictorial enough to include in his rendering of the house's setting. His treatment here may have been consciously in the mid-eighteenth-century, or earlier, English vein of featuring ruins in picturesque scenery, with overtones of the gothic mood that Dr. Garden intended at Otranto. Fraser's published sketch of Sheldon Church is well known, but what is not so well known are the ones that he made of Sheldon Church and Sheldon House from several different angles. The one of the church shows gothic windows (when the actual windows were rounded at the top), which further invites the point that he was more interested in a gothic mood of ruins in landscape than in merely recording that particular church.[40]

Two additional points can be made about the Fraser sketches. They illustrate that the several country seats surrounding Charleston comprised an identifiable genre of country house living of interest to a painter like himself sensitive to varied landscape settings, and that the owners generally appreciated a simplified, natural landscape. It is not surprising that his sensitivity to open landscape also impelled him to take an interest in gardening. On that subject, he once wrote (in 1845) that he preferred the word "Gardening" over "Horticulture," as "Gardening" was the word always used by the best English writers: "Swift, Addison, Cowley in his beautiful poem addressed to Mr. Evelyn, Sir William Temple, Horace Walpole and Cowper." He added: "Man longs, amidst the lines and angles, and the artificial ornaments of even a palace, to behold the unmeasured variety of nature."[41]

In an address at the dedication of the Magnolia Cemetery in 1851, a cemetery located on a plantation on Charleston Neck and appropriately named Magnolia Umbra,[42] he revealed also a sense of landscape that included the expressive or meditative, this time in the form of tombs, moss, and dark oak trees. His sketches reveal his taste for hilly and rolling land, but in this instance he was pleased chiefly with the stillness of tidal waters. "In a section of country not remarkable for any variety of scenery, or for any striking features of landscape beauty . . . greater undulation of surface would scarcely be desirable, it being already sufficiently varied to favor the meandering course of the water, which flows beneath yon moss-hung oaks, even to the limits of your enclosure."

University of South Carolina

~~~~~~
——————————————NOTES——————————————

1. David Ramsay, *Ramsay's History of South Carolina, from its First Settlement in 1670 to the Year 1808* (Newberry, S.C., 1858), II, pp. 127-130. For Mrs. Lamboll's garden, see Elise Pickney, *Thomas and Elizabeth Lamboll: Early Charleston Gardeners* (Charleston, S.C., 1969). Shecut wrote that Mrs. Lamboll laid out her flower and kitchen garden "upon the European plan" about 1750 and that it was the first of its kind in Charleston: J. L. E. W. Shecut, *Shecut's Medical and Philosophical Essays* (Charleston, S.C., 1819), p. 42. See also Martha Logan, *A Treatise on Gardening* (Charles Town, S.C., 1772).

2. For a recent survey of botanical gardening in South Carolina, see Richard Beale Davis, *Intellectual Life in the Colonial South, 1565-1763* (Knoxville, Tenn., 1978), III, pp. 1217-1220.

3. John Bartram, "Diary of a Journey through the Carolinas, Georgia, and Florida, from July 1, 1765, to April 1, 1766," *Transactions of the American Philosophical Society*, XXXIII, pt. 1 (December 1942), pp. 3, 21. Laurens's Charleston garden was in the area now bounded by Anson, Laurens, East Bay, and Society streets.

4. David Ramsay, *Ramsay's History*, p. 128.

5. *Ibid.*

6. See Hunter Dickinson Farish, ed., *Journal & Letters of Philip Vickers Fithian, 1773-1774: A Plantation Tutor of the Old Dominion* (Charlottesville, Va., 1957).

7. Philip M. Hamer et al., eds., *The Papers of Henry Laurens* (Columbia, S.C., 1968-   ).

8. *Ibid.*, V, p. 9.

9. For these gardens, see Blanche Henrey, *British Botanical and Horticultural Literature before 1800* (London, 1975), II, pp. 157, 158, 274, 640. For H. Laurens's interest in European gardens, see H. Laurens to James Laurens, Apr. 15, 1772, Hamer et al., eds., *Laurens Papers*, VIII, p. 271.

10. See Edmund and Dorothy Smith Berkeley, *Dr. Alexander Garden of Charles Town* (Chapel Hill, N.C., 1969), pp. 242ff.

11. Quoted in the *London Chronicle*, June 2, 1774; Alexander Garden to John Ellis, July 13, 1771, Hamer et al., eds., *Laurens Papers*, VII, pp. 553-554.

12. Foreword by J. Kirkland Moore (Athens, Ga., 1980).

13. *South Carolina Historical Magazine*, IX (January 1908) pp. 56-57; *ibid.*, XXIX (October 1928), p. 334. Robert Squibb also had a nursery on the east side of Meeting Street in the village of Romney. Emma B. Richardson, *Charleston Garden Plats* (Charleston, S.C., 1943), p. 13. His Charleston garden was on the south side of Tradd Street between present-day Legare and Lenwood.

14. Squibb, *Gardener's Calendar*, p. x.

15. Manigault Papers, South Caroliniana Library, University of South Carolina, Columbia, S.C.

16. Ramsay, *History*, II, p. 129; Charles Fraser, *Reminiscences of Charleston* (Charleston, S.C., 1854), p. 64.

17. *SCHM*, XXIX (January 1928), pp. 8-11; Marguerite Duval, *The King's Garden* (Charlottesville, Va., 1982), pp. 126-139; François, duc de la Rochefoucault-Liancourt, *Travels through the United States of North America, The Country of the Iroquois and Upper Canada, in the Years 1795, 1796, and 1797*, 2nd ed. (London, 1800), II, pp. 434-435. See also Richardson, *Charleston Garden Plats*, p. 24 and plate on p. 23; Henry Savage, Jr., *Lost Heritage* (New York, 1970), pp. 179-235; and David H. Rembert, Jr., "The Carolina Plants of André Michaux," *Castanea, The Journal of the Southern Appalachian Botanical Club*, XLIV (June 1979), pp. 65-80.

18. Alicia Hopton to John Laurens, June 17, 1771, William Gilmore Simms Collection of Laurens Papers, Kendall Whaling Museum, Sharon, Mass.

19. H. Laurens to J. Laurens, Nov. 6, 1771, Hamer et al., eds., *Laurens Papers*, VIII, p. 34.

20. Eliza Lucas to Miss Bartlett [ca. 1743] in Elise Pinckney, ed., *The Letterbook of Eliza Lucas Pinckney, 1739-1762* (Chapel Hill, N.C., 1972), p. 61.

21. Arthur Raleigh Humphreys, *William Shenstone; An Eighteenth-Century Portrait* (Cambridge, 1937), pp. 6, 86.

22. George C. Rogers, Jr., *The History of Georgetown County, South Carolina* (Columbia, S.C., 1970), pp. 257-259. William Shenstone wrote Gov. William Henry Lyttelton, Nov. 13, 1756, while the latter was in South Carolina, and described himself as occupied "as usual in the little embellishments of my Ferme ornée, from which, during the summer season, I derive much tranquil Amusement." Hennig Cohen, *The South Carolina Gazette, 1732-1775* (Columbia, S.C., 1953), p. 69.

23. Hamer et al., eds., *Laurens Papers*, VIII, p. 111. Laurens had purchased Mepkin plantation on June 5, 1762: *Ibid.*, III, p. 100.

24. Charles Fraser, *A Charleston Sketchbook, 1796-1806* (Charleston, S.C., 1940), nos. 35, 36, 37.

25. For a discussion of Otranto, see Berkeley and Berkeley, *Dr. Alexander Garden*, pp. 236-239.

26. Rochefoucauld-Liancourt, *Travels*, II, pp. 428-429.

27. Ralph Izard Collection, Robert Scott Small Library, College of Charleston, Charleston, S.C.

28. *Ibid.*

29. Rochefoucauld-Liancourt, *Travels*, II, pp. 435-438.

30. Dr. John Farquharson to Gabriel Manigault, June 24, 1789, Manigault Papers.

31. Drayton Hall is now a property of the National Trust.

32. Rochefoucauld-Liancourt, *Travels*, II, p. 438. Thirty years ago Hennig Cohen wrote: "The trend away from formalism encouraged by Shenstone was more appropriate to a region where parks could be made to utilize a natural body of water on one side and virgin forest on the other. Middleton Gardens, while still formal, used the natural setting; at Magnolia the departure from formalism was even greater": *South Carolina Gazette*, p. 67.

33. Fraser, *The Charleston Sketchbook*. It is conceivable that Fraser may have been influenced by the paintings of Salvator Rosa and Claude Lorrain. Joseph Allan Smith, who must have gained his enthusiasm for Italy by listening to Ralph Izard's accounts of his visit to Pompeii and Herculaneum in 1775, spent fifteen years in Europe and brought back a large

collection of art, including a number of copies of works by Rosa. George C. Rogers, Jr., "Preliminary Thoughts on Joseph Allan Smith as the United States' First Art Collector," in David Moltke-Hansen, ed., *Art in the Lives of South Carolinians: Nineteenth-Century Chapters* (Charleston, S.C., 1979), chap. 1. As for Lorrain, Fraser himself wrote a poem in praise of Claude Lorrain:

> and with classic grace
> Italia's scenes portray'd—the sombre arch,
> The consecrated grove—the slumbering lake,
> The azure mountains mingling with the sky
>
> *Charleston Sketchbook* (Charleston, S.C., 1845), p. 46.

34. See pages h, i, j, and n in Fraser's second sketchbook at the Charleston Museum, Charleston, S.C., and *Charleston Sketchbook*, nos. 32, 33, 34.

35. See pages p, r, s, t, and u in Fraser's second sketchbook and *Charleston Sketchbook*, nos. 7, 12.

36. Rochefoucault-Liancourt, *Travels*, II, pp. 435-436.

37. Page n in Fraser's second sketchbook.

38. Frederick Fraser (1762-1816) had married Mary DeSaussure and lived in Prince William parish. See *Charleston Sketchbook*, no. 8.

39. "Horseshoe Bridge" can be found in the sketchbook in the Cohen Deposit, Winthrop-Fraser Papers, South Carolina Historical Society, Charleston, S.C.

40. Page s in Fraser's second sketchbook. On the subject of picturesque gothic ruins, see John Dixon Hunt, "Emblem and Expressionism in the Eighteenth-Century Landscape Garden," *Eighteenth-Century Studies*, IV (Spring, 1971), pp. 294-317 and Edward Malins, *English Landscaping and Literature, 1660-1840* (London, 1966).

41. Fraser, "Gardening," *Charleston Sketchbook*, pp. 172, 176.

42. *SCHM*, XIX (January 1918), pp. 22-23.

Landscape Archaeology: A Key to Virginia's Cultivated Past

William M. Kelso

Not many would doubt the historical value of archaeology's more spectacular discoveries—the Rosetta Stone, Pompeii, Tutankhamen's Tomb, or Tikal have few skeptics. Even unearthing the more recent American past has gained respectability through such efforts as that of the National Park Service at Jamestown, Virginia, and currently through Colonial Williamsburg's discovery and interpretation of one of Virginia's early seventeenth-century Indian massacres. But the value of digging to discover the landscape designs of early American domestic estates, by comparison, might seem dubious. Even if it is possible to recover a landscape design through archaeology, how important can that be to historical inquiry or to historical preservation? Recent research in Virginia, however, not only proves the value of understanding the full setting of the estates, but also demonstrates how worthwhile and essential a part of the reconstruction process archaeology can be.

Virginia's plantation estates, like their British models, were a complete environment, house and setting, culture and nature usually playing complimentary architectural roles. But during the 1800s, after practically a full one hundred years of neglect in the tidewater and piedmont sections of Virginia, plantation "grounds" quickly disappeared, often, it seems, without trace. Consequently, restoration efforts of the first half of the twentieth century, as successful as they were in preserving the fabric of the grand mansions, were often forced to conjure up whatever landscaping seemed conveniently and attractively "colonial revival." Since then, re-planted boxwoods and other plants have grown into trees, in many cases obscuring the very houses, vistas, and contours the designs were originally intended to enhance. But who can blame the last generation's historical landscape architects? Historical record of the cultivated surroundings of most of the restored estates did not exist, and except for attempts to trace the more obvious architectural garden details like brick walkways and walls, little consideration was given to the potential of archaeological research.

Since the 1960s, fortunately, the methods of historical archaeology have become refined, and the process of recovering, reconstructing, and explaining the buried material remains of the American past has come of age. By applying the principle of natural soil stratigraphy—whereby earth and artifacts are uncovered and recorded carefully by separate layers in the order in which they were originally deposited—even fragile signs of long vanished wooden fences or planting beds can be dated and recorded. Archaeological detection of fences and gate locations begin to unravel the logic and design of the divided garden space within. By finding traces of walkways, planting beds, and terracing, archaeology can define the skeleton of original landscape schemes, literally laying out full-scale maps on the ground that have not survived in documents. And wherever historical plans do exist, the archaeological discoveries can clarify their meaning. That is precisely what archaeological research has been able to do at Carter's Grove and Kingsmill plantations near Williamsburg, Virginia, and more recently at Monticello, near Charlottesville.[1]

I   Carter's Grove

Located six miles southeast of Williamsburg on the James River, the Carter's Grove site, after a rather colorful period of occupation by early planters in the seventeenth century, was owned in the eighteenth century by Robert "King" Carter who purchased the 1,288 acres in the 1720s for his daughter. It was Carter's grandson, Carter Burwell, who inherited the property and after coming of age built the brick mansion house and probably its flanking dependencies by 1755. Carter Burwell died soon after, and his son and grandson managed and periodically lived on the property until it was sold in 1838.[2]

Virtually no maps and very few records of the plantation survive. Initially, it was decided that the area surrounding the original house and two flanking outbuildings, the "office" and "kitchen," would be hand-tested by digging two-foot-square test holes at ten-foot intervals, recording the soil layers, and defining concentrations of eighteenth-century artifacts. This had the advantage of disturbing as little as possible of the modern landscape in the immediate environs of the house, yet at the same time providing a glimpse of the subsurface. On the other hand, plowed fields surrounding the mansion site, already disturbed to a depth of as much as fifteen inches, could be tested with an earth grader every twenty feet to reveal any undisturbed archaeological remains below the plow zone. It was during the mechanical trenching that the archaeological evidence of the "lost" garden first came to light.

Removal of the plow zone in a test trench between the mansion and the river revealed a double line of dark soil stains in the subsoil with parallel narrow dark streaks[3] (*Plate 27*). It soon became obvious that these were holes dug to seat support posts for a fence or fences and for planting ditches. Subsequent excavation tracing the lines completely through four ninety degree turns clearly indicated that the fences enclosed a three-acre rectangular tract directly centered on the mansion and its three-tier advance terraces.

Remnants of cedar posts and darker brown soil stains suggested that the posts had been roughly cut logs from six inches to one foot in diameter—nothing very ornamental. Furthermore, since the lines of smaller holes intersected and, in some cases, disturbed the earlier fill in the line of larger holes, we concluded that there had been two garden fences in the eighteenth century, the one with the smaller posts being the later. Discoveries of artifacts such as tobacco pipes, pottery, and wine bottle glass inside the holes even helped us date the two fences: the first one from soon after 1740, and the second sometime after 1769, the date when English creamware of the type found in the later postholes was first imported to Virginia. Similarly, artifacts indicated that the first fence had disappeared sometime between about 1760-1780 and the second before about 1835. Although this process of discovery is slow, tedious, and expensive, it provides reliable evidence and is enormously helpful to the garden historian, for whom chronology is vital in defining a succession of garden styles and shapes.

Irregular spacing of the postholes also revealed where gates had been located, with excavation inside the fence lines confirming gate positions through discovery of sand or natural clay paths leading to them. Another important discovery was a central "alley" and other sand walkways just inside and along the fence lines or across the entire rectangular enclosure, all of which divided the lower two-thirds of the garden into intriguing planting beds seventy-five feet by one hundred. Excavation of one of the planting beds also showed that as much as two feet of subsoil had been originally excavated and replaced with humus. The same excavation failed to show similar beds at the south end of the enclosure, however, although an intermediate fence line was found contemporary with the second period fence line. We surmised from this that the southern end of the enclosure may have been relegated to livestock grazing or to some field crop, notwithstanding the incongruous visual effect such use would have had upon the garden scene.

One of the most attractive features of the gardens immediately south of the main house was the three-tiered terrace flanked on both sides by sharp slopes. We excavated a central "ramp" of sand, but no steps, down the terrace slope from the south lawn next to the house, as well as a six-foot-wide crushed oystershell "walk" up through the south lawn from the terraces to the house. Although we tested intermittently on the terraces and south lawn for stains remaining from any planting patterns, we found none.

Although there is a hint in the records that Carter's Grove had a decorative and functional garden in some form, the discovery of the formally laid out rectangular garden with its symmetrical planting beds, walkways, gates, ramp, and terraces became one of the most unexpected and pleasant surprises of the archaeological survey. As so often happens, too, the archaeological discoveries raised a different set of questions regarding the historical records; often what seemed like insignificant phrases read before the digging took on considerable new meaning afterward. Before the archaeology, for example, Nathaniel Burwell's purchase in 1765-1766 of "1500 Garden Pails" and "840 fence rails and 921 stakes" was only vaguely interpreted; later we realized this purchase comprised part of a major rebuilding of Carter Burwell's enormous garden fence line or "paling."[4] Seen in light of the 1,400-foot fences found archaeologically, it is clear that Burwell was rebuilding his father's garden enclosure; this confirmed the archaeological plan and chronology. Eight years after the discovery and reconstruction of the garden a map came to light containing a drawing (*Plate 28*) of the south front of Carter's Grove; it shows the ramp and an arrangement of plants on the terraces, very evident as late as 1881.

The reconstructed garden paling itself today makes a considerable impact on the south front. Not a fence in the modern sense, the wooden palings of the colonial period often appear to have been similar to fort stockades, 10-foot-high solid barriers quite capable of keeping the largest and most athletic animals like cattle and deer, and the smallest and more elusive creatures like groundhogs and rabbits, out of the cultivated areas. Certainly the huge postholes found at Carter's Grove are indicative of such massive height, and contemporary records consistently show that such imposing garden barriers were the norm both in England and America.[5]

Although our archaeology failed to find evidence of the kinds of plants growing at Carter's Grove in the eighteenth century—and the documents are equally mute—the following description of a "Mr. Pratts" garden near Philadelphia, written in 1800, fits so precisely the Carter's Grove garden plan found archaeologically that it could be interpreted as one, not improbable, version of Burwell's garden design:

> Saturday 19th . . . Mr. Pratts garden for beauty and elegance exceeds all that I ever saw—It is 20 rods long—and 18 wide An ally of 13 feet wide runs the length of the garden thro' the centre—Two others of 10 feet wide equally distant run parrallel with the main alley. These are intersected at right angles, by 4 other alleys of 8 feet wide—Another alley of 5 feet wide goes around the whole garden, leaving a border of 3 feet wide next to the pales—This lays the garden into 20 squares, each square has a border around it of 3 feet wide—Likewise the border of every square is decorated with pinks and a thousand other flowers, which is impossible for me to describe. The remaining part of each square, within the border, is planted with beans, pease, cabbage, onions, Betes, carrots, Parsnips, Lettuce, Radishes, Strawberries, cucumbers, Potatoes, and many other articles—Without the pales stand a row of trees upon three sides of the garden—These consist of Pear, Peach, apple, cherry, and mulberry trees. Within the pales, on the out border, are planted, Quince, snoball, Laylock, and various other small trees, producing the most beautiful flowers—
> The beauty, Taste, and elegance which attends it, is perfectly indescribable—
> It is an enchanting prospect, and carries the spectator, into an extacy, which he cannot describe—The effluvia arising from the various flowers—sweetens the air.[6]

II Kingsmill

Kingsmill plantation, Carter's Grove's neighbor to the west, was also a Burwell family James River estate. It was built for Lewis Burwell, Nathaniel Burwell's uncle, during the period 1728-1736. It is conceivable that

Nathaniel even went to live at Kingsmill when his father suddenly died in 1756, leaving him, in his minority, in his uncle's care. Naturally the question arises whether Lewis Burwell's landscaping design at Kingsmill in the 1730s and 1740s at all influenced his brother's and nephew's ideas at Carter's Grove. Until archaeology was carried out at Kingsmill in 1975, that question was unanswerable. All that remained of the buildings and gardens were two flanking outbuildings of brick and traces of three terraces between the site of the house and the river. A hint of an influence is evident in a sketch dating from 1781.[7] Thanks to archaeology, we now know that that influence was considerable.[8]

Soil stains at Kingsmill left from the major fencepost holes enclosing a three and one-half-acre rectangular space on the south front of the mansion site were quickly uncovered; as at Carter's Grove, gate locations defined by shorter spaces between posts signaled major crosspaths and a central alley delineating three areas of one hundred feet by one hundred sixty: the immediate front lawn and terraces with two sets of planting beds below. Repair and replacement posthole stains were also found along the fence line enclosing the lower planting beds, suggesting a relatively long life for the fence and therefore the garden. Excavations also determined that granite steps descending the terraces dated to the original eighteenth-century construction.

The two major brick dependencies already mentioned were not aligned wings of the mansion but were built at right angles to the north front of the house forming a forecourt. Excavations in this forecourt area unearthed something of a formal garden, a parterre defined by the remains of a serpentine walkway, central approach walk, fences, and planting hedges (*Plate 29*). Brick walks connected a central gate and the flanking outbuildings, but occasional concentrations of crushed shell indicated that the brickwork was only the foundation of a shell surface. Soil stains left from fence postholes were found conforming to the curvilinear course of the northern path, but supporting evidence suggested unmistakably that the original fenceposts were ornamental brick pillars in rather an extravagant style.[9]

As these and other details of the plan revealed themselves, it became evident that the aligned forecourt and garden on each front with work areas to the side were identical in many respects to the plan of the grounds found at the Governor's Palace in Williamsburg. The similarities of the two plans strongly suggest that Lewis Burwell drew much of his inspiration for the Kingsmill plan from what he saw at the Palace. Fortunately, what the Palace garden looked like is particularly well documented.

III Monticello

The landscape schemes of the Williamsburg area, especially of the Palace, were so familiar to the last governor to live there, Thomas Jefferson, that they may well have had an impact on his landscaping ideas at Monticello.[10] Recent archaeological and historical studies at Monticello are attempting to come to terms with the extent to which Jefferson was influenced by the landscape designs of the colonial Virginia-British estates of his time, and with the nature and degree of his originality as a garden designer. What makes this archaeological project particularly exciting is that the discoveries are actually being used to reconstruct Monticello's famous gardens.

Copious landscape plans for Monticello survive so that archaeology at first seemed an unnecessary luxury. Because most of the visual remains of the well-documented fences, planting squares, walls, orchards, and vineyards had disappeared, however, the Thomas Jefferson Memorial Foundation undertook archaeology. The results have proven archaeology to be invaluable not only for providing physical details for reconstruction but also for its ability to more clearly interpret Jefferson's notes and sketches.

Learning from our experiences at Carter's Grove and Kingsmill, we started the excavations at Monticello in 1979 by testing the gardens' major architectural features: fences, planting squares, and terraces (*Plate 30*). Guided by an insurance map of 1796, notes of 1806-1811, a plan of the property made in 1809, and two detailed orchard planting maps, the digging quickly showed that archaeological remnants of the major garden elements had survived.[11] The major problem became how best to study the enormous garden-orchard area, some eight acres in all, and how to "read" the soil, a natural red clay quite unlike the contrasting dark and light sandy loam of the Carter's Grove-Kingsmill area.

Obviously, concentration on such key features as the fence line limited the area to dig, and the tested area began to reveal clues. For example, we soon discovered that although it was extremely difficult to see postholes along the garden fence line, either remaining fragments of the locust posts or stones used to wedge the posts fast in the holes marked where the posts had been. Once a regular spacing pattern and alignment was detected, the relatively faint color and the textural differences of the soil stains could also be seen. In this manner, excavations uncovered over 850 feet of paling that Jefferson directed his man Watkins to build in 1808:

> His first work is to pale in the garden, with a paling 10. feet high. . . . they are to be of the size usual in strong garden paling. I do not know what that is. there will be 3. to each pannel and consequently 900. in all.
> The pales are to be of chestnut, riven, and strong; 5. f. 3. I long . . . I suppose they will be generally from 5. to 7. I. wide, and should be so near as not to let even a young hare in.[12]

Fence line excavations along Monticello's original south approach road known as Mulberry Row presented another set of problems. More than one set of fence postholes was found, along with a complex stratigraphy and artifacts associated with an adjacent series of Jefferson-period craft shops, servants' quarters, and utilitarian outbuilding sites (*Plate 31*). Although the Foundation's policy was to study and restore only those garden elements postdating 1809, the date after which the Monticello house reached its present form, it became impossible to understand the 1809 landscape without thoroughly excavating all soil levels and building sites, even those turning out to be part of an earlier period. In fact, one of the most significant results of the Monticello excavations has been the discovery that so much of what had been constructed during the first forty years of Jefferson's development was changed at the time of or soon after his retirement from the presidency in 1809. Of equal value has been the discovery of the complexity of the landscape schemes, including their inter-relatedness to the house and outbuildings.

Excavation along the southern wall line of the outbuildings along Mulberry Row made it clear that two major periods of fences dating to Jefferson's time once stood there. They were easily identified as earlier and later by determining their relative position in related soil strata and the dates of associated artifacts. But which of these represented the 1809 line that was so well described by Jefferson became of paramount importance for future reconstruction, particularly in light of the fact that gates, so significant to understanding divisions in the enclosed gardens, were in this case in different locations in each line. Surprisingly, it was the subsequent excavation of two Mulberry Row foundations described in 1796 as a "smokehouse and a dairy" and a "storehouse for nailrod and other iron" that proved to be the strongest evidence for dating the lines.[13] Once uncovered, the remains of the smokehouse/dairy and storehouse (*Plate 32*) proved that the earliest fence line used the south walls of the two adjacent structures as a part of the enclosure. The later line of fence postholes, on the other hand, ran continuously through the same area, even penetrating and therefore *postdating* the earth floor and life of the smokehouse/dairy. Consequently, "paling either touching or passing very near to each house . . . along Mulberry Row" described in the insurance plat of 1796 and the earliest fence line found archaeologically are likely identical.[14] By the same reasoning, it could be determined that the later fence line represented the remains of the 1809 paling. These seemingly inconsequential conclusions, in light of Jefferson's 1806-1811 notes on his garden layout and other archaeological evidence found later on the slope, will eventually allow an accurate reconstruction of the garden.

Jefferson's garden notes and sketches during 1806-1811 demonstrate that the garden laid out and planted after that period was considerably different from that which he had laid out earlier. This was chiefly the result of a new eighty by one thousand foot leveled platform south of and parallel to Mulberry Row. This enormous feature, laid out under the direction of the overseer Edmund Bacon between 1806-1809, established platforms on three southwest to northeast levels. It was achieved by cutting into the relatively gentle natural mountain slope and simultaneously moving the excavated dirt to the rear, behind a stone retaining wall. Although the slope leading down from the Mulberry Row level, just below the fence lines, had eroded considerably over the years, and the stone retaining wall was buried in the slope below, there was every reason to believe that once these and other key elements of the original platform garden plan could be revealed archaeologically, Jefferson's meticulous description of the location and cultivation of the border beds, planting beds, walkways, and even a decorative garden "pavilion" would permit reconstruction with an extraordinary degree of accuracy.

Excavations into the eroded Mulberry Row slope uncovered the original brick-lined edge of a northwest border bed, and analysis of the deposition of cultivated soil at other strategic points along the base of the slope defined the location and extent of the beds to the southwest. These features in turn isolated the northwestern extent of the platform garden layout, the original grade, and the exact center of the platform. To the southwest across the platform at the center, the location and probable nature of a "terras" between the "upper" (southwestern) and "middle" platforms was also uncovered. On the same line, farther to the southwest, the digging also uncovered a stone foundation connected to the remains of the stone retaining wall, a feature that, in light of some very precise building specifications noted by Jefferson in 1807 and 1810, proved to be the remains of a key element in his landscape scheme: "the Pavilion at the center of the long walk."[15] Jefferson intended to build this pavilion, which eventually became his garden retreat, out of brick and upon a foundation of "large stones to a sufficient depth," twelve feet, six inches square with "Tuscan" arches on all four sides and a "pyramidal roof" with a "Chinese railing." A visitor in 1827, the year after Jefferson died, described the structure as a "temple . . . which was a favourite spot with him to read and sit in"[16] (*Plate 33*). Excavations below and in front of the long garden wall revealed enough brick and stone in place to suggest that a stair leading down from the pavilion platform to the slope was once part of the pavilion plan as well.

When we turned our attention to the orchard/vineyard area southwest of the wall, we sought to confirm (if possible) the plans Jefferson carefully drew in 1778 and 1811. Hoping that the planting of orchard trees and their eventual decay would leave soil stains and that numerous terraces suggested in the records could be archaeologically detected, test trenches were made by backhoe to remove the regularly plowed depth of the soil. The last of five cuts revealed two- to three-foot diameter discolorations at twenty-five-foot intervals extending on a line northwest to southeast on the sunny southwest slope (*Plate 34*). Without doubt these were the tree holes. Another line of holes at a right angle to this line, with the holes at forty-foot intervals, clarified still further Jefferson's orchard planning. In all, fifty-seven stains or holes were seen to form a tree planting grid that conformed to both the 1778 and 1811 plans.[17] In his plans Jefferson specified what trees went into what holes, so that we are now in the process of replanting his orchard of two centuries ago with extraordinary precision. His vineyard, too, has unfolded to us through some rows of holes for vine-supporting stakes.

So from soil stains and surviving foundations, archaeology defined the enclosed garden at Monticello for reconstruction. But how did that space harmonize with the house, the Mulberry Row buildings, and the yards in between? Naturally the shapes and positions of the various craft structures and log slave houses must have comprised a major element of the landscape, although apparently not an attractive one. In 1809 Margaret Bayard Smith remarked on her visit to Monticello:

> Upon approaching the house on the first circuit road [Mulberry Row], we passed the outhouses of the slaves and workmen. They are all much better than I have seen on any other plantation, but to an eye unaccustomed to such sights, they appear poor and their cabins form a most unpleasant contrast with the palace that rises so near them.[18]

Aesthetically pleasing or not, excavations are proving that the rustic slave houses and workshops with their animal yards between them were a dominating feature of the south side of the mountain for at least forty years. We must remember that Jefferson, after all, used the long terraced garden and southwestern slopes for practical landscaping and gardening. In that context, the workshops and slave houses do not seem impossibly out of place. In any case, the ornamental grounds were up near the house and not unduly interfered with by the practical areas to the south, especially since a tall solid paling separated the two large areas.

Still, the creation of the platform and enclosed garden by 1809 marked the beginning of Jefferson's final landscape plan which, as the archaeology and documents suggest, spelled doom for most of the wooden structures along Mulberry Row. He apparently realized their negative visual effect, as Smith did; and perhaps Jefferson may have improved the slaves' quarters as an expression of concern for their well being generally. In any event, by the time the 1809 plat of the mountaintop was made, most of the seventeen wooden buildings identified on the insurance map of 1796 had gone.[19]

After the rehabilitation of Mulberry Row by the removal of the wooden buildings, it was not at all necessary to screen it from the house. Instead of a tall solid paling to hide it, then, Jefferson chose to construct a type of ha-ha to encircle and protect the formal west lawn, a type of barrier that left what must have become a more manicured version of Mulberry Row clearly in view.[20]

In 1823 a visitor remarked:

> As we approached the house we rode along a fence which was the only one of the kind I ever saw. Instead of being upright, it lay upon the ground across a ditch, the banks of the ditch raised the rails a foot or two above the ground on each side of the ditch, so that no kind of grazing animals could easily cross it, because their feet would slip between the rails. It had just the appearance of a common post and rail straight fence, blown down across a ditch.[21]

This was probably the ha-ha five hundred yards in length constructed and mentioned but not specifically located in the records in 1814.[22] The 1823 description, however, makes it clear that the barrier was along the approach road, that is, Mulberry Row. Accordingly, test trenches were made at right angles to and north of that road in the hope of intersecting any of the backfilled ditches. Stains representing ditch backfill were found

168

in each of three test trenches, and the subsequent excavation of the darker fill revealed a four foot wide, two foot, eight inches deep trench traced, at the time of this writing, over a distance of 612 feet. There is every reason to believe that this is what remained of the 1823 ha-ha even though the relatively narrow and shallow ditch appears to represent the remains of a very minor barrier, hardly capable of "keeping grazing animals" of any size or ambition off the formal west lawn. But the earth piled on each bank and the horizontal wooden fence could well have created a substantial cattle guard indeed.

As the Monticello excavations continue into other areas on the mountaintop, there is every reason to believe that other key landscape features like the course of original roads, decorative planting designs, other supportive craft buildings and servants' quarter sites, and probably other improvements now lost to the records will appear. Although many features of Jefferson's complex landscaping at Monticello may never be reconstructed, knowledge of their existence will add another dimension to his practical and architectural genius.

Thomas Jefferson Memorial Foundation, Charlottesville

NOTES

1. The author conducted the excavations of these sites as follows: exploratory excavations at Carter's Grove plantation directed by Ivor Noël Hume, on contract with the Colonial Williamsburg Foundation, 1970-1971; excavations at Kingsmill plantation under a grant from Anheuser-Busch, Inc., to the Virginia Historic Landmarks Commission, 1972-1975; and excavations at Monticello for the Thomas Jefferson Memorial Foundation with support from the National Endowment for the Humanities, 1979-1982.

2. The exploratory excavations at Carter's Grove discovered the first evidence of what Ivor Noël Hume's subsequent excavations have proven to be a fascinating and dramatic early seventeenth-century settlement there known as Martin's Hundred. Ivor Noël Hume, *Martin's Hundred* (New York, 1982). For the historical background to Carter's Grove, see Mary A. Stephenson, *Carter's Grove Plantation: A History* (Williamsburg, Va., 1964).

3. The archaeological description here and what follows is taken from William Kelso, "A Report on Exploratory Excavations at Carter's Grove Plantation, James City County, Virginia (June 1970-September 1971)," unpubl. report, Colonial Williamsburg Foundation, Williamsburg, Va.

4. Burwell Ledger 2, 1764-1776, June 1765, 1766, Research Department, CWF.

5. A description of the paling at Monticello discussed later in this article was used as a model for the reconstructed Carter's Grove fence. Another example of such a massive paling is in the birdseye view of Llanerch, Denbighshire, painted in 1662, now in the Mellon Collection, Yale University, New Haven, Conn.

6. Lewis Beebe, MS Journal, 1776-1801, Historical Society of Pennsylvania, Philadelphia.

7. Lt. Col. John Simcoe, "Rebels dislodged from Williamsburg Landing," 1781, Research Library, CWF.

8. For views of Kingsmill in 1972 and a summary of the archaeological excavation, see William M. Kelso, "An Interim Report on Historical Archaeology at Kingsmill, the 1975 Season," Virginia Research Center for Archaeology, Williamsburg.

9. This evidence includes a base of what was probably a brick pillar, fragments of carved Portland stone that possibly were part of a decorative urn, and a 1778 reference to "taking down pillers." Humphrey Harwood, Ledger B, fol. 10, Research Dept., CWF.

10. Jefferson often visited the neighboring plantations in the Williamsburg area, and legend has it that Rebecca Burwell refused his offer of marriage at Carter's Grove.

11. Frederick Doveton Nichols, *Thomas Jefferson's Architectural Drawings*, 4th ed. (Charlottesville, Va., 1978), nos. 133, 225, 127, 234. The 1806-1811 notes are in a private collection.

12. Edwin Morris Betts, ed., *Thomas Jefferson's Garden Book, 1766-1824* (Philadelphia, 1944), p. 377.

13. Nichols, *Jefferson's Architectural Drawings*, no. 133.

14. *Ibid.*

15. *Ibid.*, no. 182, p. 1.

16. *Ibid.*; Ralph D. Gray, ed., "A Tour of Virginia in 1827: Letters of Henry D. Gilpin to his Father," *Virginia Magazine of History and Biography*, LXXVI (October 1968), p. 467.

17. Nichols, *Jefferson's Architectural Drawings*, nos. 127, 234.

18. Margaret Bayard Smith, *The First Forty Years of Washington Society* (New York, 1906), p. 68.

19. Nichols, *Jefferson's Architectural Drawings*, no. 225.

20. Jefferson Memorandum, James Monroe Law Library, n.d., Jefferson Papers, Massachusetts Historical Society, Boston; Jefferson to Martha Jefferson Randolph, June 6, 1814, in Betts, ed., *Jefferson's Garden Book*, p. 533.

21. William Hooper, "Descriptive Visit to Monticello, September 20, 1823," Thomas Jefferson Memorial Foundation Library, Monticello.

22. Jefferson Memorandum.

The Temple in the Garden: Thomas Jefferson's Vision of the Monticello Landscape

William L. Beiswanger

Thomas Jefferson was twenty-five in 1768 when he began the development of Monticello, his mountaintop estate in the piedmont of Virginia. The improvement of the grounds, as well as the design, construction, and remodeling of his house, became a life-long preoccupation spanning more than fifty years. Had we been visitors to his aerie in 1809, we might have shared the wonder expressed by Margaret Bayard Smith when Jefferson told her of the improvements he planned—"the roads, the walks, the seats, the little temples"; they "seemed to require a whole life to carry into effect," she remarked.[1]

Mrs. Smith reminds us that most of Jefferson's ideas for garden embellishments were to remain only in his imagination. This was true of the more than twenty designs for garden structures known to us from surviving manuscript notes and drawings, for it is almost certain that only one was constructed—a pavilion that came to a ruinous end during Jefferson's lifetime and is now being re-created with the aid of the historian's research and the archaeologist's trowel. But the drawings and notes seem ample compensation for all that was unrealized or lost, for perhaps nowhere else in Jefferson's remarkable creative endeavors do we find such a wealth of ideas derived from architectural, historical, and literary sources.

The earliest record of his ideas for the improvement of the grounds is found in a three-page section of the pocket memorandum book that he kept for the year 1771.[2] The memoranda include an idea for a graveyard to be located in "some unfrequented vale in the park" and "among antient and venerable oaks" interspersed with plantings of "gloomy evergreens."

The scene was inspired partly by a passage which Jefferson then quoted from Nicholas Rowe's popular play, *The Fair Penitent*:

> No sound to break the silence, but a brook,
> That bubbling, winds among the weeds: no mark
> Of any shape had been there,

Unless a skeleton of some poor wretch,
Who had long since, like me by love undone
Sought that sad place out, to despair and die in.

Jefferson also transcribed this passage, as well as the key words, "unfrequented vale," from act 2, scene 1, into his literary commonplace book, his repository of poetic quotations.[3] There he also wrote, after "some poor wretch," the phrase, "who had long since, like me by love undone."

In this setting he proposed to create a labyrinth to enclose the area set aside for burials. In the notes he sketched two diagrams: the first showing the central area reached through a simple labyrinth with straight paths—not described in the text; the second showing a circular area of about sixty feet in diameter approached through a narrow spiral walk, four feet wide, lined with either an untrimmed hedge of cedar or, as an alternative, a hedge of holly on a low stone wall. The constricted path would have compelled us to walk alone and seems intended to prolong and dramatize the experience in the labyrinth, where thoughts might have turned to reflections on mortality. By way of a release from this melancholy scene, at the exit the view is directed on "a small and distant part of the blue mountains."

In the center of this enclosure would be erected a small gothic temple sheltering an altar of stone with sides of turf and illuminated only by "the feeble ray of an half extinguished lamp." The graves about the temple would be marked by various monuments including urns set upon pedestals and, over the resting place of "a favorite and faithful servant," a pyramid of rough stone. Jefferson noted that the temple should be gothic "of antique appearance," but we do not know if he had any specific example in mind.

A second woodland temple was planned at a mountainside spring north of the house. Again, Jefferson was specific about the setting:

> A few feet below the spring level the ground 40 or 60 f. sq. let the water fall from the spring in the upper level over a terrace in the form of a cascade. Then conduct it along the foot of the terrace to the western side of the level, where it may fall into a cistern under a temple, from which it may go off by the western border till it falls over another terrace at the Northern or lower side.[4]

Within sight of the temple and close to the spring would be placed "a sleeping figure reclined on a plain marble slab, surrounded with turf," and on the slab the pseudo-classical inscription long associated with grottoes:

> Huius nympha loci, sacri custodia fontis,
> Dormio, dum blandae sentio murmur aquae.
> Parcemeum, quisquis tangis cava marmora, somnum
> Rumpere, si bibas Sive lavere, tace.[5]

About the spring were to be planted beech and aspen trees with a vista opened to the millpond and Rivanna River below and, as the notes indicate, perhaps to the neighboring village below and to the west.

It was over the cistern that Jefferson intended to construct a two-story structure against the hillside with the ground floor room arched on the three exposed sides and an exterior stair leading up the back of the building to a second story chamber lighted by "spacious" windows in three of the walls. Each room was to be an eight-foot cube and the entire building was to be raised two feet above the cistern, which Jefferson said might serve as "a bath or anything else." A table and a few chairs would be the only furnishings and the sound of an Aeolian harp concealed under the building would complete the scene.

The unique feature of the temple design is the roof, which he noted may be "Chinese, Graecian, or in the taste of the Lanthern of Demosthenes," known today as the Choragic Monument of Lysicrates. The distinctive dome of the Lysicrates monument is covered with a fish-scale pattern and capped with a large finial in the form of an upright floral ornament.

With some certainty we can say that the source was the early and imperfect view in Jacob Spon's *Voyage d'Italie* (Amsterdam, 1679)—a work that he had in his library and cited when designing another garden structure in 1779.[6] Although Jefferson chose to model his temple only in part on that famous Greek structure, it is significant that he did so one year after the earliest known version of the building was constructed as a garden feature at Shugborough, Staffordshire, by James Stuart.[7]

The temple design was abandoned, however, after Jefferson reconsidered the problem of leveling the steep ground around the spring. He noted that a better idea would be a grotto formed in the hillside, with sides and arched ceiling of clay covered with moss and spangled with translucent pebbles and shells. The floor would also be paved with pebbles and the spring made to enter at a corner of the grotto high on the wall and to trickle down or fall from a spout into a basin. Jefferson noted that it would be more appropriate to place the sleeping figure in this cavern reclining on a couch of moss with the Latin inscription translated into English:

> Nymph of the grot, these sacred springs, I keep
> And to the murmur of these waters sleep;
> Ah! spare my slumbers! gently tread the cave!
> And drink in silence, or in silence lave!

Indeed, these ideas and sentiments are derived conceivably from Pope's description of his grotto at Twickenham, discussed by John Dixon Hunt in his essay elsewhere in this volume.[8] Jefferson owned the Warburton edition of Pope's *Works* and recommended it to his friend, Robert Skipwith, in a book list in 1771.[9]

The several ideas in the 1771 memoranda were never executed and in 1773 a simple square plot enclosed by a fence was instead established for the graveyard. Nevertheless, these conceptions are significant as some of the first expressions of mature ideas on landscape gardening recorded in America—ideas which were inspired by literary associations and probably influenced by several important works on the theory of landscape gardening, including William Shenstone's essay "Unconnected Thoughts on

Gardening" and Thomas Whately's *Observations on Modern Gardening* (1770). Shenstone's essay, to which was added "a Description of The Leasowes," his *ferme ornée,* was published in his collected *Works* (London, 1764), which were purchased by Jefferson in 1765.[10] We know that he consulted this work, for on the page following his memoranda on the improvement of the grounds he copied lines from Shenstone's verses in an exercise in English prosody.

Although he did not acquire Whately's influential *Observations on Modern Gardening* until 1778, Jefferson knew of the work by 1771—just one year after its publication—and recommended it in the book list he prepared for Skipwith. Jefferson thought so highly of the book that he obtained a second copy in Paris just before he toured some of the English gardens in 1786. He stated that while Whately's descriptions

> in point of style are models of perfect elegance and classical correct-
> ness, they are as remarkeable for their exactness. I always walked over
> the gardens with his book in my hand, examined with attention the
> particular spots he described, found them so justly characterised by
> him as to be easily recognised, and saw with wonder, that his fine
> imagination had never been able to seduce him from the truth.[11]

Apart from these works on theory it appears that during this early period Jefferson derived much of his inspiration for the landscape from literary associations. The poems of Ossian, which began to appear in 1760, were one important influence. Passages from *Fingal, an Ancient Epic Poem, by Ossian the Son of Fingal, Translated from the Gaelic* (1762) are found in Jefferson's literary bible on the page following the extract from Nicholas Rowe's *The Fair Penitent,* and lines from *Temora, an Ancient Epic Poem* (1763) appear in other sections of the book.[12] Jefferson shared the belief of most of his contemporaries that these works were a translation by James Macpherson of the epic poems of a third-century Celtic bard. The poems enjoyed a sensational popularity, not only in Great Britain but also on the Continent. They stirred readers' emotions with scenes of terror, gloom, obscurity, and infinity. It would be making too much of the influence of Ossian were it not that Jefferson acknowledged his admiration for the work and that it reveals a side of his personality that was receptive to sentimental and fantastic ideas fostered by literary associations. In 1773 he wrote to Charles McPherson of Edinburgh hoping to obtain directly from his relative, James Macpherson, transcriptions of the poems in the original Gaelic. He, like most of the world, was unaware that James Macpherson was the author of the poems. In the letter he confessed,

> These peices have been, and will I think during my life continue to be
> to me, the source of daily and exalted pleasure. The tender, and the
> sublime emotions of the mind were never before so finely wrought up
> by human hand. I am not ashamed to own that I think this rude bard
> of the North the greatest Poet that has ever existed.[13]

The 1771 memoranda also suggest that Jefferson associated life at Monticello with the rural life of the ancients as celebrated in the writings of Cicero, Horace, and Pliny the Younger. He chose as an inscription in Latin, intended for a stone or metal plate fastened to a tree near the grotto, selected lines from Horace's famed second epode (here translated):

> Blessed is he—remote, as were the mortals
>   Of the first age, from business and its cares—
> Who ploughs paternal fields with his own oxen
>   Free from the bonds of credit or of debt
> His life escapes from the contentious forum,
>   And shuns the insolent thresholds of the great
> Free to recline, now under aged ilex,
>   Now in frank sunshine on the matted grass,
> While through the steep banks slip the gliding waters,
>   And birds are plaintive in the forest glens,
> And limpid fountains, with a drowsy tinkle,
>   Invite the light wings of the noonday sleep.[14]

Apparently Jefferson's enthusiasm for his ideas reached his friends. A Mrs. Drummond residing near Williamsburg, Virginia, responded:

> Let me recolect Your discription, which bars all the Romantic, Poetical, ones I ever read . . . No pen but Yrs., cou'd, (surely so butiful discribe) espeshally, those few lines, in the Miltonic Stile. Thou wonderful Young Man, so piously entertaining, thro out that, exalted Letter. Indeed I shal' think, Spirits of an higher order, inhabits Yr. Aerey Mountains,—or rather Mountain, which I may contemplate, but never can aspire too.[15]

It is unfortunate that Jefferson's letter to Mrs. Drummond is lost, but the celebration of rural pleasures is very much evident in the August 1771 letter to Robert Skipwith. He concluded:

> But whence the necessity of this collection? Come to the new Rowanty, from which you may reach your hand to a library formed on a more extensive plan. Separated from each other but a few paces, the possessions of each would be open to the other. A spring, centrically situated, might be the scene of every evening's joy. There we should talk over the lessons of the day, or lose them in Musick, Chess, or the merriments of our family companions. The heart thus lightened, our pillows would be soft, and health and long life would attend the happy scene.[16]

During the period before his departure for Europe on a diplomatic mission in 1784, Jefferson continued to familiarize himself with the principles of classical architecture and the rules for proportioning the architectural orders. This particular interest in the orders is evident in several studies for an observation tower for the mountain that adjoins and rises about four hundred feet above Monticello (*Plate 35*). Jefferson called the mountain Montalto, and although title to the land was recorded in 1777, his interest in the site, at least for its visual effect, is known to date from 1771 when he noted in his memorandum book for March 24 that he was to receive from Edward Carter as payment for legal services "as much of his nearest mountain as can be seen from mine, and 100 yds beyond the line of sight."[17]

The first of these study drawings was for a tower exhibiting in each of the five stories a different example of the Roman orders.[18] The notes on the verso explain that the tower was to be one hundred feet high, the walls constructed of stone, and a window framed at each level in both the front and back walls, but those windows in the front "so much lowest as to direct the line of sight to Monticello." The orientation of the broad side toward Monticello as well as the fact that the columns and entablatures were to appear only on the "front" and the profiles cut merely out of plank indicates that Jefferson was interested primarily in viewing the structure in silhouette from the vantage point of Monticello. The tower therefore would have functioned as a "sham" or eye-catcher such as had been common in English landscape gardens for most of the century.

Jefferson subsequently altered the design of this tower (*Plate 36*)[19] to bring it into line with classical principles and changed the uppermost story to conform to a design of an octagonal cupola in James Gibbs's *Book of Architecture* (London, 1728), plate 31, figure 2. He acquired Gibbs's work in December 1778;[20] although he may have had access to a copy before that time, it is likely that these two studies date after the purchase.

Further revisions in the specifications were noted, but he concluded with the remarkable proposal:

> A Column will be preferable to any thing else. It should be 200 f. high, and have a hollow of 5.f. in the center for stairs to run up. On the top of the capital a ballustrading.[21]

The column would have towered more than six hundred feet above Monticello and nearly twelve hundred feet above the valley below. This was also a common feature in the English landscape garden such as the "Column of British Liberty" at Gibside, in Durham, dating from the mid-eighteenth century (140 feet high); the column designed by Capability Brown for William Pitt in 1765 at Burton Pynsent, in Somerset;[22] and, of course, the octagonal column at Stowe (115 feet high) "intended by Lord Cobham as a prospect tower from which to survey the landscape achievements of a lifetime."[23] Jefferson and John Adams visited Stowe on their tour of English gardens in 1786. Adams recorded in his diary, "I mounted Ld. Cobhams Pillar, 120 feet high, with pleasure, as his Lordships Name was familiar to me, from Popes Works."[24] Although Jefferson does not mention Cobham's column in his own account, one suspects that he joined Adams in mounting the circular staircase to take in the commanding view of several counties and, if so, perhaps reflected on what might have been had he carried out his own visionary idea.

Two other drawings for the Montalto observatory have survived.[25] The specifications for one of them indicate that the tower (*Plate 37*), excluding the crowning battlemented parapet, was to be 120 feet high and constructed in four stories, each a cube (excluding the extra height of parapets) diminishing in size toward the top. The single room in this massive structure would be in the top story and measure ten feet by fifteen, lighted by three windows and heated by a fireplace. This chamber was to be raised "4 feet above that of its gallery" and vaulted to support two feet of earth—the purpose of which is never explained.

Jefferson's design has been acclaimed "as an amazingly daring excercise combining scientific and visual functions at once, in order to escape from historicism, and expecially from traditional Georgian trimmings, into the realm of abstract geometrical forms."[26] Whether Jefferson's design was a conscious attempt to express abstract geometric form or, on the other hand, was conceived principally as a structural solution for a tall building probably will never be known. It is important to recognize, however, that if Jefferson was moving toward "abstract cubism" in his studies for an observatory in the late 1770s, it is equally true that "abstract cubism" is not an important consideration in any of his later designs for garden structures—even after his opportunity to study French examples during the period 1784-1789.

With few exceptions one can turn to the books on architecture in Jefferson's library to discover a source for each of his ideas for garden structures. In many cases he copied the designs, only simplifying them when a change of scale was necessary or the construction was too involved. His drawing of a domed temple (*Plate 38*) was based directly on Lord Burlington's pavilion at Chiswick illustrated in William Kent's *Designs of Inigo Jones* (1727), which Jefferson purchased in Williamsburg in December 1778.[27] The ink drawing exhibits some of Jefferson's finest draftsmanship and shows by a composite both the interior space and exterior form. Notes on the verso identify the design as a study for the remodeling of the south pavilion, which was constructed in 1770 and was eventually to terminate the promenade connected to the south wing of the house. The dome was to be adapted to the existing square plan and the details drawn not only from Kent's work but also from Palladio's *Quattro Libri dell'Architettura*, Gibbs's *Rules for Drawing the Several Parts of Architecture*, *The Builder's Dictionary* (1734), and Spon's *Voyage d'Italie*.[28] In a note at the end of the specifications dated April 23, 1779, Jefferson decided that it would be better to retain the pavilion "on the old plan" and suggested:

> Build such a temple as that in Jones pl. 73 on the point of land between the meadow and intended fish pond in the park.[29]

An important early example of what appears to be an imaginative adaptation of a published design is Jefferson's drawing of a garden temple and dovecote, dating from about 1779 (*Plate 39*), perhaps related to the improvements for Monticello planned in the spring of that year.[30] The design may have been based on a small pavilion published in James Gibbs's *Book of Architecture*, plate 77 *(Plate 40)*. It was within the roof that Jefferson planned the dovecote with access holes in the frieze, and on the verso of the drawing he gave the proportions of the entablature and roof, carefully basing it on the module of Palladio's Tuscan order. He broke from Palladio's proportions in one instance, however, and increased the projection of the abacus to prevent rats from threatening the doves' habitation. The reference to a north-south orientation suggests that Jefferson had considered the axis of the temple in relation to a given site, but the location is not known.

If it is true that Jefferson's design is a reworking of Gibbs's idea, then it suggests that Jefferson was reacting to neo-Palladianism and moving toward an expression of purer classical design that goes well beyond the simplification of neo-Palladian forms. In some ways Jefferson's design is truer to the stepped roof forms of antiquity such as the representations suggested by scholars for the Lion Tomb at Cnidus and the Mausoleum at Halicarnassus that Jefferson undoubtedly knew from another of Jacob Spon's imperfect views.

Despite the disruptions of the Revolutionary War, Jefferson continued with the construction of his house and his plans for the improvement of the grounds. In 1778 he acquired two important books on English landscape gardening that may have inspired some of his ideas from this period: Thomas Whately's *Observations on Modern Gardening*, which he had long wanted, and George Mason's *Essay on Design in Gardening* (London, 1768). This second book seems to have been written principally to supplement Shenstone's "Unconnected Thoughts on Gardening" but was overshadowed by Whately's more comprehensive treatise that appeared two years later. Nevertheless, one cannot help but think that Jefferson responded warmly to Mason's comment:

> In this country [England] the spirit of liberty extends itself to the very fancies of individuals: independency has been as strongly asserted in matters of taste, as in religion and government. . . . Yet to this whimsical exercise of caprice the modern improvements in gardening may chiefly be attributed.[31]

The war had severely curtailed the book trade, so when Jefferson heard that copies of these works were available from the library of Samuel Henley, who left Williamsburg for England at the outbreak of the Revolution, he made special arrangements to acquire them with the persistence of a true book collector.[32] Henley, who has been described as one of the new men of the Enlightenment, came to Virginia in 1770 and lectured at the College of William and Mary on ethics and the laws of nature and nations as well as on "elementary ideas of poetry." He had corresponded with William Gilpin—a central figure in any discussion of the picturesque—on the nature of the picturesque in Virgil and Milton.[33] Jefferson knew Henley, who was a near contemporary, and it is conceivable that Henley was partly responsible for the "furor hortensis" at Monticello.

Perhaps the one person in Virginia who, from firsthand experience, could have best informed Jefferson on the art of landscape gardening was Lord Botetourt, who arrived in Williamsburg in October 1768 as the newly appointed governor of the colony. Lord Botetourt had taken a personal interest in the improvements of his English estate, Stoke Gifford, near Bristol. At this dramatic site overlooking the vale of Berkeley, Thomas Wright, noted for his landscape designs and garden embellishments, began work about 1749 and contributed to the improvement and maintenance of the park and buildings until the early 1780s.[34] In his *Essay on Design in Gardening*, Mason mentioned that the woods at Stoke were among the "juster models of artificial disposition,"[35] and in his second edition (London, 1795) he elaborated:

> The management of them gave me, more than anything I had seen, an
> idea of what might be done by the internal arrangement of a wood.[36]

Wright's achievement at Stoke has been called "a perfect integration of landscape and architecture."[37] With his experience at Stoke Gifford, Botetourt would have been a reasonable person for Jefferson to seek out regarding landscaping. Disappointingly, however, there is no indication that Jefferson was on the same intimate terms with Lord Botetourt that he had been with Governor Francis Fauquier and his intellectual circle, or that his dealings with him were anything more than what one would expect between a governor and a burgess.

It should perhaps not go unnoticed that in October 1769 Jefferson entrusted his friend James Ogilvie with the task of obtaining estimates for executing the columns, entablatures, and other molded work for Monticello in stone from two builders in England. One was Thomas Paty in Bristol who is known to have worked at Stoke Gifford and whose name does not seem otherwise to appear in the records of transactions between the colony and England.[38] Did Jefferson single Thomas Paty out and did he do it at the recommendation of Botetourt?

The most novel of Jefferson's ideas for garden structures were those planned in conjunction with the house. By the fall of 1772 he had begun to envision a plan that would combine the dependencies directly relating to the main house in two L-shaped wings attached to the cellars.[39] By constructing the wings in the slope that falls off on both sides of the house, Jefferson would be able to have level access to the rooms on the outer section of the "L" while preserving an almost uninterrupted view of the mountaintop from the garden front rooms of the dwelling. The scheme was unique in American building and recalls some of Palladio's designs for villas but with the important distinction that Jefferson's scheme provides access to the dependencies, not from a courtyard, but from outside the wings. The flat roofs would become promenades that would appear as extensions of the main floor of the dwelling, and from these terraces there would be fine views of the gardens, the plains below, and the mountains beyond (*Plates 41 and 42*). Jefferson's concept of the promenade parallels the suggestion made by Lord Kames for an artificial walk elevated high above the plain—a walk that would be airy, extend and vary the prospect, and elevate the mind. Kames published his idea in the essay "Gardening and Architecture" in his *Elements of Criticism* (Edinburgh, 1762)—another work that Jefferson recommended to Robert Skipwith in 1771.

At each end of the promenades Jefferson planned to construct a two-story pavilion entered from the terrace level through a Tuscan portico. In the angles of the terraces he proposed to build matching temples. No fewer than five designs for these temples were considered between the time the dependencies were first planned and their construction after 1800. Most of the designs date from the period preceding Jefferson's departure for Europe in 1784.

The earliest idea was to build a nearly exact copy of the Chinese *Ting* illustrated in William Chambers's *Designs of Chinese Buildings* (plate VI, figure 2).[40] Chambers claimed that he had taken his design from a building that stood in the middle of a small lake in a garden at Canton and chose it as a particularly fine model of the type of *Ting* found in gardens. His description, which suggests a parallel between elements of Chinese form and Palladio's architectural orders, must have appealed to Jefferson, who was then well immersed in the intricacies of proportions in classical architecture.[41] But Jefferson concluded his page of notes on the design with the thought, "I think I shall prefer to these Chinese temples, 2. regular Tuscan ones, of the height of the Outchamber . . . or perhaps, to both the Monoptery in Vitruv."[42] The choice of the monopteros may have been prompted by Chambers's observation that the plans of certain Chinese structures were similar to the monopteral temple form,[43] although the ultimate source of the idea came from plates 34 and 35 in Claude Perrault's *Architecture de Vitruve*.[44]

The last idea considered before his departure for Europe was a scheme for octagonal structures, shown on the drawing of the terrace level (*Plate 42*). Unlike the earlier designs, these temples were to be enclosed. The roofs were to be in the form of domes similar in proportion and detail to the house and garden temple at Chiswick illustrated in Kent's *Designs of Inigo Jones*. The walls were to be of brick twelve feet high. The architectural order for the interior of the north octagon was to be Ionic with modillions from Palladio (Book I, plates 18-22). Each building would have a fireplace with the flue to "issue at the sides of the octagon, about half way up, and have an iron flue of two or three feet to deliver the smoke that far from the wall."[45]

The visual effect of the juxtaposition of the temples with the mass of the house—to say nothing of his plan (later abandoned) to construct a number of obelisks twenty-two and one-half feet high on the terraces to convey smoke from the fireplaces in the rooms below—certainly was unique in American design and seems clearly a product of his imagination.[46]

By 1784 when Jefferson departed for Europe, his ideas on landscape gardening were well established and were surprisingly little altered in suceeding years. His celebrated tour of English gardens with John Adams in 1786 broadened the theoretical base of his ideas and provided the opportunity for critical study of landscape effects described in Whately's book. Although to point out all that Jefferson saw or even what is known to have pleased him is beyond the scope of this essay, several comments on what he observed are pertinent. Certainly the structures that he saw in the gardens in the English landscape style on the Continent should not be considered any less important an influence on Jefferson than English examples. Designs of the "fantastic" and "sentimental" such as the hermitage at Wilhelmsbad, Hanau, Germany, where he saw "A good figure of a hermit in plaister, coloured to the life, with a table and book before him, in the attitude of reading and contemplation" genuinely impressed him despite Whately's criticism of such theatrical effects.[47] In the same park, a sentry box, "Covered over with bark, so as to look exactly like the trunk of an old tree," was considered "a good idea" which "may be of much avail in a garden."[48] Certainly the Column House at le Desert de Retz, the country estate of M. de Monville, is known to have excited his imagination. This structure, in the form of a broken fluted column, was four stories high with oval rooms arranged around a central spiral staircase. Jefferson wrote in his famous "Head and Heart" dialogue: "How grand the idea excited by the remains of such a column! The spiral staircase too was beautiful."[49] Fantasies such as these were published in numerous pattern books during the last half of the eighteenth century. Several of these appear in Jefferson's want list of books made up before departing for Europe: "Halfpenny's Geometrical paling & Chinese Lattice," "Decker's Chinese & Gothic Architecture," "Halfpenny's Chinese & Gothic Architecture," and "Halfpenny's Gothic Temples."[50] Added to these was a search for Father Attiret's "Account of the Emperor of China's Gardens near Pekin," published in Robert Dodsley's edition of *Fugitive Pieces* (London, 1765). Except for *Fugitive Pieces*, there is no record that any of these works was acquired and it is not known whether Jefferson knew of them only from publisher's lists or other references, or whether he had actually seen copies.

Jefferson also admired the Roman monuments in the south of France like those at St. Rémy and the Maison Carrée, which he called "the most precious the most perfect model of antient architecture remaining on earth; one which has received the approbation of near 2000 years."[51] These were to appeal to Jefferson's strong antiquarian interests and were later to play a major part in his scheme for embellishing the grounds at Monticello.

Jefferson returned to America in 1789 and for nearly twenty years remained almost constantly in public life. The affairs of state, the operation of his plantations, and the extensive remodeling of his house led to further postponement of landscape improvements. In 1806, near the close of his presidency, he wrote to William Hamilton of Philadelphia:

> Having decisively made up my mind for retirement at the end of my present term, my views and attentions are all turned homeward. I have hitherto been engaged in my buildings which will be finished in the course of the present year. The improvement of my grounds has been reserved for my occupation on my return home.[52]

The landscape that he had envisioned was a *ferme ornée* where the "attributes of a garden" would be interspersed among the "articles of husbandry" associated with a plantation.[53] His notes and drawings have been studied at Monticello with a view to re-creating, at least on paper, his plan for this complex landscape. The result at this stage of research is the site plan (*Plate 43*). The house is at the center of a leveled area of elliptical shape beyond which the ground gradually slopes down to a road called a roundabout which circumscribes the mountaintop and measures almost exactly one-half mile in length. The lawns, flower garden, shrubbery, and the more ornamental planting of clumps of trees are within this area. Progressively lower on the hillside are three other roundabouts connected by oblique roads, some of which are designated "1 in 10" or "1 in 20"—references to the rate of descent. On each side of the roundabouts Jefferson intended to distribute the features of his *ferme ornée*, showing, in effect, how areas for hogs, chickens, and cows could coexist with the more refined aspects of the landscape. From the roads these features would appear as a series of episodes, artfully arranged. To the southeast, benefiting from that exposure, is the vegetable garden plateau laid out on an heroic scale and, below that, the principal orchard and vineyards. A second orchard, blooming slightly later, is shown on the north slope, and a grove of about eighteen acres on the steep and generally rocky western slope. Below the fourth or lowest roundabout are the parks (including the deer park), the woodlands that occupy the sections to the northwest and southwest, and (off to the northeast and east) the cultivated fields.

Many of Jefferson's ambitious ideas for the grounds were not realized. Among them was a proposal, recorded in a memorandum headed "General ideas for the improvement of Monticello," to tap a spring located high on Montalto and bring the water by cascade to the base of the mountain where it would be conveyed by pipes up the Monticello slope to small ponds located on the lawn near the west front of the house.[54] The cascade was to be visible from Monticello through a vista. Another scheme was to construct a bridge over the main road where Montalto and Monticello meet so as to join the two pleasure grounds without the interruption of public traffic.

One senses that wherever possible Jefferson exploited function for aesthetic purposes. An example of this is the area between the second and third roundabouts where he intended to establish grass and clover patches (some of which were to be experimental) to supply fodder for the animals; it also seems to serve very well as a glade between the grove and the "timber zone."[55]

Jefferson's general approach to designing landscapes was expressed succinctly in the letter to William Hamilton in which he theorized about an American equivalent of the English landscape grounds. Although he acknowledged that it is to England "without doubt we are to go for models in this art," he made this distinction:

> Their sunless climate has permitted them to adopt what is certainly a beauty of the very first order in landscape. Their canvas is of open ground, variegated with clumps of trees distributed with taste. They need no more of wood than will serve to embrace a lawn or a glade. But under the beaming, constant and almost vertical sun of Virginia, shade is our Elysium. In the absence of this no beauty of the eye can be enjoyed. This organ must yield it's gratification to that of the other senses; without the hope of any equivalent to the beauty relinquished. The only substitute I have been able to imagine is this. Let your ground be covered with trees of the loftiest stature. Trim up their bodies as high as the constitution and form of the tree will bear, but so as that their tops shall still unite and yield dense shade. A wood so open below will have nearly the appearance of open grounds. Then, when in the open ground you would plant a clump of trees, place a thicket of shrubs presenting a hemisphere the crown of which shall distinctly show itself under the branches of the trees. This may be effected by a due selection and arrangement of the shrubs, and will I think offer a group not much inferior to that of trees.[56]

In the spirit of this landscape, Jefferson planned an entirely new set of garden buildings. In the notes, "General ideas for the improvement of Monticello," he proposed to construct a model of the Lantern of Demosthenes "at the Point"—perhaps the site where in the 1770s he planned a waterfall and a version of the domed temple at Chiswick. He also revived the idea of constructing a temple at each angle of the promenades. Once again he changed his mind, ruling out the octagonal structures—a decision perhaps motivated by his firsthand observations at Chiswick, where he criticized the dome of the main house for its "ill effect, both within and without."[57] He chose, instead, the Chinese pavilion that he had seen in the Menagerie at Kew Gardens in 1786 and knew from illustrations in his copy of Chambers's lavish folio, *Plans, Elevations, Sections, and Perspective Views of the Gardens and Buildings at Kew* (London, 1763).

There is also an intriguing reference to "a turning Tuscan temple 10.f. diam. 6. columns. proportions of Pantheon" to be built "at the Rocks" (an unidentified location).[58] For this, Jefferson may well have turned to the plate of the Temple of Eolus in the volume on Kew Gardens, where Chambers explains what was meant by "turning":

> On an eminence, stands the Temple of Eolus . . . within the columns is a large semicircular nich, serving as a seat, which revolves on a pivot, and may with great ease be turned by one hand to any exposition, notwithstanding its size.[59]

An idea that recalls the graveyard scheme from 1771 is a spiral labyrinth, shown in a sketch with a garden pavilion or seat in the center. Jefferson suggested that the labyrinth be planted with a variety of shrubs to form a thicket with the tallest shrubs in the center. He may have had this spiral configuration in mind when he added the note several lines later:

> The Broom wilderness on the South side to be improved for winter walking or riding, conducting a variety of roads through it, forming chambers with seats, well sheltered from winds, and spread before the sun. A temple with yellow glass panes would suite these, as it would give the illusion of sunshine in cloudy weather.[60]

A more ambitious proposal was to construct four small pavilions, each exhibiting a different style of architecture, along the southeast walk of his vegetable garden. He planned to shade the long walk, which overlooks the orchard and vineyards, with an arbor covered principally with grape vines but with the sides "quite open." The four temples, called "boxes," were to be spaced regularly along the outer edge of the path and form alcoves where one could retire from the hot sun. Jefferson's idea resembled what he saw at Stowe where two recesses terminated a long, straight terrace walk overlooking the countryside. He noted that the two recesses were "like the bastion of a fort" and that

> In one of these is the temple of Friendship, in the other the temple of Venus. They are seen the one from the other, the line of sight passing, not thro' the garden, but through the country parallel to the line of the garden. This has a good effect.[61]

Some of the most interesting designs for Jefferson's garden terrace were taken from Friedrich Meinert's *Die Schöne Landbaukunst* (Leipzig, 1798) which Jefferson purchased in 1805. With the exception of a structure in the gothic style, the three other garden buildings cited in the notes are related in style to designs identified with the visionary architects Ledoux and Boulée in France and Friedrich Gilly in Germany (*Plate 44*).

Other structures he considered for the garden plateau were models of the Pantheon in Rome, a model of cubic architecture—possibly the Maison Carrée at Nîmes which Jefferson regarded as the finest example of cubic architecture—and a specimen of Chinese architecture. No sources were cited for the last two, however, and the notes conclude with the thought,

> But after all, the kitchen garden is not the place for ornaments of this kind. Bowers and treillages suite that better, and these temples will be better disposed in the pleasure grounds.[62]

Specifications for those temples that he had decided to build are recorded in a later memorandum.[63] With the exception of a gothic structure, none of the three other designs from Meinert was considered. Instead, Jefferson decided to build models of some of the classical structures he most admired: the Maison Carrée, the Choragic Monument of Lysicrates, and the Pantheon. The "model" of the Maison Carrée was to measure twelve feet long, nine feet wide, and nine feet high and require six thousand bricks to construct. The Pantheon, or "Rotunda" (the term he used after lining our Pantheon), was to be fourteen feet in diameter and ten feet, six inches high to the top of the wall. It would require sixty-five hundred bricks. He also wanted an example of Chinese architecture, but a source was not cited and bricks were not requested. Meinert's gothic structure was still considered for a "Gothick model" to be constructed in stone at the graveyard, with detailing based on examples from other works as well.[64]

The location of these structures was not specified by Jefferson except for the gothic temple at the graveyard. Although he noted that bricks had been ordered for four of the buildings, the only temple we know that he constructed was not among these designs. In 1812 he entered in a workman's account a payment for "laying 7000 bricks in temple."[65] This was undoubtedly the temple that was constructed on the high central section of the massive stone wall which retained the one thousand-foot-long vegetable garden plateau. From Jefferson's specifications it is known that the structure was brick, twelve feet, six inches square, with an arch in each wall enclosed with sash (two operating sash below the impost and a fixed light above), and a roof of pyramidal shape concealed by a Chinese railing.[66] The order for the building was Palladio's Tuscan. Unhappily, the pavilion had collapsed by 1827, which recent archaeology suggests was owing to a poorly laid foundation on fill and perhaps to its precarious location at the outer edge of the wall; but a visitor who was taken to the site in that year was told that it had been a favorite spot for Jefferson to read and sit.[67] From this retreat Jefferson could have surveyed the orchard and vineyards below and the mountains and plains beyond. The panorama of about 180 degrees took in what is called his "sea view." The temple is now being reconstructed based on the evidence found by William Kelso, who elsewhere in this volume describes his archaeological work, and on Jefferson's detailed specifications.

When Margaret Bayard Smith visited Monticello in 1809, she found that Jefferson's enthusiasm for his ideas to embellish the grounds had not diminished. She recorded in her diary:

> Mr. J. explained to me all his plans for improvement, where the roads, the walks, the seats, the little temples were to be placed. There are two springs gushing from the mountain side; he took me to one which might be made very picturesque. As we passed the graveyard, which is about half way down the mountain, in a sequestered spot, he told me he there meant to place a small gothic building,—higher up, where a beautiful little mound was covered with a grove of trees, he meant to place a monument to his friend Wythe . . . I looked on him with wonder as I heard him describe the improvements he designed in his grounds, they seemed to require a whole life to carry into effect, and a young man might doubt of ever completing or enjoying them.[68]

There are some general observations that can be made about what these designs, spanning nearly half a century, tell us regarding the development of Jefferson's thinking about architecture and garden art. Literary and romantic associations inspired much of Jefferson's early ideas, but an important parallel interest were designs that could be called historically and archaeologically accurate. Clearly this antiquarian interest is evident in the measures he took to copy faithfully (at least on paper) the Chinese *Ting* from Chambers's *Chinese Designs*, which he must have accepted as an accurate example of Chinese architecture. The choice of Perrault's monopteros must have been influenced also by a belief that it was the most accurate reconstruction of that temple form based on Vitruvius's text. But by 1800 there is a noticeable emphasis on structures as symbols. His suggestion to George Washington and later to Robert Mills that the Choragic Monument would make an ideal monument to the Revolution reflects the belief that antique forms could serve as symbols of American democracy.[69] What appears to underlie this preference for the classical buildings he most admired, the Choragic Monument of Lysicrates, the Pantheon, and the Maison Carrée, rather than Meinert's neoclassical designs, is the belief that these monuments were the best visual approach to the ancient world and inspired the strongest emotional and intellectual associations.

It seems clear that by the end of Jefferson's long life he had embraced the philosophy that beauty is a mere indulgence unless the aesthetic experience is worked out in moral consequences.[70] It is this view which explains, in part, his interest in a work by his friend, Comte Constantin François de Volney, entitled *Les Ruines; ou Méditation sur les Révolutions des Empires* (Geneva, 1791). The work opens with a sublime reverie and a vision amid the ruins of the buildings of Palmyra, and although it should be quickly pointed out that Jefferson is not known to have indulged in the popular eighteenth-century art of building ruins, the significance here is that Volney's work coincides with a changing appreciation of ruins at a time when revolutionary political ideas were ripening at the end of the century. Ruins were beginning to be regarded as no longer playful reveries but as universal symbols that could "stimulate the intellect and cause the spectator to reflect about the passage of time, the meaning of history, and the destiny of man."[71]

It would be misleading, however, to leave the impression that Jefferson became fixed on this concept. Charm and invention always had their appeal, as is evident in a family story about Jefferson entertaining Volney at Monticello:

> Jefferson was a very systematic man, and could always be relied upon to appear at mealtime, but one day dinner was long kept waiting for his visitor, M. Volney, and himself, who were out walking. It afterwards appeared that the two philosophers had been detained by the labor of damming up a little stream in order that they might design a picturesque waterfall.[72]

Thomas Jefferson Memorial Foundation, Charlottesville

NOTES

1. Margaret Bayard Smith, *The First Forty Years of Washington Society* (New York, 1906), pp. 73, 75.

2. 1771 Memorandum Book, Coolidge Collection, Massachusetts Historical Society, Boston.

3. Gilbert Chinard, ed., *The Literary Bible of Thomas Jefferson: His Commonplace Book of Philosophers and Poets* (Baltimore, 1928), p. 188.

4. Memorandum Book.

5. For the classical origin and subsequent appreciation of the sleeping nymph and the epigram, see Otto Kurz, "Huius Nympha Loci," *Journal of the Warburg and Courtauld Institutes*, XVI (July 1953), pp. 171-177.

6. The reference to Spon is on the verso of a drawing listed as no. 91 in Frederick Doveton Nichols, *Thomas Jefferson's Architectural Drawings*, 4th ed. (Charlottesville, Va., 1978).

7. J. Mordaunt Crook, *The Greek Revival* (London, 1972), pp. 12, 13, 97.

8. George Sherburn, ed., *The Correspondence of Alexander Pope*, (Oxford, 1956), II, pp. 296-297.

9. Jefferson to Robert Skipwith, Aug. 3, 1771, in Julian P. Boyd et al., eds., *The Papers of Thomas Jefferson* (Princeton, N. J., 1950-   ), I, p. 78.

10. The purchase was recorded on Oct. 11, 1765, in the *Virginia Gazette* Daybooks, 1764-1766, Alderman Library, University of Virginia, Charlottesville. See Emily Millicent Sowerby, *Catalogue of the Library of Thomas Jefferson* (Washington, D. C., 1952-1959), II, for an identification of Jefferson's second copy of this book and others mentioned in this article.

11. "Notes of a Tour of English Gardens," Boyd et al., eds., *Jefferson Papers*, IX, p. 369.

12. Chinard, ed., *Literary Bible*, pp. 188, 189, 192-193, 202-204.

13. Jefferson to Charles McPherson, Feb. 25, 1773, Boyd et al., eds., *Jefferson Papers*, I, pp. 96-97. For a discussion of the influence of Ossianic poetry on Jefferson, see William H. Peden, "Thomas Jefferson: Book Collector" (Ph.D. diss., University of Virginia, 1942).

14. The translation is from Edward George, Lord Lytton, *The Odes and Epodes of Horace. A Metrical Translation into English* (New York, 1870), pp. 456, 458. It should be noted that Jefferson's version is not written in couplets.

15. Mrs. Drummond to Jefferson, Mar. 12 [1771], Boyd et al., eds., *Jefferson Papers*, I, pp. 65-66.

16. *Ibid.*, p. 78.

17. The land transfer was recorded on Oct. 15 in Jefferson's 1777 memorandum book.

18. Nichols, *Jefferson's Architectural Drawings*, no. 65.

19. *Ibid.*, no. 66.

20. The purchase was entered in Jefferson's memorandum book on Dec. 2, 1778.

21. Nichols, *Jefferson's Architectural Drawings*, no. 66.

22. Barbara Jones, *Follies & Grottoes* (London, 1974), p. 90.

23. Dorothy Stroud, *Capability Brown* (London, 1975), p. 52.

24. L. H. Butterfield, ed., *The Adams Papers*, (Cambridge, Mass., 1961), III, p. 186.

25. Nichols, *Jefferson's Architectural Drawings*, no. 126, p. 93.

26. Buford Pickens, "Mr. Jefferson as Revolutionary Architect," *Journal of the Society of Architectural Historians*, XXXIV (December 1975), p. 269.

27. Nichols, *Jefferson's Architectural Drawings*, no. 91.

28. Jefferson owned five editions of Palladio's work. The sumptuously illustrated Leoni editions of 1715 and 1742 were acquired before 1783, and at least one of those editions was probably in his library by 1769 when he referred to details when preparing specifications for the house. Fiske Kimball, *Thomas Jefferson, Architect* (Boston, 1916); 1767 memorandum book.

29. The location may have been the one described in his garden book on Mar. 10, 1779. Edwin Morris Betts, ed., *Thomas Jefferson's Garden Book, 1766-1824* (Philadelphia, 1944), p. 86.

30. Nichols, *Jefferson's Architectural Drawings*, no. 92. Jefferson's specifications were used in constructing a full-scale model for the exhibit "The Eye of Thomas Jefferson" held at the

National Gallery of Art, Washington, D. C., in 1976. For further discussion of the dating and the source for this and the preceding drawing, see my contribution to entry 572 in the exhibit catalog edited by William Howard Adams.

31. Mason, *Essay on Design in Gardening*, pp. 26-27.

32. Boyd et al., eds., *Jefferson Papers*, II, pp. 198-199; VIII, pp. 11-14.

33. Fraser Neiman, *The Henley-Horrocks Inventory*, Botetourt Publications, No. 1 (Williamsburg, Va., 1968), pp. 6, 8. Although Henley apparently was not writing to Gilpin on strictly picturesque subjects, the fact that Henley knew Gilpin's work at a time when none of the tours had been published suggests that he might have been familiar with the circle of friends who were aware of Gilpin's interests and who were instrumental in encouraging him to publish the tours.

34. Thomas Wright, *Arbours & Grottos*, with a catalog by Eileen Harris (London, 1979).

35. Mason, *Essay on Design in Gardening*, p. 50.

36. *Ibid.*, p. 127.

37. Wright, *Arbours & Grottos* (unpaginated).

38. An undated manuscript in the hand of James Ogilvie entitled "Valuation of Masonry by Thomas Patty Mason in Bristol," Jefferson Papers, Mass. Hist. Soc.

39. Kimball, *Thomas Jefferson, Architect*, pp. 125-127.

40. William Chambers, *Designs of Chinese Buildings, Furniture, Dresses, Machines and Utensils* (London, 1757). For Jefferson's detailed proportioning of his version of this building, see Nichols, *Jefferson's Architectural Drawings*, no. 119.

41. Chambers, *Designs*, pp. 6-7 and preface.

42. Nichols, *Jefferson's Architectural Drawings*, no. 119.

43. Chambers, *Designs*, p. 7 and preface.

44. 2nd ed. (Paris, 1684). For Jefferson's modifications of the order from the Corinthian in Perrault to the simpler Tuscan, see Nichols, *Jefferson's Architectural Drawings*, no. 111.

45. Nichols, *Jefferson's Architectural Drawings*, nos. 56 verso, 60 verso, and 117.

46. See Jefferson's notes on the verso of no. 56, *ibid.*

47. "Memorandums on a tour from Paris to Amsterdam, Strasburg, and back to Paris 1788. March. 3," Boyd et al., eds., *Jefferson Papers*, XIII, p. 17. For Whately's criticism, see *Observations on Modern Gardening* (London, 1770), p. 120.

48. "Memorandums," p. 17.

49. Jefferson to Maria Cosway, Oct. 12, 1786, Boyd et al., eds., *Jefferson Papers*, X, p. 446.

50. Kimball, *Thomas Jefferson, Architect*, pp. 91-92 and fig. 233.

51. "Hints to Americans travelling in Europe," Boyd et al., eds., *Jefferson Papers*, XIII, p. 274; Jefferson to James Currie, Jan. 28, 1786, *ibid.*, IX, p. 240.

52. July 1806, Jefferson Papers, Library of Congress, Washington, D. C.

53. Jefferson, memorandum to his overseer, Edmund Bacon, Feb. 1, 1808, Mass. Hist. Soc.

54. Nichols, *Jefferson's Architectural Drawings*, no. 171. The "General ideas for the improvement of Monticello" are the first two pages of a fourteen-page notebook. The earliest date in the notebook is Sept. 4, 1804. Other dates are 1805, 1806, and 1807. Based on the similarity of paper type to other dated examples, the first two pages on landscape improvements could have been begun while Jefferson was in Europe. There is no internal evidence to prove that, however.

55. Nichols, *Jefferson's Architectural Drawings*, nos. 129, 197.

56. Jefferson to Hamilton, Jefferson Papers, Lib. Cong.

57. Boyd et al., eds., *Jefferson Papers*, IX, p. 369.

58. *Ibid.*

59. Fiske Kimball speculated in *Thomas Jefferson, Architect*, p. 169, that Jefferson's drawing of a monopteros with the hours marked on the architrave and frieze (Nichols, *Jefferson's Architectural Drawings*, no. 183) may have been the study for the "turning" temple, but this is unlikely since the Doric rather than the Tuscan order appears in the drawing, and the proportions of the Pantheon are not followed. It is quite conceivable that the drawing is a design for a mantel clock similar in style to those known in France as a *pendule à cercles tournants*.

60. Nichols, *Jefferson's Architectural Drawings*, no. 171.

61. Boyd et al., eds., *Jefferson Papers*, IX, p. 371.

188

62. Nichols, *Jefferson's Architectural Drawings*, no. 171.

63. *Ibid.*, no. 182, p. 3. For a discussion of the many published architectural sources that were consulted by Jefferson when planning these temples, see William L. Beiswanger, "Thomas Jefferson's Designs for Garden Structures at Monticello" (M.A. thesis, University of Virginia, 1977).

64. See Robert Mitchell's last plate, "Design to elucidate the Style of Gothic Architecture," in *Plans, and Views in Perspective* . . . (London, 1801); Wilhelm Gottlieb Becker, *Neue Garten-und Landschafts-Gebaüde* (Leipzig, 1798-1799); and Becker, *Porte-feuille des Artistes* (Leipzig, 1800), plate 30.

65. Miscellaneous manuscripts, Mass. Hist. Soc.

66. Nichols, *Jefferson's Architectural Drawings*, no. 182, p. 1.

67. Ralph D. Gray, ed., "A Tour of Virginia in 1827: Letters of Henry D. Gilpin to his Father," *Virginia Magazine of History and Biography*, LXXVI (October 1968), p. 467.

68. Smith, *First Forty Years*, pp. 73, 75.

69. Jefferson to Robert Mills, Mar. 3, 1826, in H. M. Pierce Gallagher, *Robert Mills Architect of the Washington Monument 1781-1855* (New York, 1935), pp. 100, 163. The idea of symbols of American democracy is discussed by Karl Lehmann, *Thomas Jefferson American Humanist* (New York, 1947), pp. 158-160.

70. H. M. Kallen, "The Arts and Thomas Jefferson," *Ethics*, LIII (July 1943), p. 282.

71. Paul Zucker, *Fascination of Decay* (Ridgewood, N. J., 1968), p. 198. Jefferson's translation of the first twelve chapters of Volney's work was incorporated in Joel Barlow's translation published in Paris in 1802: Sowerby, *Catalogue of the Library of Jefferson*, II, p. 20.

72. Frank R. Stockton, "The Later Years of Monticello," *Century Magazine*, XXXIV (September 1887), p. 657.

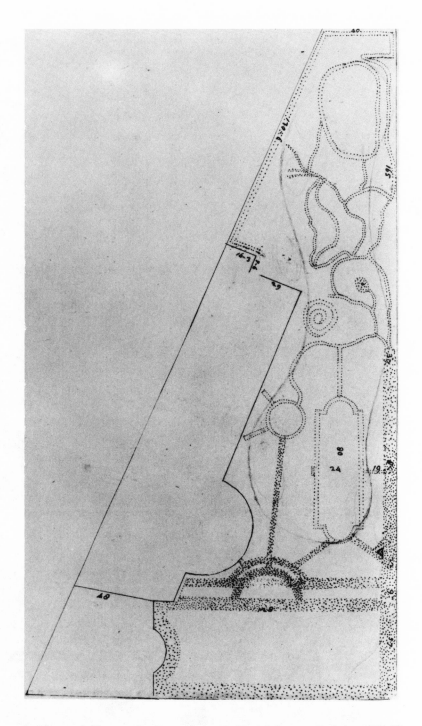

1. Thomas Jefferson, plan for *gardens at the Hôtel de Langeac*, Paris (ca. 1785-89). (Courtesy of the Howard C. Rice, Jr. Collection, Thomas Jefferson Memorial Foundation).

2. William Birch, *Solitude* (ca. 1784-89). From Alice Lockwood, *Gardens of Colony and State* (1932), vol. I, p. 346.

3. William Birch, *Woodlands* (ca. 1787-89). From Alice Lockwood, *Gardens of Colony and State* (1932), vol. I, p. 348.

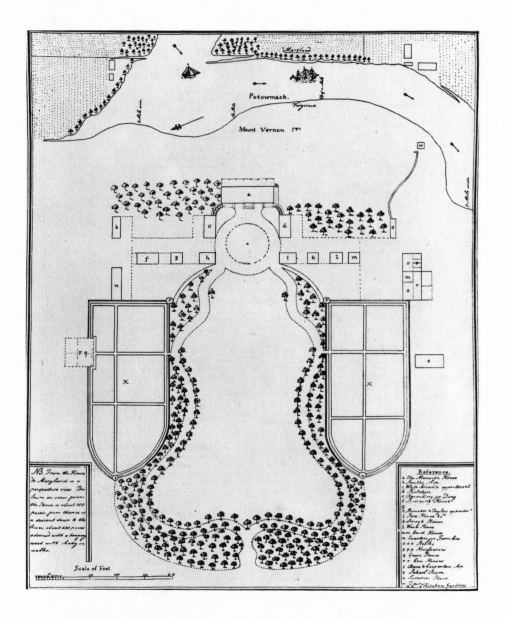

4. Samuel Vaughan, plan of the *gardens at Mount Vernon* (1787). (Courtesy of the Mount Vernon Ladies' Association of the Union).

5. Benjamin Latrobe, *Sedgeley* (1799). (Courtesy of the Philadelphia Museum of Art: Fairmount Park Commission).

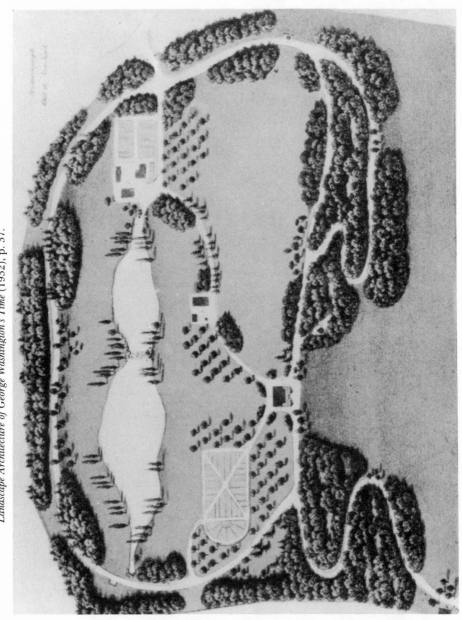

6. Plan of the gardens at Duanesburgh, New York (ca. 1800). From *Colonial Gardens: The Landscape Architecture of George Washington's Time* (1932), p. 37.

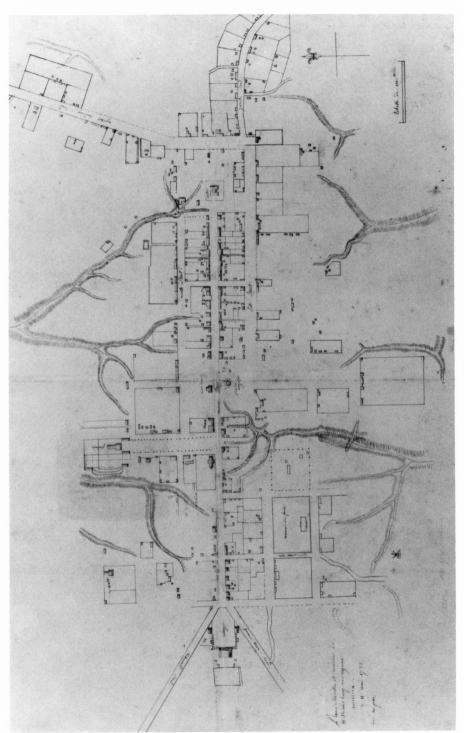

7. *Frenchman's Map* of Williamsburg (ca. 1781-82). (Swem Library, College of William and Mary. Photo: Courtesy of the Colonial Williamsburg Foundation).

8. *Governor's Palace and green.* Williamsburg. (Photo: Courtesy of the Colonial Williamsburg Foundation).

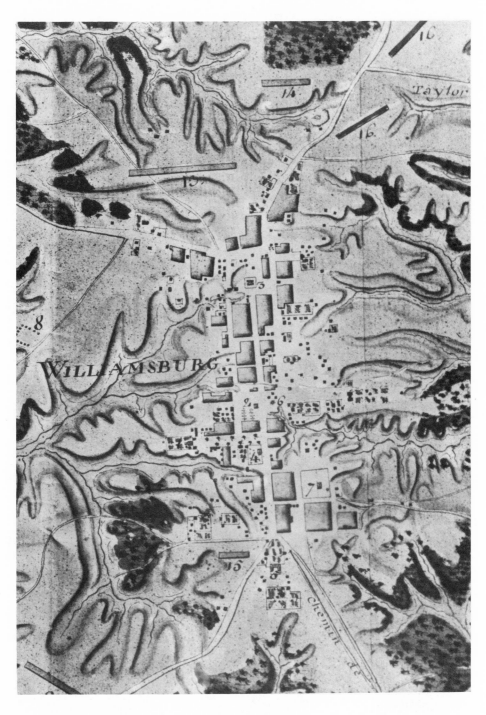

9. *Rochambeau Map* (ca. 1782). Custis's garden had disappeared by the date of this map. (Courtesy of the Library of Congress).

10. Charles Bridges, *John Custis* (ca. 1735). (Courtesy of Washington and Lee University).

11. Charles Willson Peale, *William Bartram* (Old City Hall, Philadelphia. Photo: North Carolina Collection, University of North Carolina).

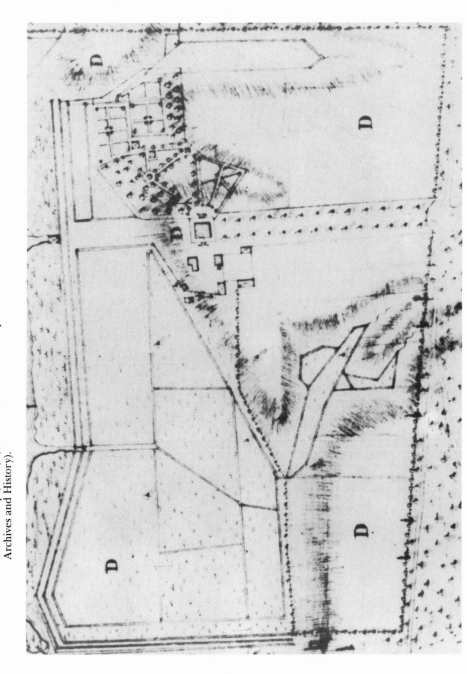

12. Plan of *Russelborough*, estate of governors Dobbs and Tryon, Brunswick Town. From the Sauthier Map (1769). (Photo: North Carolina Department of Cultural Resources, Division of Archives and History).

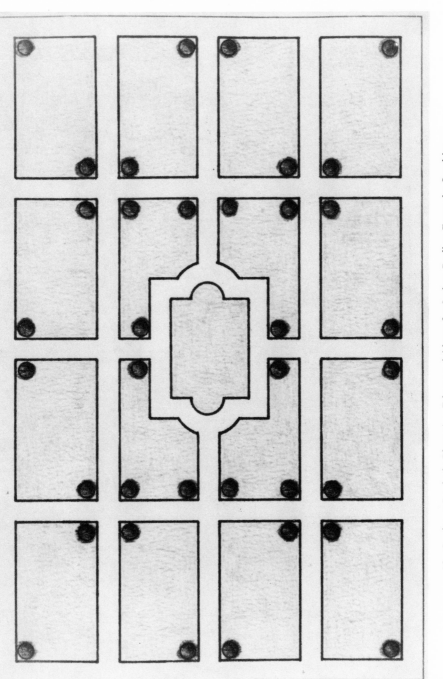

13. *Garden at Pembroke Plantation*, Edenton, laid out for Joshua Bodley. From the Sauthier Map (1769). (Photo: North Carolina Department of Cultural Resources, Division of Archives and History).

14. *Garden at Hayes Plantation*, Edenton, seat of Samuel Johnston, governor 1787-89. From the Sauthier Map (1769). (Photo: North Carolina Department of Cultural Resources, Division of Archives and History).

15. Anon., *The Hermitage*, on Prince George's Creek near Wilmington, seat of John Burgwin. Drawing (ca. 1795-1805). (Photo: National Society of the Colonial Dames of America in North Carolina).

16. Henry Pelham, 1775 map showing *Brattle Street*, Cambridge (detail). Aquatint (London: June 2, 1777).

17. Anon., *The South West Prospect of the Seat of Colonel George Boyd at Portsmouth, New Hampshire* (1774). Oil on canvas (detail). (Lamont Gallery, Phillips Exeter Academy).

18. *View of the seat of the Hon. Moses Gill Esq. at Princeton, in the County of Worcester, Massa.ts.* Detail of engraving in *Massachusetts Magazine,* IV (November, 1792).

19. Anon., *Thomas Banister House*, Brookfield (late 18th century). Oil on panel (detail). (Private collection).

20. Unidentified *formal garden plan* (late 18th century). Pen-and-ink drawing. (McIntire Collection, Essex Institute, Salem, Massachusetts).

21. Asher Benjamin, plan of *formal garden for the Jonathan Leavitt House,* Greenfield (1797). Pen-and-ink drawing (fragment). (Asher Benjamin Collection, Society for the Preservation of New England Antiquities, Boston).

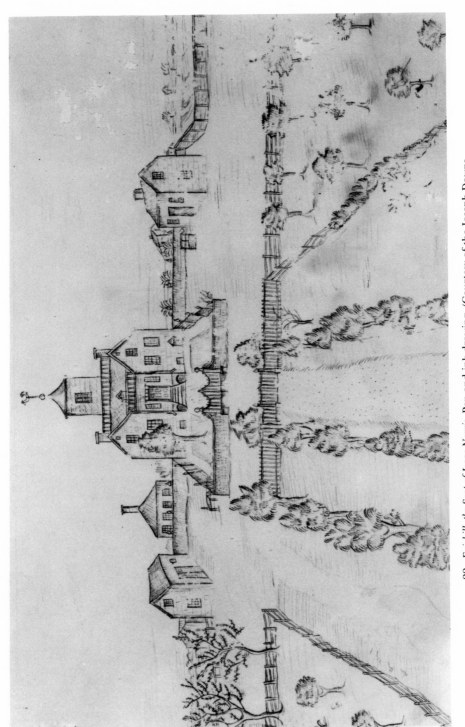

22. *Fairhill, the Seat of Isaac Norris.* Pen-and-ink drawing. (Courtesy of the Joseph Downs Manuscript Collection, Henry Francis du Pont Winterthur Museum).

23. John Nancarrow, *Plan of the Seat of John Penn, Jr.* (ca. 1784). Pen-and-ink drawing. (Courtesy of the Historical Society of Pennsylvania).

24. Charles Fraser, *A View on Mepkin*. Sketchbook. (Carolina Art Association, Gibbes Art Gallery, Charleston).

25. Charles Fraser, *Rice Hope*. Sketchbook. (Carolina Art Association, Gibbes Art Gallery, Charleston).

26. Charles Fraser, *Sheldon*. Sketchbook. (Charleston Museum).

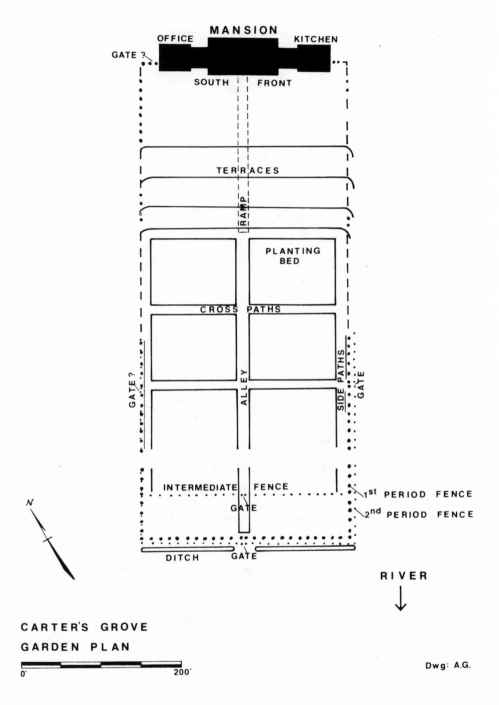

27. Archaeological plan of *Carter's Grove garden.*

28. *South front of Carter's Grove with terraces and ramp.* From Smith and Stroup, "Map of the Vicinity of Yorktown, Virginia" (Philadelphia, 1881). (D.A.R., Yorktown Chapter).

29. *North front garden, Kingsmill.* Excavation of kitchen building and mansion foundation (background), curvilinear brick walk foundation, planting ditch, and postholes for replacement fence (left). (Virginia Historic Landmarks Commission).

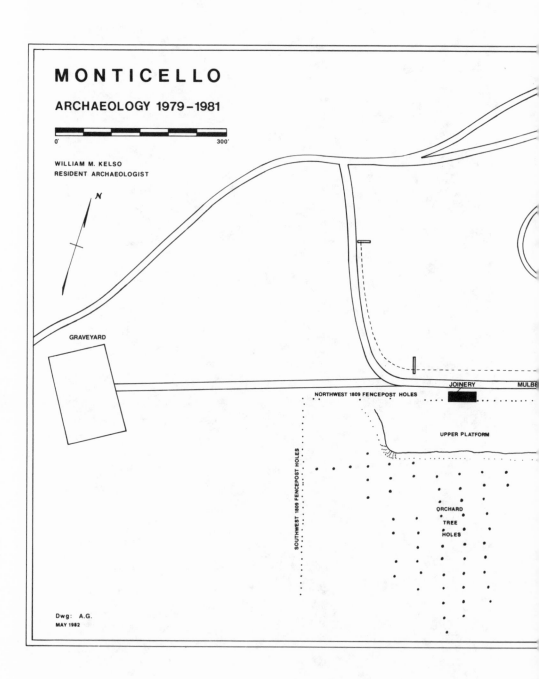

MONTICELLO

ARCHAEOLOGY 1979–1981

0'   300'

WILLIAM M. KELSO
RESIDENT ARCHAEOLOGIST

N

GRAVEYARD

JOINERY   MULBE

NORTHWEST 1809 FENCEPOST HOLES

UPPER PLATFORM

SOUTHWEST 1809 FENCEPOST HOLES

ORCHARD
TREE
HOLES

Dwg: A.G.
MAY 1982

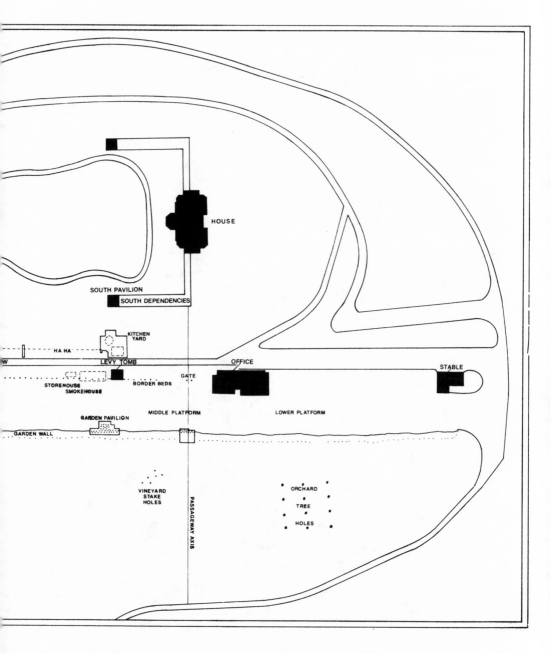

30. Archaeological plan, *Monticello*. (Thomas Jefferson Memorial Foundation).

31. A section of a succession of *original fenceline postholes* excavated along the northwest edge of the garden at *Monticello*. (Thomas Jefferson Memorial Foundation).

32. Remains of a *smokehouse/diary* (background) and a *storehouse* (foreground) at *Monticello*. (Thomas Jefferson Memorial Foundation).

33. Conjectural reconstruction of the *Monticello garden pavilion* based on archaeological remains and Jefferson's specifications. (Thomas Jefferson Memorial Foundation).

MONTICELLO
RECONSTRUCTION OF GARDEN PAVILION
0'   5'

34. Aerial photograph showing original *orchard planting holes* (white dots left center) and the western section of the 1809 *garden fenceline postholes* (dots extreme left) at *Monticello*. (Thomas Jefferson Memorial Foundation).

35. *Montalto at Monticello* from the kitchen garden plateau. (Photo: Edwin Roseberry).

36. Study for an *observation tower for Monticello*. (Massachusetts Historical Society).

37. Study for an *observation tower for Monticello*. (Massachusetts Historical Society).

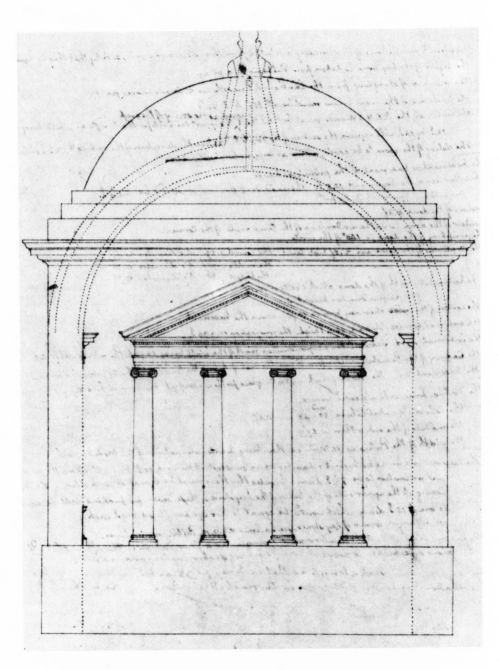

38. Design for a *temple for Monticello* (ca. 1779). Based on plate 73 in William Kent, *Designs of Inigo Jones* (1727). (Massachusetts Historical Society).

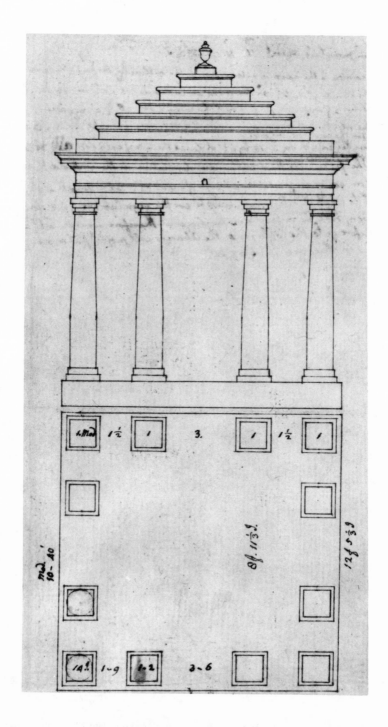

39. Design for a *dovecote for Monticello* (ca. 1779). (Massachusetts Historical Society).

40. *Garden pavilion.* From James Gibbs, *Book of Architecture* (1728).

41. *The north terrace, dependencies and pavilion at Monticello.*

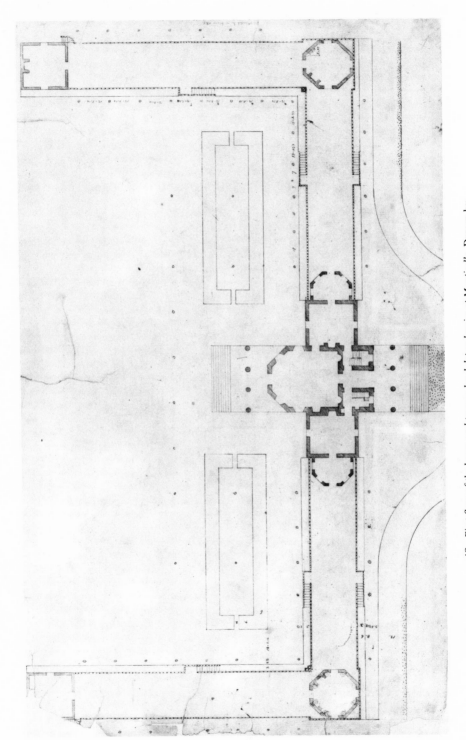

42. *First floor of the house and terrace-level dependencies at Monticello.* Drawn by Jefferson before 1784. (Massachusetts Historical Society).

43. Jefferson, concept for a *"ferme ornée"* for Monticello. (Author's study drawing).

44. *Temple* design. From Friedrich Meinert, *Die Schöne Landbaukunst* (1798), plate 38.